MUSIC Made Simple

The Made Simple series
has been created
especially for self-education
but can equally well
be used as
an aid to group study.
However complex the subject,
the reader is taken
step by step,
clearly and methodically,
through the course. Each volume
has been prepared by experts,
taking account of
modern educational requirements,
to ensure the most
effective way of
acquiring knowledge.

In the same series

MUSIC   Made Simple

Peter Dimond, MA

MADE SIMPLE
BOOKS

Made Simple
An imprint of Butterworth–Heinemann Ltd
Linacre House, Jordan Hill, Oxford OX2 8DP

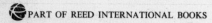PART OF REED INTERNATIONAL BOOKS

OXFORD   LONDON   BOSTON
MUNICH   NEW DELHI   SINGAPORE   SYDNEY
TOKYO   TORONTO   WELLINGTON

First published 1982
Second edition 1987
Reprinted 1978, 1989, 1991

ISBN 0 7506 0474 3

Printed in England by Clays Ltd, St Ives plc

Foreword

This book is designed to be used by both the serious music student and the amateur who wishes to know more about his hobby.

Most chapters are divided into two parts. Such chapters may be taken as a whole, or the book may be used by following all the first or second parts in succession. The first part of each chapter places composers in their historical and stylistic contexts and deals with the repertoire of music, its structure, and the instruments which play it. The second part of each chapter is devoted to the rudiments of music and to the theoretical basis of composition. Very little previous knowledge is assumed. In these sections the reader is first introduced to the elements of music and then taken step by step through the standard eighteenth-century harmonic practice which forms the basis of four-part and two-part writing. Suggestions are also given for melodic writing; and exercises are included for most of the techniques, to which the answers are given in Appendix V. Most chapters include suggestions for further reading.

It may be objected that to teach composition without a parallel course of aural training is of limited value – and the present book may well be used in conjunction with aural training – as the student should be able to hear what he writes. On the other hand few, if any, public examinations test that ability. Aural examinations test the ability of the student, to a limited extent, to hear what somebody else has written, but a candidate may pass or fail a composition examination solely on his ability to put agreeable harmony on paper. There does, then, seem to be a widespread and tacit acknowledgement that a knowledge of harmony is in itself of some value, just as there seems to be some value in writing tolerable French or classical Greek without necessarily being able to think in those languages. However, no one would deny that a student's musical training is incomplete until he can hear what he writes.

In writing this book my thanks are due to several people. I am deeply indebted to Mr Paul Roberts who suggested that the book should be written at all. My next debt is to Mr Ivan Rendell who succeeded in transcribing my illegible music examples into acceptable manuscript copy. I am grateful to Mr Robert Postema for his guidance in the preparation of the book; to Miss Louise Bloomfield who undertook the arduous task of editing it; and to Mrs Anne Totterdell for help in preparing the index. The responsibility for the completed work is entirely mine.

PETER DIMOND
Haselbury Plucknett
August 1981

Contents

1

INTRODUCTION

Stylistic Periods of Western Music History

It is convenient to divide the history of Western Music into stylistic periods. These are usually distinguished as follows: Medieval, Renaissance, Baroque, Classical, Romantic, Twentieth century. Western music originated to a large extent in the early Christian Church where it was customary to chant parts of the services. The style of the chant (Plainchant or Plainsong) was established by Pope Gregory I (*c.* 540–604). Gregorian chant is still sung today. During the *Middle Ages* the music of the Church began to develop independently of the needs of the liturgy and eventually became an art form in its own right. Early in the fifteenth century a mood of experiment, expansion and rejuvenation began to affect the peoples of Europe and particularly of northern Italy. Since the mid-nineteenth century this new cultural period has been called the *Renaissance*. The spirit of the Renaissance greatly affected the course of music and both in the earlier and in the later parts of the period there arose composers of outstanding ability, such as **Josquin Desprès**, **Byrd**, and **Palestrina.**

The *Baroque* period was ushered in with the arrival of opera. During this period also instrumental and orchestral music was written independently of any functional purpose. Baroque music culminated in the dominating figure of Bach and ended with his death in 1750. But even before that date the style of music had changed in the direction of simplicity and directness of appeal. To people of the nineteenth century the style appeared *Classical* in its emphasis on elegance and fine proportion; it is seen at its most effective in the music of Haydn and Mozart and was the style inherited by Beethoven. During the course of Beethoven's career in the first quarter of the nineteenth century the element of *Romanticism*, which is perhaps present in all music, became the dominant one and gave its name to the music of the rest of the century. The Romantic period formally ended in the first decade of the twentieth century although Romanticism has continued to play an important part in the century's musical thinking. *Twentieth-century* music is written in a diversity of styles, none of which has become dominant; but this has not prevented the musical life of our own day from proceeding with a vigour which is perhaps unequalled in any other period of musical history.

These then are the *musical styles* and their approximate dates, which in most cases overlap.

Medieval 1100–1425	Classical 1740–1820
Renaissance 1425–1600	Romantic 1810–1900
Baroque 1600–1750	20th century 1900–the present day

Medieval Music

The music of the Middle Ages may be divided into three distinct phases each of which roughly corresponds with a particular type of musical composition.

1

1. *Organum* From about 900–1200 the practice was established of adding from one to three other parts to the single line of the Gregorian chant. This practice was known at the time as *organum*. The added parts moved to a large extent parallel with the original chant. This produced some combinations of sound which were considered disagreeable at the time, a fact which provided the basis for the development of organum during the period.

Towards the end of the period there arose in Paris a group of composers who have become known as the *Notre Dame School*, since they were active at the time of the building of Notre Dame Cathedral (1163–1257). Two of the most important and progressive members of this group were **Léonin**, who was active from about 1150–1180, and **Pérotin** (*c*. 1160–1240). These two between them wrote examples of organum for the whole of the church's year.

2. *Conductus* Organum is based on a line of plainchant which is held by the tenor part (Latin: *tenere* = to hold). During the twelfth century a new type of composition emerged where the tenor part consisted of either a newly composed or else a non-church (secular) musical line. To this line either two or three parts were added and allowed to move more freely than in the case of strict organum. This method of composition became known as *conductus*. Singers of organum felt that they were moving forward independently of each other; those of conductus tuned together in harmony.

3. *Ars Nova* In 1320 the French composer and theorist **Philippe de Vitry** (1291–1361) wrote a lengthy article in which he distinguished between modern music (*Ars Nova*) and old-fashioned music (*Ars Antiqua*). Ars Nova was characterized by a greater variety of rhythm and an increased independence in the part writing. Above all the new style gave prominence to the form of composition known as the *motet*. A motet is a short sacred piece of music for unaccompanied singing in two, three, or four parts. It is based on an existing melody which is sung by the tenor. The other parts not only have their own independent music but often their own words as well. The motet remained an important form of composition throughout the medieval and Renaissance periods, during which time it attracted the attention of the foremost composers. A particular form of the composition, known as the *isorhythmic motet*, was perfected by **Guillaume de Machaut** (*c*. 1300–1377). This was normally in three parts closely woven around the tenor; the rhythmic pattern is repeated to different sections of a plainchant. Machaut's outstanding composition is his Mass. It was written about 1360 and is possibly the first complete setting of the Mass by a single composer, and possibly the only one before the mid-fifteenth century.

The Renaissance Period

By the beginning of the Renaissance period music had developed many forms and was written in a variety of styles with important centres in England, the Netherlands, France, and Italy. During the *earlier Renaissance period* (*1400–1500*) choral polyphony first began to flourish; composers began also to control the use of dissonance, and established the means by which a discord could be placed on an accented beat both for expressive purposes and to carry the music forward. In choral music the tenor part ceased to be the only one to carry the fixed tune (*cantus firmus*). The parts themselves began to be inter-related by means of imitation. The finest music was still written for the Church but composers increasingly turned their attention to writing music to accompany functions other than religious ones; for Renaissance music was above all *functional*. But the outstanding feature of Renaissance music is the composer's attitude towards his text and his concern with the rhythms and emotional content of the words which he is setting.

The earlier Renaissance period produced several outstanding composers. One of the most influential was the Englishman **John Dunstable** (*c.* 1380–1453) whose work was well-known on the Continent. In particular Dunstable's individual harmonic style affected the later music of the French/Flemish **Guillaume Dufay** (*c.* 1400–1474) who developed the devices of canon and imitation.

At Dufay's death the leadership of the Netherlands School passed to **Johannes Ockeghem** (*c.* 1430–1495). Ockeghem's professional ability as a manipulator of the elements of music in composition was outstanding. His work was very influential. One of his pupils was Josquin Desprès (*c.* 1440–1521), a prolific composer of great importance. Josquin wrote several fine French *chansons* and over 100 Masses, but it is in his motets that his ability is most fully apparent. He has a fine sense of melody which he is able to weave into imitative passages of some complexity but always to purely musical ends. He is a master at producing unity out of variety.

Josquin stands at the end of the earlier Renaissance period. The late Renaissance also, at the end of the sixteenth century, produced music of outstanding quality.

PART ONE: MUSIC IN ITALY 1550–1600

In 1550 there were two main centres of Western music: Italy and England. Italy was coming to the end of the period we now know as the Renaissance; Michaelangelo, one of the last and greatest of Renaissance figures, died in 1564. The Renaissance was concerned with the rebirth of learning connected with the Classical civilizations of Greece and Rome. There had been a rebirth of literature; of sculpture and of architecture; and, to a certain extent, of painting. But as yet there had been no attempt to revive the music of the ancient civilizations. Instead, music in Italy in 1550 was dominated by two traditions: a school of composers who came from the Netherlands; and the music of the Roman Catholic Church.

The church of *St Mark in Venice* united these two traditions. This cathedral church was the only important Christian building to be designed in the shape of a Greek cross instead of a Latin one. This means that the transept – the aisle which goes across the church – is exactly halfway along the building's total length so that there is just as much of the church at the altar end as there is at the congregation end. This made the usual relationship of choir and congregation impossible. The result was that St Mark's had two choirs placed opposite one another on balconies at each end of the transept, each choir with its own organ and organist.

It was therefore possible to write music which made use of the striking effect of having two choirs perform alternately. This applied also to the two organs and even to the instrumental groups. This effect is known as *antiphony*. It happened also that northern Italy at this time was particularly rich in outstanding composers. And so this accident of architecture had a great influence on later sixteenth-century music.

Willaert

In 1550 the director of music at St Mark's was a Netherlands composer, **Adrian Willaert** (1490–1562). Willaert was a prolific composer and many of his choral works make use of the antiphonal possibilities of the Cathedral. He was equally famous in his day as a teacher. He attracted pupils from all over Europe and made Venice one of the two great centres of Italian music. The other centre was at Rome. At Venice he founded a school of music which immediately attracted outstanding performers and composers throughout Europe. Willaert died in 1562. As a result of his initiative it is possible to speak of a Venetian School during the latter part of the sixteenth century.

Lassus

An even more important Netherlands composer was **Orlando di Lasso** (1538–1594). (This form of his name is Italian; he is known equally by the Latin form of Orlandus Lassus.) He was born in Mons. As a young choirboy his voice was of such beauty that he is said to have been carried off three times by talent scouts looking for likely recruits for the choirs of the aristocratic households of Europe. At the age of fourteen he arrived in Italy, having accompanied the Netherlands army there. He spent eight years in Italy and eventually became director of music at the church of St John Lateran in Rome. He finally settled in 1557 in Munich at the court of Duke Albert V of Bavaria. Duke Albert was anxious to make his musical establishment as great as any in Europe and the reputation of Lassus at this time was such that he was considered the right person for this job. Lassus was a prolific composer and his works today fill sixty large volumes. He could write outstanding music in every form then available. Lassus's music is frequently of great beauty and it is often tinged with melancholy. Towards the end of his life he appears to have suffered a mental breakdown and it is this proneness to depression which is heard in the music.

Polyphony

In addition to the Netherlands' composers the other great influence on music during the Renaissance period was the Roman Catholic Church. One of the Church's outstanding contributions to music was the art of singing *plainsong* or *plainchant*. This is a method of chanting the words of a service by all the voices together in unison. The Chant moves gently up and down and takes its rhythm from the accent of the words. It is an art which lends itself to great subtlety of performance and from a devotional point of view allows the partakers of the service to concentrate on the meaning of the words they are singing.

From the art of plainchant there developed the style of music known as *polyphony*. Polyphony means 'many voices'. This method of writing music is the combining together of two or more melodies so that they make musical sense. A round, for example 'Three Blind Mice', is a very simple form of polyphony. The style is, however, capable of great complexity. When we sing a round the various parts imitate one another exactly, that is, they all sing the same music and there is clearly a limit to the number of times we can repeat the round before losing interest. Sixteenth-century polyphony also used this device of imitation but the music is kept alive by the fact that the imitations are not exact while each part may have stretches of independent melody. An old word for a note is 'point'. When two lines of melody are performed together the notes ('points') run against one another. This is known as 'counterpoint'. The means by which sixteenth century polyphony proceeds is therefore called *imitative counterpoint*.

The main Roman Catholic service is the Mass. It became customary to set the complete service to music so that the music itself became known as a *Mass*. Another important vocal form was the motet (see p. 2), sung in Latin and not part of the Mass. It is in two, three or four parts and is based on an existing melody which is sung by the tenor. Parts other than the tenor have not only their own independent melodic line but often their own words as well. The English counterpart to the motet is the *anthem*. Both the Mass and the motet were usually set using polyphony and by the early sixteenth century in Italy vocal polyphonic writing had become extremely complex. The result of this was that it was no longer possible to distinguish individual words as they were being sung; but one could hold that this did not much matter since they would be quite clear to God. However this may be, Renaissance composers on the whole reacted extremely sensitively to the words they were called upon to set to music and there was a general feeling in the early sixteenth century that vocal music should become simplified.

The Reformation

Indeed, the desire for reform was rife throughout the Roman Catholic world, not only in music but in most of the matters with which the Church was concerned. During much of the fifteenth century the Church had been at odds with itself and was discredited in the eyes of those who viewed it from without. The climax of the discontent came in 1517 when a religious revolt against the Church was staged by Martin Luther.

Luther was himself a priest. He was also a very able scholar, being in 1517 a professor of theology. In addition he was a competent musician, and sang and composed with distinction. He was thus equipped not only to argue about the abuses from which the Church suffered but also to make provision for reforming the church's music.

Luther brought matters to a head in 1517 by assembling ninety-five complaints against the Church, mainly to do with the way in which it raised money, and posting them up in public. This was the beginning of the movement known as the Reformation. It was a movement born of protest and the church which arose from it became known as the Protestant church. Starting in Germany it spread very rapidly, but not to Italy.

Martin Luther had decided views on what sort of music he wanted the Church to have. He believed that the congregation should be allowed to take part in singing the words of the service and to sing them in their own language rather than in Latin. This meant that the music of the reformed church had to become simple and capable of being performed by non-musicians. Polyphony was not suitable for this. Luther therefore introduced what we would recognize as hymn tunes, known as *chorales*; and the chorale became the basis of Lutheran church music. It is believed that Luther himself wrote some of the earliest chorale tunes. A very well known one is Ein' Feste Burg (A Mighty Fortress) which appears at the end of this chapter.

The Roman Catholic Church was aware of the need to reform itself and it eventually reacted to the success of Lutheranism by setting up a standing committee of its dignitaries in the town of Trent in Northern Italy. This Council of Trent lasted from 1545 to 1563. The Council was naturally concerned mainly with religious matters but since music played such an important part in both the existing and the new forms of worship the Council made suggestions for the reform of Roman Catholic music also. Polyphonic settings of the Mass were to be simplified so that the words could be heard by the listener. The effect of the Council's decision upon the leading Catholic composers of the sixteenth century was immediately apparent.

It is not surprising that the other main centre of musical activity in Italy in the sixteenth century was Rome, since the musical establishment of the Vatican was of great importance. For many centuries the Popes had had their own choir, the Papal Choir which consisted of thirty-two singers, in the Sistine Chapel; composers at Rome constantly supplied this choir with music. The outstanding composer of the sixteenth century, not only at Rome but throughout Europe, was Palestrina.

Palestrina

Palestrina (1525–1594) is the name of the place where the composer was born; his own names were Giovanni Pierliugi. Palestrina is perhaps the most important of all composers in the sixteenth century. His life was centred upon Rome. Unusually for a Renaissance musician he never travelled more than about fifteen miles from the centre of his activity. He became, and still is, the established composer of the Roman Catholic Church; and the Papal Choir of the Sistine Chapel has remained the supreme interpreter of Palestrina's music. In his youth Palestrina studied the music of the Netherlands composers but his own style has a purity and effortlessness which is difficult to imitate and impossible to surpass. In this respect he has been both the delight and envy of most subsequent composers.

It is not, therefore, surprising that when the Council of Trent wished to reform the music of the Church it was to Palestrina that they turned. Polyphony was to be simplified and the words of the Mass were to be audible. The Council pointed to an existing Mass of Palestrina as an indication of what they wanted. This work we now know as the *Missa Papae Marcelli* (The Mass of Pope Marcellus). In this Mass there are passages of pure chordal writing interspersed with the polyphony. During the latter part of the sixteenth century this alternation of polyphony and harmony became more and more common and indeed it can be very effective if music which is proceeding in a complex manner suddenly becomes very direct.

Palestrina's music is entirely for voices singing unaccompanied. This is known as *a capella* singing. But Palestrina would not have objected to a discreet organ accompaniment to the voices. He wrote 90 Masses and over 500 motets. As a man Palestrina was extremely astute and took care to ensure that the Popes for whom he worked took notice of his music. In one work each time the setting of the words 'Behold the Great High Priest' occurs Palestrina had a picture of the Pope set in the first letter.

His later life was clouded by the death of his wife and of his two sons, as a result of a plague. He married again, however – a lady who had a monopoly in the production of the fur clothing which was much worn by the civil and ecclesiastical dignitaries of the time. Palestrina devoted the profits from this trade to the development of property.

As Willaert was the leader of the Venetian School and attracted musicians from other parts of Europe and in particular from the north, so the Roman School and Palestrina attracted musicians particularly from Spain. The most important Spaniard who worked in Rome was **Thomás Luiz de Victoria** (or Vittoria) who was born about 1540. He refused to write any music except for the Church on the grounds that God gave him musical ability for the sole purpose of praising him by means of it. His music is generally quite emotional and not without a characteristically Spanish flavour.

Palestrina's music was nearly all for the Church, but he did write some secular vocal music as well, in the form known as the *madrigal*. The madrigal was the most important secular form in the sixteenth century.

The Madrigal

The singing of madrigals as a hobby became popular in Italy in the early part of the sixteenth century and has never gone out of fashion since then. Madrigal music is in two or more parts, and was intended to be sung with one person to each part. There is no accompaniment. Today when performing vocal music it is usual for the singer to have all the parts printed on the page in front of him so that it is possible to see exactly when to come in and what effect one's part has in relation to all the other parts. An orchestral performer today plays from music which contains only his own part: sixteenth-century madrigal parts followed this practice and were usually printed in *part books*. This method was sometimes elaborated by printing books arranged in such a way that four people sitting on different sides of a table could read from a single copy; aristocratic and courtly persons, particularly the men, were expected to be able to sing a part at sight.

The point of a madrigal is that the music is in some way expected to match the feeling or subject matter of the poem being set. This is a further instance of the careful attitude which the Renaissance composers adopted towards their texts.

It was the Venetian School under Willaert which first revived the madrigal using French and Italian popular songs as a starting point. Polyphony and imitative writing were used as well as straightforward chordal writing, but the melody in a madrigal usually stayed in the top part of those singing at any one time. Other madrigal composers associated with Willaert are **Cipriano de Rore** (1516–1565) and **Jacques Arcadelt** (*c.* 1510–1568) whose madrigal 'The gentle white swan sings when it dies' is quite popular today. But the most outstanding Italian madrigal composer of the late sixteenth century is **Luca Marenzio** (1553–1599).

Marenzio came from northern Italy and worked for a time in Venice. His travels took him to Bavaria, to Orlando di Lasso, and even to Poland. He died in Rome. Nearly 200 of his madrigals were published in his lifetime. His fame derives from his ability to interpret his text in such a way that it also makes excellent musical sense in its own right. The following are examples of the ways in which a madrigal composer might handle his text, all of which are used by Marenzio. At a mention of 'heavens' or 'mountains' music goes up; 'arch' produces a melodic curve and 'sea' a wavy kind of melody. 'Day' is represented by open notes which, except for their outline, are white, while 'night' produces a lot of black notes; these also indicate 'hell'. Many of these examples are interesting as they show that the composer was writing just as much for the performer, who could see the effect on the printed page, as for the listener, who might not be able to link the sound he was hearing with what it looked like on paper. All of the above are *literal* renderings of the text. Emotional renderings are also general throughout most madrigal writing. 'Joy' and 'happiness' are easy enough to convey in music but in the sixteenth century words such as 'martyrdom', 'sadness', 'pain', 'cruelty', and 'tears' often result in grinding discords and unexpected turns of harmony.

Instrumental Music

Unaccompanied vocal music, both religious and secular, played a most important part in the sixteenth-century Italian composer's output. But there was a further development in music at this time which assumed ever-increasing importance as the century progressed, and in the following century ousted vocal music from its supreme position. This was instrumental music. Instruments have been used functionally for many centuries; that is, to accompany dancing, hunting, entertainment, eating, and the performance of various rituals. But in the sixteenth century in Italy instrumental music began to be performed for its own sake. There was an enormous variety of instruments available, for instrumental groups had not become standardized. Many of them subsequently fell into disuse but most of them are again made today.

Two composers are particularly associated with this development: **Andrea Gabrieli** (1510–1586) and his nephew **Giovanni Gabrieli** (1557–1612). Both men wrote in all the forms available at the time; they wrote both Masses and madrigals; they wrote both polyphonically and harmonically; they wrote both vocal and instrumental music. Both of them were highly original composers. They came from Venice. Andrea became second organist at St Mark's in 1566. About twenty years later he was made first organist and his nephew became second organist. When Andrea died Giovanni became first organist and held the post until his death. Both were famous for their organ playing. From our point of view it is the originality of their works which stands out; for both composers made use of the antiphonal possibilities of St Mark's. The *Sonata pian' e forte* by Giovanni Gabrieli is often performed today. It uses a wind group and a string group, which sometimes play together but more often in opposition to one another. As the title implies – 'pian' e forte' means 'soft and loud' – great play is made of echo effects and contrasting dynamics.

The sound of the brass for which the Gabrielis wrote is a familiar one today, for brass instruments have undergone little basic structural alteration for several centuries. In particular the trombone, or *sackbut*, has remained largely unaltered, since the principal on which it works, that of the sliding tube, was already perfected. *Trumpets* in the sixteenth century were available in more sizes than is common today and the sounds were produced without the help of valves. In addition to these two brass instruments, Gabrieli used a very common sixteenth-century instrument which later went out of fashion. This was the *cornett*. The cornett was made of wood or ivory and was derived from the shape of an animal's horn. The sound was made in the same way as that of a trumpet or trombone, with the player engaging his lips against a mouthpiece. In the sixteenth century the cornett was made in several sizes and was treated as a member of the brass family.

The Viol

The stringed instruments for which Gabrieli wrote were the family of *viols*. The violin existed at this time but had not yet developed into the instrument we know today. The viol, although it is played with a bow, belongs to a different family. There were three different sizes of viol in common use, all of which were held between the legs when played. As the Italian word for *leg* is *gamba* the instrument became known as the *viol da gamba*.

The viol has six strings against the violin's four and the fingerboard has gut frets on it as does a guitar. The tuning of the strings also uses the same intervals as the guitar although not at the same pitch. The method of playing the viol also differs from that of the violin, a viol bow being held from underneath with the palm of the hand upwards which means that the instrument can be played only between the knees. The wood of a violin bow curves inwards towards the hair while that of a viol arches away from the hair. This means that it is much easier to play more than one string at the same time on a viol than on a violin. The actual sound of a viol is different from that of a violin; the structure of the viol causes the sound to be less striking but also, since the fingers are put down just behind the frets, every note has the clear sound of an open string. Violin players commonly use *vibrato* when playing; that is the fingers are pressed on to the string rather as if they were trying to push a drawing pin quickly into it. This effect, which is used for expressive purposes, is not used on the viol. Altogether then, the sound of the viol is sweeter and smoother than that of the violin. The antiphonal effect between strings and brass which Gabrieli was aiming at in the *Sonata pian' e forte* has a much greater impact using the viol family than it would have with the violin family.

With the retreat from polyphony in the sixteenth century and the great importance of the madrigal in the secular and, to some extent, in the spiritual sphere; and with the advance of instrumental music as the century progressed, the course of music began to develop more and more in the direction of a style which was dramatic, simple, and harmonic. In the event, however, the change to the new style was both abrupt and decisive. The man who was at the forefront of this musical revolution was both an important composer in his own right and one of the most influential musicians in the history of music – **Claudio Monteverdi** (1567–1643).

A full consideration of Monteverdi's achievement must be reserved for a later chapter. Here it may be said that he was born in northern Italy, at Cremona. When he was sixteen, in 1583, his first book of madrigals appeared and from the first it became apparent that the composer was carrying the Renaissance concern with the words to its logical conclusion; the text was more important than the music. The climax of Monteverdi's new ideas came in 1605 with the publication of this fifth book of madrigals. By then he was working for the Gonzaga family at the court of Mantua. The last thirty years of his long working life were spent as director of music at St Mark's in Venice. When he died the style of music then being written made Renaissance music scarcely recognizable.

PART TWO: HOW TO WRITE DOWN MUSIC

Example 2.1 shows a section of a keyboard. You will notice that the black notes are grouped regularly in twos and threes and that they come between the white notes without displacing them.

2.1

If you move from *any* note to the one immediately next to it, whether from white to black, from black to white, or from the two possible white to white notes, you move the interval of a *semitone*. A semitone is the basic unit of difference of pitch in western music.

The pattern of black and white notes repeats itself up and down the keyboard. If you move from any note to the note having the same position in the next pattern up or down you move an *octave*. An octave is divided into twelve equal semitones. Two consecutive semitones form a *tone* (or *whole tone*).

A *scale* is an arrangement of tones and semitones within an octave.

Western music inherited from ancient Greece via the Middle Ages a number of eight-note scales. These were known as *modes*. Twelve modes were possible but not all were in use. During the period we have been considering in this chapter, the number of modes had to a large extent been reduced to two. We know these modes as the *major* and *minor scales*.

On the keyboard the notes are given names using the first seven letters of the alphabet: A–G. The letter names are applied as shown in Example 2.2.

C|D|E|F|G|A|B|C|D|E|F|G|A|B|C|D|E|F|G|A|B|C|D|E|F|G|A|B|C|D|E

2.2

The black notes derive their names from their relationships to the white notes next to them. If you wish to refer to a black note a semitone *above* a white note you add the word 'sharp' to the name of the white note; if you wish to refer to a black note a semitone *below* a white note you add the word 'flat' to its name. This means that all black notes can be referred to in two ways: i.e. C sharp = D flat; D sharp = E flat; F sharp = G flat; G sharp = A flat; A sharp = B flat. The symbol for sharp is ♯ and the symbol for flat is ♭. So C♯ = D♭, etc.

In order to cancel a previous sharp or flat, one more symbol is necessary. This is called a *natural* sign; its symbol is ♮.

These three symbols are called *accidentals*.

If you use an accidental with the letter name of a note you place the symbol *after* the letter, e.g. C♯ B♭ F♮: if you use an accidental with an actual note the symbol is placed *before* the note – see Example 2.3.

                                                                    2.3

How to Form a Major Scale

A major scale may be formed starting from any note within the octave; i.e. from any note on the keyboard. To form the scale, start on any note and move upwards (to the right) using the following intervals: Tone, Tone, Semitone, Tone, Tone, Tone, Semitone. This will bring you to the note an octave above the starting point. For example, if you start on C the move of a Tone will take you to D; another Tone to E; a Semitone to F; a Tone to G; a Tone to A; a Tone to B; and the final semitone up to the C an octave above the starting point.

In forming a scale there must be one note of each letter *contained in the octave.* This happens automatically in the major scale of C, which consists of the notes CDEFGAB. However, in all other scales, when moving Tone, Tone, Semitone, Tone, Tone, Tone, Semitone, at least one black note will have to be used and at least one accidental will have to be used in order to preserve the sequence of letter names.

The scale of *A major*, for example, must consist of the notes ABCDEFG. Moving a tone from A takes you to B; a tone from B takes you to the black note between C and D. This must be a C of some sort in order to preserve the letter sequence. It can therefore only be C♯. A semitone from this C♯ lands on D; a tone from D gets to E; a tone from E gets to the black note above F = F♯; a tone from F♯ gets to the black note above G = G♯; a semitone from G♯ arrives at the top A. The scale of A major therefore consists of A B C♯ D E F♯ G♯. Here is an example of a scale which starts on a black note and includes flats. It is the scale of B♭ major.

$$B♭ \quad C \quad D \quad E♭ \quad F \quad G \quad A \quad B♭$$
$$T \quad T \quad S \quad \quad T \quad T \quad T \quad S$$
$$T = tone; \ S = semitone$$

Exercises

1. Write out the letter names of the scale of G major. Start on G and move upwards Tone, Tone, Semitone, Tone, Tone, Tone, Semitone. One note will have to be sharpened.
2. Now try the scale of D major.
3. Now write down the scale of E♭ major.

Writing Down Music

The system of writing down music is surprisingly economical and quite logical. A great deal of music is written down in *short score*; for this two sets of five lines are used. Each set of five lines is known as a *stave* or staff (see Example 2.4). Notes are placed above and below the lines, on the lines, and in the spaces between the lines; notes so placed are all white notes. The higher or lower the pitch of a note is, the higher or lower it appears on the sets of five lines. Surprisingly, these two sets of five lines together represent over three octaves of pitch. Notes higher or lower than this are placed on additional small lines above and below the two sets. These additional lines are called *ledger lines*.

2.4

There is one ledger line possible between the two sets of five lines. If the sets of lines are printed a little further apart this same ledger line can attach itself either below the top five or above the lower five, but it always houses the same note. This is *Middle C*, shown in Example 2.5. If you sit at the

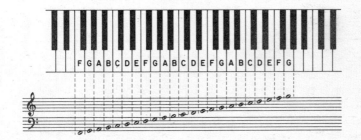

2.5

middle of a keyboard the C right in front of you is Middle C; it is frequently near the lock of the piano. The economy of our system of notation can be seen from Example 2.6 where the notes of the keyboard are related to the sets of five lines. The two sets of five lines are distinguished from each other by symbols called *clefs*. Above Middle C is the *treble clef* and below it is the *bass clef*. The treble clef is formed on the note G above Middle C and is also

2.6

known as the G clef (see Example 2.7). The bass clef is formed on the note F
below Middle C and is also known as the F clef. This clef may be written in

2.7

two forms (see Example 2.8). Notice the two dots which follow it. The scale
of C major in the treble clef is notated as shown in Example 2.9 and in the
bass clef as in Example 2.10. All other scales contain accidentals.

2.8

C D E F G A B C

2.9

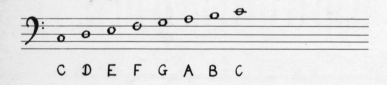

C D E F G A B C

2.10

Here is a simplified version of Luther's chorale 'Ein' Feste Burg' ('A Mighty Fortress') mentioned on page 6 above. The sign ⌢ above a note is called a *fermata*, and means that the performer must pause on that note. This sign is called a 'fermata' from the Italian verb *fermare*, to stop. The names of the notes have been added below the first line.

Exercise

Add the names of the notes on the second and third lines of Example 2.11.

C C C G B C A G C B A G A F D C

2.11

Suggested Further Reading

Blume, F. *Renaissance and Baroque Music* (London: Faber, 1975).
Palisca, Claude V. *Baroque Music* (New Jersey: Prentice-Hall, 1968).
Stevens and Robertson, eds. *The Pelican History of Music, Vol 1* (London: Penguin, 1960).
Volumes in the *Oxford Studies of Composers* series: Arnold, Denis: *Marenzio* 1969. Roche, Jerome: *Palestrina* 1971.

3

PART ONE: MUSIC IN ENGLAND 1560–1625

During the late sixteenth and early seventeenth centuries music in England rivalled that of Italy and in some ways surpassed it. The Reformation had a much more pronounced effect on English music than on Italian music. The reasons for this are to be found firstly in the excellence of English composers of the time and secondly in the course which the Reformation took in England. The reformation of the Church in England was hastened by a quarrel between Henry VIII and Pope Clement VII. As a result Henry utilized the reforms of Martin Luther and founded the Church of England with himself, and not the Pope, as its head. So securely were the foundations of the new church laid that its organization remains almost unchanged today.

The Reformation in England

However, there then were a number of active composers who had grown up in the Roman Catholic tradition and whose music was for that church. The names of the three most important all begin with the same letter: they are **Christopher Tye** (*c.*1500–1573), **John Taverner** (*c.*1495–1545), and **Thomas Tallis** (*c.*1505–1585). Of these Tallis was both the most long-lived and the most important. He died in 1585 aged about eighty. He is perhaps best known for his canon sung to the words 'Glory to thee my God this night'. But an excellent work of Tallis is a motet for forty singers, each singing a different part. The motet's Latin title is 'Spem in alium nunquam habui' which may be translated 'I have never put my trust in any but God'. The forty singers are divided into eight groups of five. Starting with one group Tallis gradually adds the others until everybody is singing; he then starts to take them away until only one group is left. If recorded stereophonically the effect is splendid.

The quarrel between Henry VIII and the Pope arose because the king was worried about creating a family so that the House of Tudor which his father had started would continue to occupy the throne of England. Consequently he married six times. These marriages resulted in three children, each by a different wife, and each of these children occupied the throne in turn. They are Edward VI, whose mother was Jane Seymour; Mary, daughter of Catherine of Aragon; and Elizabeth I, daughter of Anne Boleyn.

Henry VIII died in 1547 and was succeeded by his son, Edward, who was then aged nine; Edward died five years later. During his reign the country was nominally a Protestant one, although anyone who was over twenty when Edward came to the throne had been born when the country was Catholic. Mary, who succeeded him, reigned from 1552 to 1558 and was a Catholic. She adopted violent methods to stamp out the new religion, for which she

16

became known as Bloody Mary. Elizabeth was a Protestant and under her the Church of England became established as the state religion. Under Elizabeth also the country became strong, wealthy, and important in many ways, particularly in literature and music. Officially during her reign Catholicism was not allowed. Elizabeth, however, was a pragmatist and when it suited her personally, or for reasons of state, she did not prevent anyone she wished from practising the old religion. This was fortunate for music, for the greatest composer of her age was, and remained a Catholic.

Byrd

He was **William Byrd** (1543–1623). He was born in the reign of Henry VIII and died at the age of eighty at the end of the reign of James I, who followed Elizabeth. Byrd is usually regarded as the equal of Lassus and of Palestrina whom he easily excels in the variety of his compositions, and although the later sixteenth century in England was particularly rich in musical talent Byrd dominates the period in which he lived.

Byrd was born in Lincolnshire, probably in Lincoln itself. He was fortunate in his musical training for he seems to have studied at the court musical establishment, known as the Chapel Royal.

Whenever the court dominates music in England the term Chapel Royal is frequently used. It refers to the actual chapel in which the sovereign's private choir performs, but is more often used to refer to the whole of the musical establishment belonging to the court. In this sense musicians are often referred to as 'Gentlemen of the Chapel Royal'. The Chapel Royal choir has existed since the thirteenth century and may be likened to the Pope's Sistine Chapel choir.

Byrd was also fortunate to have had as a teacher Thomas Tallis and although Tallis was nearly forty years older than Byrd, this was the beginning of a professional partnership which lasted until Tallis's death. Byrd was recognized in his day as a composer but he was also highly acclaimed as a keyboard performer. At the age of twenty, in spite of being a Roman Catholic, he was made organist of Lincoln cathedral. He also knew how to keep his head at court, for six years later, in 1569, the Queen made him a Gentleman of the Chapel Royal and joint organist to the Chapel with Tallis. However, he did not give up his post at Lincoln until three years later, and during this time someone else must have performed his duties since he could not often have made the 120-mile journey, travelling on horseback.

In 1575 the Queen further favoured Byrd and Tallis by giving them a licence to print and sell music paper. This caused resentment at the time but was probably done in order to ensure that the paper was printed at all.

Music Printing

The introduction of music printing resulted in one of the great revolutions in the history of music. Before the invention of printing copies of both literature and music had to be individually hand-written. In the case of literature it was possible to secure several copies at once by dictating the text to a group of writers, particularly in the monasteries. With music this was not practicable; and until music could be printed the number of scores available was severely limited and confined mostly to the church. At the very beginning of the sixteenth century, however, an Italian called Petrucci succeeded in printing music. The process was costly, for each page had to go through the presses three times, once each for the staves, notes, and words. Even so, Petrucci's editions are masterpieces of the printer's art. By the time of the monopoly given to Tallis and Byrd in 1575, it was possible to print music in a single impression and, given the proper stimulus, it could be produced in large quantities. The results of music thus appearing in general circulation are incalculable. Scores were available beyond the confines of the church and used by a wide section of society. As music became available in the home a new style evolved which drew both on popular folk music and on the prevailing church style which combined austerity with richness.

Byrd's first printing venture with Tallis in 1575 was to publish a collection of thirty-four pieces for church choir which they had each composed over some years, with the title *Cantiones Sacrae*. But Byrd had by this time also written a quantity of non-church, or secular music. Like many other English composers of his day he was well aware of developments in other parts of Europe, for in spite of the difficulties of travel musicians seem to have embarked upon lengthy European journeys with apparent unconcern. Byrd himself did not travel abroad but was in correspondence with his foreign colleagues. In 1588 he collected together and published various songs, madrigals, and settings of the Psalms which he called 'Psalms, Sonnets and Songs of Sadness and Piety'. This time he was the sole publisher for Tallis had died in 1585; no doubt some of the sadness expressed in the title was occasioned by the loss of the colleague and master with whom he had worked for nearly forty years.

The English Madrigal

Byrd's madrigals in this collection herald one of the most splendid episodes in English music, the *age of the English madrigal*. But there was also a more immediate spur to the craze for the writing and singing of madrigals which exploded in 1588. This was the publication later in that year of a collection of music from across the Alps, *Musica Transalpina*, a work which consists of fifty-seven madrigals by composers throughout Europe. This was compiled by an enthusiastic amateur singer called Nicholas Yonge. The title is not strictly accurate, for some of the madrigals are by Flemish and French composers as well as by Palestrina, Lassus, and Marenzio. Two of the set are by Byrd himself.

This outstanding period of madrigal composition in England lasted almost exactly thirty years, the last collection of any consequence being published in 1618. Even during this short time it is possible to divide the period of madrigal-writing into three; English composers started by copying Italian models and using for their texts translations of Italian poems; soon the madrigals became more English in feeling, being melodious and somewhat rustic rather than courtly; finally the form lost its inspiration and expressed itself in merry *part-songs*. It is also possible throughout the whole period to make a distinction between the Ballet, the Canzonet, the Part-Song, and the Madrigal. But examples of all these forms are found in *The English Madrigal School*, a standard collection of about 900 pieces made by E. H. Fellowes and published between 1913 and 1924. For both amateur and professional singers. Fellowes's collection provides an inexhaustible supply of music of varying standards of difficulty and ranging in emotion from the lighthearted to the intensely sad. Today, there are several other easily accessible collections of madrigals.

There are only a few really outstanding composers of English madrigals although there are dozens of first-class pieces by lesser composers; for instance, in many collections appear Francis Pilkington's 'Amyntas with his Phyllis fair', John Benet's 'Weep, O mine eyes' and John Ward's 'A Satyr once'. But there are four composers in particular associated with the English madrigal; they are **Morley** (1558–1603), **Weelkes** (*c*.1575–1623) (pronounced as it looks), **Wilbye** (1574–1638), and **Gibbons** (1585–1625).

Madrigal Writers

Thomas Morley may be said to be the founder of the English Madrigal School. He was a pupil of Byrd and a Gentleman of the Chapel Royal. His dates are the same as those of Elizabeth's reign. His first book of madrigals was published in 1594 and the first one in the book, 'April is in my mistress' face' is very well known. This shows admirably Morley's lighthearted and careful way of writing. Morley is also remembered for two other musical enterprises: first, he was the author of a book called 'A Plain and Easy Introduction to Practical Music'. The book is far from plain and not very easy, but in it he suggests that if you cannot sing a madrigal at sight you are not educated. This caused people to buy and study the book in order not to be thought ignorant! In 1601 Morley also collected twenty-six madrigals as a compliment to Queen Elizabeth and called them 'The Triumphs of Oriana'. Each madrigal ends with the words 'Long Live fair Oriana'. This the Queen failed to do, for she died in 1603 before the set was published.

It is possible to argue that Thomas Weelkes and John Wilbye are the greatest of all madrigal writers, whether English or Italian. Their music expresses the emotions of the poems in a way which is difficult to surpass. Weelkes's way of doing this was to use daring harmonies which can still cause surprise 400 years later, for example in 'O Care, thou wilt despatch me' from the set of 1600. He was a Londoner and died in the same year as Byrd, 1623. He published his first set of madrigals as a young man in 1597.

Wilbye came from Norfolk where he seems to have lived in style in the houses of the great. He became a landowner himself and lived on until 1638. His first set of madrigals came out a year after those of Weelkes, in 1598. Two well-known ones are 'Weep, O mine eyes' and 'Adieu, sweet Amaryllis'.

Orlando Gibbons' death in 1625 marks the end of this period of English music. As a madrigal writer Gibbons is chiefly known for 'The Silver Swan'. But he is also remembered as the first composer whose church music was entirely for the Church of England, for the splendid flowering of music in England around 1600 included an upsurge in the writing of religious music. This was based both on the tonality which was becoming established by the emergence of the major and minor scales and on a polyphonic style of the highest excellence.

Anglican Church Music

It took about half a century after its foundation for the Church of England to give rise to music of such quality. When the Church was first established, prayer books were issued to accompany the new forms of worship. These prayer books did not at first allow for much music but gradually the church began to generate a music of its own. The Psalms were put into verse and set to music; these were issued under the name of *psalters*. We would think of them as hymn books, and one of them contains the well-known setting of Psalm 100, 'All people that on earth do dwell'. Another development was the *anthem*. This was music written especially for the choir. It is a peculiarly English form of music and is capable of being infinitely adapted for use in the services. If an anthem includes parts for solo voices it is usually known as a *verse anthem*. In addition to Psalms and anthems the *responses* were set to music; Tallis's settings are often used today. Finally, the main parts of the service, the *canticles*, were set in a way parallel to the settings of the Roman Mass. A simple setting of the canticles was known as a *Short Service* whilst a more elaborate polyphonic setting was called a *Great Service*.

Among the many composers writing for the Church around the turn of the century whose music is still used today may be mentioned **Thomas Tomkins**. He was a pupil of Byrd and organist of Worcester cathedral. He wrote seven Services and over a hundred anthems. But the contribution of Orlando Gibbons to English church music places him among its foremost composers. About two dozen verse anthems of his survive. They are polyphonic in texture and are accompanied as often by strings as by an organ. Perhaps the best-known of these is 'This is the Record of John'. Gibbons' hymn tunes are also in frequent use, nine of them appearing in the *Ancient and Modern* Hymn Book. Byrd also wrote for the new Church, producing about five dozen anthems, a Great Service, and four Short Services, all in the rich polyphonic style of the late sixteenth century.

Byrd also continued to write for the Roman Catholic Church and in 1605 published three Masses, one in three parts, one in four parts, and one in five parts. The music here marks a high point in late sixteenth-century polyphony, being intensely expressive; the final section of the four-part Mass, 'Dona Nobis Pacem', is a fine example of Byrd's deeply felt but restrained emotion. Also in 1605 Byrd published a set of Latin motets which includes the well-known 'Ave Verum Corpus', a meditation on the body of Christ. This short work is well worth studying both for the beauty of the music and for the way in which Byrd expresses the words in the music. For example, the highest note occurs only twice, at the words 'Mary' and 'Jesus'; when Byrd sets to music the words 'water and blood flowed down' all the voice parts move downwards; the words 'Have mercy upon me' ('Miserere mei') are accompanied by an expressive device known as a *false relation*, much liked by English composers. Here an accidental which occurs in one part is immediately cancelled in another part. This causes the music to become astringent at that point.

In Italy, Renaissance music stopped in 1600. One of the reasons why it continued as late as 1625 in England was that composers of the calibre of Byrd and Gibbons were still writing in the Renaissance style.

Keyboard Instruments and Musical Forms

One of the results of the advent of music printing was an upsurge of music in the home; one of the main forms that this took was the singing of madrigals, but at the same time instrumental music came into its own, an ensemble of viols being particularly favoured. Madrigal publishers took advantage of this by stating that the parts could be either sung or played on viols.

Domestic keyboard instruments also flourished. Keyboard stringed instruments are of two main types depending upon whether the string is struck or plucked. In the first group are the *clavichord* and, eventually, the *piano*; in the second are the *virginal* and, as its name implies, the *harpsichord*.

The clavichord is a very simple instrument and a very personal one; its sound scarcely carries beyond the hearing of the player. Its main feature is that when the key is pressed down a metal plate at the other end of it hits the string directly. This allows the player to use vibrato so long as the string is sounding. The strings of the clavichord run at right angles to the keys; this results in the overall shape of the instrument being oblong.

The virginal is also oblong and the strings also run at right angles to the keys. The instrument may have two keyboards side by side, each activating strings tuned to different octaves. In this case the instrument is called a *pair of virginals*. The strings are plucked by a plectrum which is attached to a small rod which is pushed up when the key is pressed down. The rods are known as *jacks*. As the jack falls back a spring mechanism prevents the plectrum from hitting the string on its way down.

The principal of the virginal is also used in the harpsichord which is, however, altogether a much grander instrument. It stands on its own legs and because the strings go in the same direction as the keys the shape is elongated, being something like that of a grand piano. The tone of the harpsichord is clear and incisive but because of the method by which the sound is produced the strings are not capable of sustained or varied sound. To overcome this the makers fitted several sets of strings which were engaged by pulling out stops producing different tonal qualities. In order to prolong the sound in slow music there grew up an elaborate system of ornamentation. Harpsichords could also be made with more than one keyboard which further increased the range of tonal quality available. An interesting convention of the time, which is used on some present-day electric pianos, was that the longer keys were black and the short ones white.

With the interest in domestic keyboard music-making there arose a breed of virtuoso player-composers. Byrd was active in this field as in most others. Another composer who achieved much fame as a virginal player was **John Bull** (1563–1628). His music reflects his ability because it is full of notes. A composer of equal virtuosity but greater competence was **Giles Farnaby** (*c*.1565–1640).

Keyboard Collections

Keyboard pieces were brought together in collections either for publication or for private use. The first such to be published was entitled *Parthenia* which came out in 1612–13. It includes pieces by Byrd, Bull, and Gibbons. The most famous collection is the *Fitzwilliam Virginal Book*. This is a collection of nearly 300 pieces of virginal music which is preserved in the Fitzwilliam museum in Cambridge. It includes music by Byrd, Bull, and Farnaby. It was not published fully until 1899.

Music for instruments, and especially for the virginal, was written in a variety of forms. The most common of these were derived from dances, often put together in contrasting pairs. A very common pair is the *pavane* and *galliard*. A pavane is a stately dance in two-time, the name being derived from the Latin for a peacock. A galliard is in three-time and is a much more energetic dance. The music for the galliard is often a transformed version of that for the pavane. When such music was used for dancing the pattern of the dance was repeated several times; at the repeats the music was varied. This resulted in sets of variations being composed independently of the dance itself. The most usual way of varying the music was to keep the chords unaltered but to decorate the melody above in such a way that it gathered more and more notes. A form of variation which repeats a bass line but alters the music above it is known as *Variations on a Ground*.

The Lute

Despite the popularity of domestic keyboard instruments by far the most important instrument of the period was the *lute*. This came to England about 1550 from France and immediately became popular. The place of the lute in society has much in common with that of the guitar today and in fact both the lute and guitar belong to the same family of instruments. But the lute differs from the guitar in several ways. Firstly its shape is different: it has a rounded back and looks something like a pear cut in half lengthways. In 1600 it had twelve strings arranged in pairs, called courses. The strings were usually made of gut although on rare occasions could even be made of silk. The fingerboard had pieces of gut, called *frets*, tied round it to mark the semitones. The frets were movable. The most individual part of the lute's shape is the box housing the pegs; this lies back at a right angle to the fingerboard. The lute is played by picking and not by strumming. The music for the instrument is written in chord symbols of some complexity representing finger shapes, known as *tablature*. The lute is a difficult instrument to play but in the hands of a good player is capable of weaving quite complicated strands of polyphony. It has a pleasing soft tone, well suited to accompanying sad or reflective songs. Towards the end of the sixteenth century the lute reached a height of popularity in England and, as in the case of the virginal, a number of excellent player-composers appeared. The most outstanding of these lutenists was **John Dowland** (1563–1626).

At the age of seventeen, Dowland started travelling about the Continent working for a variety of courtly and royal personages. He did not settle until twenty-five years later when he came to live in London. When he died the great days of lute playing in England were over and the instrument was not revived until the middle of our own century when a similar upsurge of makers, composers, and players has come to the fore.

It is fitting to close this chapter with some remarks about William Byrd as a person, since he dominates so much of it. He was twice married and had two sons and three daughters; his sons did not prolong his name after the second generation. In 1577 he came to live at the village of Harlington, which is now on the doorstep of London Airport. After fifteen years he moved to Stondon Massey in Essex, where he stayed for the rest of his life. He died there, but it is not known where he is buried. Much of Byrd's spare time from a busy life was spent in pursuing lawsuits, an activity which seems to have been something of a hobby with him. There were six of them altogether, well documented, and they concern his property. Some of these legal cases he managed to keep going for many years.

PART TWO

Key Signatures (Major Scales)

The scale of G major has one accidental, F♯.

If you are composing in the key of G, therefore, every time you come to an F it will have to be sharpened (see Examples 3.1 and 3.2). As it is much easier to put the sharp once and for all at the beginning of the stave than to have to keep writing it out, that has become the custom. Accidentals which are placed immediately after the clef determine the key and are called the *key signature*.

3.1

3.2

3.3

3.4

3.5

3.6

The accidentals are repeated at the beginning of each line of music. The key signature of G major is thus as shown in Examples 3.3 and 3.4. There is another F♯ on both the treble and the bass clefs, but these are not used for the key signature (see Examples 3.5 and 3.6). You can figure out that:

D major has two sharps: F♯ and C♯
A major has three sharps: F♯ C♯ and G♯
E major has four sharps: F♯ C♯ G♯ and D♯

You will see that the sharps build up in a constant pattern. They are placed on the staves as follows:

The scales may now be written out without using accidentals. For instance E major looks like Example 3.15.

Keys with Flats in them

If you start at the note F and work up Tone, Tone, Semitone, Tone, Tone, Tone, Semitone, you will find that the B will have to be flattened.

The scale of *F major* has one flat, B♭. Examples 3.16 and 3.17 thus show the *key signature* of F major. The major scale which has two flats is B♭. They are B♭ and E♭, as shown in Examples 3.18 and 3.19. The major scale which has three flats is E♭. They are B♭, E♭, and A♭. The key signatures for E♭ major are shown in Examples 3.20 and 3.21. The major scale which has four flats is A♭. They are B♭, E♭, A♭, and D♭.

F G A Bb C D E F   3.16

F G A Bb C D E F   3.17

Bb   Eb   Bb   3.18

Bb   Eb   Bb   3.19

Eb   Ab Bb   Eb   3.20

Eb   Ab Bb   Eb   3.21

To Identify a Major Scale from a Key Signature

The last *sharp* of the key signature is the note below the keynote.

For instance, the last sharp in the key signature of D is C♯. D is the note above this.

The last *flat* but one is the same as the key itself. For instance, the last flat but one in the key signature of E♭ (B♭ E♭ A♭) is E♭ itself.

Degrees of the Scale

In C major the first note is C, the second is D, the third is E, and so on. In D major the first note is D, the second is E, the third is F♯, and so on. When writing and talking about music, it is useful to have a way of referring to the order in which the notes come without reference to their names. The names given to the notes in a scale in order are called the *degrees of the scale*. They are as follows, and are quickly learnt:

1st degree (keynote)	*tonic*
2nd degree	*supertonic*
3rd degree	*mediant*

4th degree	*subdominant*
5th degree	*dominant*
6th degree	*submediant*
7th degree	*leading note*

In C major for instance the *tonic* is C, the *mediant* is E, the *dominant* is G. In E♭ the tonic is E♭, the mediant is G, the dominant is B♭. You may find it useful to work the following exercises.

Exercises

Write down:
1. the tonic and dominant of D major
2. the supertonic and mediant of F major
3. the leading note and subdominant of B♭ major
4. the dominant, submediant and tonic of E major

Note Values

So far we have been dealing with the *pitch* of notes. Pitch is the positioning of a note in any scale in relation to all other notes, and depends on the speed of vibrations which cause it; the faster the vibrations, the higher the note. We now come to deal with the *length* of them. Incredible as it may seem, most music can be written down by using only five different note values, although more are available. The blacker a note looks, the shorter it is in relation to the others. Notes are given either English or American names; the English are historical, and the American are logical. So far most of the notes we have used have looked like this: ♩

In English this is a *minim* ♩   two minims make a semibreve ○
half a minim is a *crotchet* ♩ ∴ four crotchets make a semibreve
half a crotchet is a *quaver* ♪ ∴ eight quavers make a semibreve
half a quaver is a *semiquaver* ♬ ∴ sixteen semiquavers make a semibreve

In America a *semibreve* is a *whole note*; a *minim* is a *half note*; a *crotchet* is a *quarter note*; a *quaver* is an *eighth note*; a *semiquaver* is a *sixteenth note*.

3.22

3.23

The stems of notes are placed up or down depending upon where they lie on the stave. Notice that the tails of quavers and semiquavers are always to the right of the note, as in Example 3.22. If two notes are written on the same stave the stem of the top one goes up and that of the bottom one goes down, as in Example 3.23. All notes can be made longer in two ways:

(i) by tying two or more notes of equal pitch together with a curve;

(ii) by putting dots after notes. This has the effect of adding half the value of the note on to itself.

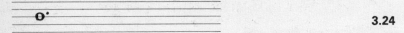

If the note lies on a line the dot is placed above the line, as in Example 3.24.

3.24

Example 3.25 shows the beginning of the National Anthem. It is in G major. The tune starts with three crotchets. The fourth note is a dotted crotchet and is followed by a quaver. The last note is a dotted minim. If you hum from the beginning very slowly and think of each crotchet as two quavers, you will feel that the dotted crotchet is equal to three quavers. If you now hum faster and think only of crotchets you will feel that the last note is equal to three crotchets.

3.25

Bar Lines

Example 3.26 is the beginning of the National Anthem again:

3.26

If you hum the tune you will feel that every third note is accented. This causes the music to fall into a series of regular pulses. This regularity is signified by a line immediately before each main accent. In this way the music is said to be divided into *bars* by *bar lines*. To show that the music has come to the end a double bar line is used. The first bar starts without a line. The beginning of the National Anthem now looks like this:

3.27

The American word for a bar is a *measure*.

Suggested Further Reading

Blom, E. *Music in England* (Penguin, 1947).
Brown, D. *Thomas Weelkes* (London: Faber, 1969).
Fellowes, E. H. *William Byrd*, 2nd ed. (Oxford University Press, 1974).
le Huray, P. *Music and the Reformation in England* (Cambridge University Press, 1978).
Stevens, D. *Thomas Tomkins* (Dover, 1967).
Volumes in the *Oxford Studies of Composers* series: Paul Doe: *Tallis*; David Brown: *Wilbye*.

4

PART ONE: MUSIC IN ITALY AT 1600

The Renaissance in Music

The Renaissance in Italy was a movement which profoundly affected all the arts. It was the result of an attempt to recreate or to copy the culture of the classical civilizations, particularly that of Greece. In this connection we speak of Renaissance Music from about 1425 to 1600. However, in the case of music it was scarcely possible to copy or recreate ancient music since the surviving examples of such music are very few and there is much speculation as to how they should be performed. Nevertheless the Renaissance did come to music. When it arrived at about 1600 its effects were somewhat startling and unforeseen. It effected perhaps the greatest revolution in the whole history of music: it caused the introduction of opera.

The idea of a play which is supported by music is very much with us today. Background music heightens and underlines dramatic points which are made visually. But when a play is entirely set to music it is the music which dominates the drama; the dramatic action in a sense waits upon the music. The *pace* at which things happen can be entirely speeded up, slowed down, or stopped by the music alone. Similarly the *intensity* with which things happen can be dictated by the music and an action can be made to seem either significant or of very little account by the music which accompanies it. One of the marks of a good opera composer is that the pace and intensity of the music and the drama are identical.

The relationship between words and music in a drama was a subject of much debate in the late sixteenth century, both in Italy and in France. In Italy the starting point was Attic tragedy, that is the plays written in Athens in the fifth century B.C. by three men in particular; Aeschylus, Sophocles, and Euripides. The plots of these writers' plays usually concentrate on a single misfortune; the characters are few in number and they carry the action swiftly forward. However, there is a further very important element in a Greek tragedy: the presence of the *Chorus*, which consists of a group of actors. By means of their speeches the playwright analyses and comments upon the course of the action which is thereby slowed down. The words of the Chorus are spoken by all members chanting together.

In Florence during the latter half of the sixteenth century a scholar of great repute called Girolamo Mei collected together everything he could find written by the Greeks about their music. He applied his results to the plays of the Attic tragedians, and came to the conclusion that the chorus parts were sung, not spoken, and were accompanied by instrumental music. There is a great deal of agreement today that he was right. However, he also reached a much more startling conclusion: that the parts of the *main actors* throughout were accompanied by, or set to, music. This was a revolutionary suggestion at the time and today is not considered to be the case, but Mei's authority as a scholar was such that his theories gained general acceptance.

These conclusions were taken up by two groups of thinkers in particular, one in France and one in Italy. In France there was founded in 1575 a group calling themselves the Society for Music and Poetry (*Académie de Musique et de la Poésie*). Their interest was in the way that the words of a play could be set to music so that they could be heard and that their sense remained clear. In Greek poetry the length of a syllable is more important than its stress. The Académie therefore paid particular attention to the length of the notes which went with the music. This method is called *vers mesurée*. The practice of setting one syllable to one note of music has remained a characteristic of French music ever since.

The Camerata

But it is the Italian group who are perhaps the best-known and most important working at the time, on the problems of words and music. They were led by a Florentine aristocrat, Count Bardi, and formed themselves into an active and somewhat rowdy discussion group. They became known merely as 'The Society' or *Camerata*, and their thinking lay in two directions. Firstly, they denounced polyphonic vocal music because, as they said, it tore the poetry to pieces and in any case the sense of it could not be heard. This was a more extreme position than the judgement of the Council of Trent earlier in the century. Secondly, influenced by the findings of Girolamo Mei, they said that music in a play should be used as a vehicle for carrying the words in their general sense; it should not seek to interpret every nuance of meaning as it went along. This was in direct opposition to the thinking of the late sixteenth-century madrigal writers. Words, therefore, should be recited when set to music; thus, what they were proposing has become known as *recitative*. This was a most important conception and one which dominated operatic music entirely for a time and has remained influential ever since. Count Bardi moved to Rome in 1592 and the Camerata broke up, but not before its ideas had started to influence the most advanced musical thinkers of the time.

A further spur to the dramatic intentions of such composers was the form of lighthearted entertainment known as the *Intermezzo*. Intermezzi consisted of collections of songs, instrumental music, and dances loosely strung together to provide entertainment between the acts of a comic play. Intermezzi which were based upon a single theme began to appear as an art form in their own right at the end of the sixteenth century.

During the 1590s all these various elements began to combine in Florence. Renaissance literary thought turned towards tragic plays in the Greek manner accompanied throughout by music. It was impossible to perform such plays using the prevailing polyphonic style. Furthermore the ideas of the Camerata and those of Mei coincided. What was wanted was a single vocal line supported by instrumental harmony. Harmonic writing was already to hand, in the madrigal style, in the direct church style suggested by the Council of Trent, and in the growing awareness of the possibilities of the major and minor modes. The triumph of this single vocal line over polyphony is generally known as the *monodic revolution*.

The Monodic Revolution

The adoption of *monody* was swift and its results surprising. In 1597, only three years after the death of Palestrina, the composer **Jacopo Peri** (1561–1633), who had been a member of the Camerata, published a play with music on the subject on the maiden Daphne who was turned into a laurel tree. What the audience saw was not a play but the first *opera*. The music to the opera is lost; this is perhaps not surprising if it was considered of less importance than the words. However, the music of the opera which Peri soon produced on the subject of *Euridice* has survived. Peri had a rival in **Giulio Caccini** (1545–1618); and the importance which was already attached to the new art form can be judged from the intrigue which surrounded Peri's production. For Caccini was so upset that Peri's *Euridice* was staged before his own version that he contrived to have some of his own music interpolated into the performance of Peri's opera. The style of Peri's music is that championed by the Camerata and consists almost exclusively of Recitative. This method of representing the mood of the words in music became known as the *stile rappresentativo*. Peri's and Caccini's *Euridice* were both produced in 1600. These events mark the beginning of the period of music which we now call the *Baroque*. It is a long stylistic period and does not end until the death of Bach in 1750.

In theory there is no reason why the musical side of the newly invented art form should not have remained as a mere adjunct to the drama. In fact, the form of opera was adopted by a composer of enormous stature and became, as a result, a vehicle for the expression of the most profound musical emotions. The composer was Monteverdi.

Monteverdi

Claudio Monteverdi (1567–1643) is now seen as one of the most outstanding figures in the history of music. He dominated musical thinking and the course of music in the abrupt transition from the Renaissance to the Baroque. He was born in Cremona, and was twenty-five when the Camerata disbanded. During the next few years composers and musical theoreticians were well aware that they had created a problem for themselves, for the polyphonic method of writing had been capable of expressing whatever emotions a composer wished to portray. But during the 1590s this style was superseded by one which concentrated on a single line of music whose purpose was to let words speak for themselves. How was this method of writing to cope with all the complex emotions and ideas which music is so precisely able to convey? It was Monteverdi's achievement to fill out the monodic style and to invest it with music of startling originality and deep expressiveness; and he lived long enough to see the style established in the hands of his successors and already entering upon a process of development. The basis of his method was a precise feeling for the *expressive possibilities of dissonance*.

Dissonance in music is one of the composer's most telling means of giving life to the music, by the creation and subsequent release of tension. During the tonal period, roughly 1600–1900, when music was largely based upon concord, its use was of immense importance.

Monteverdi started his career by writing madrigals and published his first collection when he was twenty. In these works he followed the example of

Marenzio but from the first he added new expressive devices, for example, making the voices chant in block chords or suddenly stopping the music as if in exclamation. Soon after 1590 he was appointed to the ducal court at Mantua where he stayed until 1612. Other books of madrigals followed the first, and by 1600 he had made sufficient impact upon his contemporaries to have become the centre of a storm of protest. For in that year his music was violently and publicly attacked by a canon of Bologna cathedral, Giovanni Artusi. Monteverdi took note of Artusi but did not alter his style of composition. In 1605 he published his *Fifth Book of Madrigals*, a collection which is often regarded as a turning point in western music. The book starts with a written Preface in which Monteverdi defends his method of writing. He calls it the *seconda prattica*, the 'second practice', 'an alternative method of writing', as opposed to the polyphonic method. As the first number in this collection Monteverdi placed a deliberately provocative madrigal, *Cruda* (= cruel) *Amarilla*. To signify cruelty Monteverdi used a startling series of discords, shown in Example 4.1.

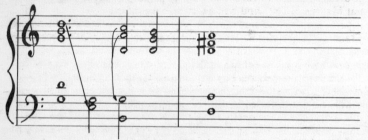

4.1

In 1607 Monteverdi turned his dramatic powers to opera and produced the first outstanding example of the form, *Orfeo*. Orfeo has the same plot as the *Euridice* of Peri with the name of the hero as the title instead of that of the heroine. The fable of Orpheus ('Orfeo' in Italian) both fascinates the composer of opera and presents him with a challenge. For Orpheus was a musician of such ability that he could tame wild animals by his singing and playing. His wife, Euridice, died from a snake bite and was taken down to the underworld. Orpheus followed her and such was the effect of his music upon those below that he was given permission to lead his wife back to the upper world. He was not to look back until they were safe above, but at the very last moment the anxiety of love got the better of him. He looked back and his wife was lost to him for ever.

Monteverdi's librettist, Alessandro Striggio, had provided him with a scenario of five acts, including a marriage celebration, scenes in the countryside, and Orpheus's visit to the underworld. For his orchestra Monteverdi used thirty-six instruments including seventeen strings played with the bow; two harpsichords; three organs; twelve wind instruments among which were four trumpets and four trombones; a harp; and two large guitars. This lavish orchestration gives the impression of immense grandeur; the rich dignity of the opera's opening heralds an entirely new era in music. At different points of the opera certain instruments are instructed to play while the rest are silent; in particular the trombones are used for the scenes in the underworld.

Trombones continued to be used in this way in opera until they became part of the regular symphony orchestra at the beginning of the nineteenth century.

For the vocal line Monteverdi took as his starting point the recitative style of Peri but in using it he succeeded in capturing the pathos and intensity of emotion of Orpheus's situation. For instance, when Euridice's death is announced the music moves slowly and with powerful dissonance expressing the stunned state of Orpheus; but as he resolves to use his powers to recover her the music quickens and mirrors his outburst of passion. Besides recitative Monteverdi uses strophic songs – i.e., songs with recurring verses, music either straight or varied, some of them derived from dances – and madrigals and instrumental interludes. An outstanding example of a varied strophic song is Orpheus's invocation to the boatman Charon to ferry him across the river of the underworld, the Styx, beginning with the words 'possente spirito' (powerful being). But this profusion of types of music is not used in a haphazard way; Monteverdi has structured each act and the whole opera so that it presents an overall balance of form and musical logic. The opera was first performed at Mantua in 1607 and was an immediate success.

Monteverdi then turned immediately to the myth of Ariadne (*Arianna* in Italian), another heroine who was parted from her lover. This opera was produced at the court in Mantua in 1608 to celebrate a wedding, which is surprising considering the subject matter. The music for this opera is lost except for one solo which is sung by Ariadne when she finds herself left alone. This *Lament of Arianna* has remained well known ever since. The music has a softness which is not dispelled by the harsh harmonies.

But it was not only in the opera house that Monteverdi adopted the style of the seconda prattica. In 1610 he presented to the Pope, Paul V, a collection of religious works including a *Mass* and music for the evening service, *Vespers*. The Mass is more conservative in style than are the operas; but the *Vespers* are set to splendidly full-blooded music and if performed stereophonically in a large cathedral have a magnificent effect.

This use of *antiphony* is derived by Monteverdi from the practice of St Mark's in Venice; and it was to St Mark's that Monteverdi was appointed in 1613. He stayed there almost thirty years, until his death. During this time he composed richly for the Church, using both the styles in the Mass and the Vespers of 1610.

He also continued to compose operas, most of which are now lost. But a work which still exists and which is important for the development of orchestral writing is *The Battle between Tancredi and Clorinda* written in 1620. The piece is laid out for four stringed instruments and accompanying keyboard. The instrumental music is quite distinct from that of the voices and provides a running commentary on the course of the battle. Near the beginning is a passage marked 'horses in action' where the music imitates the galloping of horses. But more important is the use of two string devices which have been the stock in trade of most operatic composers ever since: *string tremolando*, where each note is played with the bow going back and forth across the string as fast as possible; and *pizzicato* where the string is plucked.

Roman Opera

The course of opera, started by Peri and effectively raised to a level of great importance by Monteverdi, moved from Florence to Rome in about 1620 and from there to Venice, altering and developing as it did so. The dominant period of Roman opera lasted from about 1620 to 1640. During this period opera developed as a spectacle with lavish stage effects. Changes of scene were frequent; stage furniture was sumptuous; and mechanical contraptions were evolved to cause, for example, people and chariots to descend from the skies or from earth into the underworld. There were two musical results of this: the role of the chorus was strengthened and the power of recitative was weakened. The distinction between *recitative* which was used for purely narrative purposes and *aria*, or song, was becoming more marked. This process was hastened by the increasing importance yielded to the *solo singer*. For it was not long after the invention of opera that singers realized that they were the most important part of it. This resulted in the cultivation of fine singing as an end in itself – *bel canto* – and also a weakening in the expressive use of music to interpret the words. There also emerged a type of male singer who dominated the Italian operatic stage for nearly two centuries: the *castrato*. The tonal quality of the voice of a castrated male is quite different from that of a female, for his voice combines the bell-like quality of a boy soprano with the fully developed power and breath control of a man. It has a wide range and great staying power, and can be trained to execute difficult music with great agility. At times in operatic history the castrato became more important than the composer himself.

Venetian Opera

In the 1630s the artistic centre of opera transferred to Venice. Unlike Florence and Rome, Venice was a republic. The result of this was that Venetian art was not the preserve of the courts or dependent upon the Pope's attitude towards it, but was available to the ordinary citizen. It is therefore no accident that the *first public opera house* was opened in Venice, at the *teatro San Bassiano* in 1637. This was a commercial venture and a very successful one – during the next sixty years, fifteen similar establishments opened in the city. When the first opera house was opened Monteverdi was still at St Mark's and aged 70. He had been writing a steady stream of stage works since *Orfeo* but since most of the music is lost we cannot trace his development. His last two works, written for the Venice opera, have survived. They are *The Return of Ulysses* (*Il Ritorno d'Ulisse in Patria*) of 1641 and *The Coronation of Poppaea* (*L'Incoronazione di Poppea*) of 1642. It is interesting to compare these works with *Orfeo* of over thirty years earlier, particularly in the light of the development of opera in Rome. In these late operas recitative and aria have become two distinct entities. The number of instruments in the orchestra has been reduced considerably, no doubt influenced by the necessity of the Venetian opera house to pay its way; the orchestra now consists mostly of strings and accompanying keyboard. There is a great deal of spectacle in the operas but Monteverdi did not follow the Roman custom of giving an important part to the chorus. Poppaea was a real person, the wife of the emperor Nero; and Monteverdi's is the first historical opera and is considered by some to be his masterpiece.

With the death of Monteverdi in 1643 the operatic tradition passed to his pupil, **Francesco Cavalli** (1602–1676). He in his turn became director of music at St Mark's in Venice. He also spent time in France at the court of Louis XIV, an important fact for the development of opera outside Italy. His work naturally includes music for the Church but it is as an opera composer that he is chiefly remembered now. About thirty of his forty-two operas have been preserved. He was possessed of a great melodic gift which admirably suited the *bel canto* style of singing. In his work, as in late Monteverdi, aria and recitative are separated. The recitative itself also shows an important development with Cavalli; in Cavalli's operas there emerged the convention of setting the narration at a fast conversational pace punctuated by chords and extemporized musical comments from the continuo player at the keyboard. This is known as *recitativo secco* (dry recitative). It is a very flexible method of dealing with the outlines of the story, for the music is completely subordinate to the verbal sense, and the performer is given full rein to act out the part he is playing. This type of recitative is distinguished from a more dramatic form with orchestral accompaniment. This is *recitativo accompagnato* or *recitativo stromentato* (instrumental) and is used to precede and set the scene for an aria which now becomes an independent and set piece of music.

A contemporary of Cavalli who was trained in the Roman tradition of opera was **Marc' Antonio Cesti** (1623–1669). He was famous in his day throughout Europe and travelled widely carrying the influence of opera beyond the bounds of Italy. A further development of opera can be seen in the work of **Alessandro Stradella** (1642–1682) who was of the generation after Cavalli. He introduced contrapuntal devices into his work, and seems to have spent a great deal of his rather short life in fleeing from a bunch of assassins, who eventually killed him, as the result of an unwise elopement in his youth.

Carissimi

The most important development in Italy during the first half of the seventeenth century was undoubtedly opera; but it was not alone. Closely allied to opera was *oratorio*. An oratorio is rather like an opera except that the ingredients are differently mixed; it is dramatic, but not acted; it has recitative and arias for solo voices, it is usually based on a Biblical text; great prominence is given to the chorus; and it has instrumental accompaniment. The composer who did more than any other to fix the form of the oratorio was **Giovanni Carissimi** (1605–1674). Carissimi drew his texts from the Old Testament and his treatment of the chorus makes it a character in its own right; for instance the storm at sea in *Jonah* and the battle sequence in *Jephtha* belong to the chorus. Carissimi's choral writing is mostly chordal rather than contrapuntal and in this way exhibits the final emergence of the *major and minor modes* as the basis of harmony. Most of Carissimi's oratorios have a Latin text. In later developments writers of oratorio used their own language.

Carissimi is also connected with the development of the *cantata*. This is a form of music which, like an oratorio, is similar to an opera but is not acted. In a cantata the emphasis is on the solo voice rather than on the chorus; in fact it is possible to have a cantata without a chorus at all. The text of the seventeenth century cantata could be either sacred or secular.

The three forms of opera, oratorio, and cantata continued to develop in Italy during the late Baroque period but by that time the centre of musical interest had shifted from Italy northwards.

PART TWO

Intervals

An *interval* is the difference in pitch between one note and another.

Names of intervals are expressed numerically: e.g., 4th, 5th, 7th.

The name of an interval is arrived at by counting upwards from the lower note.

The lower note is counted as 1.

The name of an interval depends entirely on the *letter names* of the notes: e.g. C upwards to G is a 5th (C D E F G); E♭ upwards to C is a 6th (E♭ F G A B C); C♯ to B♭ is a 7th (C D E F G A B).

Because any note may be affected by an accidental the type of an interval may alter, but not its name: e.g., C to G is a different sort of 5th from C♯ to G or from C to G♭.

The following names are used for different types of intervals: *major*; *minor*; *perfect*; *augmented*; *diminished*.

Only three of these names can be applied to any one interval.

The basic names of intervals are as they are found in any major scale.

Using the scale of C major the intervals are as shown in Example 4.2.

2ND   3RD   4TH   5TH   6TH   7TH   OCTAVE

4.2

tonic–supertonic	= major 2nd	tonic–mediant	= major 3rd
tonic–subdominant	= *perfect* 4th	tonic–dominant	= *perfect* 5th
tonic–submediant	= major 6th	tonic–leading note	= major 7th

If a major interval is decreased by a semitone it becomes minor.

If a minor interval is decreased by a semitone it becomes diminished.

If a perfect interval is decreased by a semitone it becomes diminished.

If a perfect interval is increased by a semitone it becomes augmented.

If a major 2nd or 6th is increased by a semitone it becomes augmented.

The table below shows all the names of intervals for reference.

Interval			Names		
2nd	major	minor		augmented	
3rd	major	minor			diminished
4th			perfect	augmented	diminished
5th			perfect	augmented	diminished
6th	major	minor		augmented	
7th	major	minor			diminished

From this table it can be seen that:

2nds and 6ths may be major, minor, or augmented
3rds and 7ths may be major, minor, or diminished
4ths and 5ths may be perfect, augmented, or diminished

Intervals greater than an octave are called *compound intervals*. It is useful to name them as far as the 13th: i.e., 8ve (octave) + 2nd = 9th; 8ve + 3rd = 10th; 8ve + 4th = 11th; 8ve + 5th = 12th; 8ve + 6th = 13th.
The interval of the augmented 4th (from F to B in C major) is known as the *tritone*: in the Middle Ages its use was shunned and it was called the 'Devil in Music' (*Diabolus in Musica*). To name an interval it is best to regard the bottom note as the *tonic* and count upwards, remembering always that the letter names of the notes determine the number of the interval. E.g. D to F♯ is a major 3rd. A to E is a perfect 5th. G to C♯ is an augmented 4th.

Exercises

1. Name the following intervals: (a) C to G; (b) D to A; (c) E♭ to B♭; (d) F to B; (e) G to B♭; (f) A to E♭; (g) B♭ to F.
2. Name the notes of the following intervals above C: (a) major 2nd; (b) minor 3rd; (c) perfect 4th; (d) diminished 5th; (e) augmented 6th; (f) minor 7th.
3. Using the same intervals as in 4.2 name the notes above B♭.

Minor Scales

It is easier to deal with minor scales practically than historically. They exist in three forms: *Harmonic*, *Melodic ascending*, and *Melodic descending*; and they may be considered in relation to the major scale on the same tonic. The *key signature* of a minor scale is the same as that of the major scale beginning a minor 3rd above the tonic, e.g.

C minor has the same key signature as E♭ major (= 3 flats), which is a minor 3rd above C.
D minor has the same key signature as F major (B♭)
E minor has the same key signature as G major (F♯)
F minor has the same key signature as A♭ major (B♭ E♭ A♭ D♭)
G minor has the same key signature as B♭ major (B♭ E♭)
A minor has the same key signature as C major
B minor has the same key signature as D major (F♯ C♯)

Given the key signature minor scales may be formed as follows:

1. They all have a minor third above the tonic: this is their distinguishing feature.
2. The *harmonic minor scale* has in addition its leading note raised a semitone, e.g., the leading note of C minor is B♮; the leading note of G minor is F♯. This means that *an accidental always has to be put before the leading note in a harmonic minor scale.*

   Another result of this raised leading note is that there is the interval of an augmented 2nd between the 6th and 7th degrees of the harmonic minor scale. Music Example 4.3 shows the minor scale of C: key signature = B♭ E♭ A♭ (as for E♭ major)

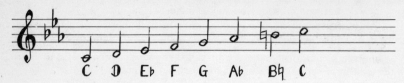

3. The *melodic minor scale ascending*, in addition to the minor 3rd, has the 6th and 7th degrees of the scale raised a semitone from those notes as they appear in the key signature, e.g., in C minor the A♭ and B♭ become A♮ and B♮. Another way of looking at this form of the minor scale is to regard it as identical with its major on the same tonic except that the 3rd is a minor one.

4. The *melodic minor scale descending*, in addition to the minor 3rd, has its 6th and 7th flattened exactly as they appear in the key signature. In fact, the key signature is taken from this form of the minor scale, which is known in America as the 'natural minor'.

Example 4.4 shows the complete melodic minor scale of C.

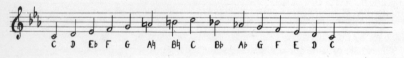

4.4

Major and minor scales formed on the *same tonic* are called *tonic major* and *tonic minor* in relation to one another.

Major and minor scales formed with the *same key signature* are called *relative major* and *relative minor* in relation to one another: e.g., E♭ is the *relative major* of C minor. C minor is the *tonic minor* of C major.

Time signatures

The beginning of the National Anthem at the end of Chapter 3 is shown in Example 3.27 on p. 28. There are three crotchets' worth of music in each bar; or, in American terminology, there are *three quarter notes* to each bar. This *three quarter notes* (¾) is the *time signature* of the National Anthem, which is said to be in '*three-four*' time. The time signature is placed at the beginning of a piece of music immediately after the key signature. It is not repeated at the beginning of subsequent lines of music (see Example 4.5). From the example of the time signature of the National Anthem it may be seen that the lower number indicates the *value* of the basic beat in the bar (in this case a crotchet) and that the upper number indicates how many of them there are (three).

Many different time signatures are possible but in practice they are limited.

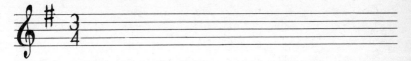

4.5

The lower number indicates usually either a minim (half note), a crotchet (quarter note), or a quaver (eighth note).

The number of beats in a bar is most often two, three or four. However each of these beats is sometimes felt to be divided into three – e.g., a bar may be made up of two, three or four groups of three quavers, each group with its own accent (see Example 4.6). In this bar there are six eighth notes in two groups of three. The time signature is therefore $\frac{6}{8}$.

A bar in $\frac{3}{4}$ time may also be divided into six quavers; but as there are three beats in the bar, one for each crotchet, the six quavers appear as in Example 4.7. A bar in $\frac{4}{4}$ time is said to be in *common time*.

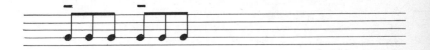

4.6

4.7

The sign ₵ is often used to indicate $\frac{2}{2}$ time or two minims to a bar. It is often casually referred to as 'cut common time'. The symbol ₵ also (and probably more correctly) refers to a time of four minims to a bar which is known as *alla breve*. The most common time signatures are $\frac{2}{2}$, $\frac{3}{2}$, $\frac{4}{2}$, $\frac{2}{4}$, $\frac{3}{4}$, $\frac{4}{4}$; and $\frac{6}{4}$, $\frac{6}{8}$, $\frac{9}{8}$, $\frac{12}{8}$. The last four of these, where the basic beat is divided into three, are said to be in *compound time*; all the others are in *simple time*.

It is also possible to refer to the number of beats in a bar as *duple*, *triple* or *quadruple* (two, three, or four).

Phrases formed by combining these terms often form the basis of examination questions but they are hardly in everyday use. They are as follows:

Simple duple time	$= \frac{2}{2} \frac{2}{4}$	Compound duple time	$= \frac{6}{4} \frac{6}{8}$
Simple triple time	$= \frac{3}{4} \frac{3}{2}$	Compound triple time	$= \frac{9}{8}$
Simple quadruple time	$= \frac{4}{4} \frac{4}{2}$	Compound quadruple time	$= \frac{12}{8}$

Rests

Silence is one of music's most potent means of expression. It is indicated by symbols called *rests*. There is a rest corresponding to every note length.

Rests are as shown in Example 4.8.

breve semibreve minim   crotchet   quaver semiquaver

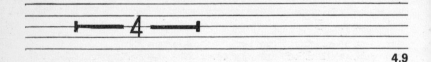

4.8

Rests may be dotted or tied together as notes are (see Chapter 3, pp. 27–8). A complete bar's rest in any time is indicated by a semibreve rest.

Rests of more than one bar are indicated as shown in Example 4.9. The number in the stave indicates the number of bars' rest. In ensemble and orchestral music it is necessary to count one's way through bars' rest in order to keep with the other players. Orchestral players who are not playing in the middle of a piece of music appear to be doing nothing; they are in fact counting bars.

4.9

Grouping of Notes and Rests

Notes and rests should be grouped in such a way that the basic pulse indicated by the time signature is clear to the eye; e.g., a $\frac{3}{4}$ bar may appear as shown in Example 4.10. In sung music it is usual to write a single note for each syllable of a word and to group the notes together only if more than one note is to be sung to a syllable.

4.10

The Brace

When two staves are used in combination, as in piano music, they are joined together for the convenience of reading by a brace, as shown in Example 4.11.

If organ music includes a part for pedals it is written as shown in Example 4.12.

4.11

4.12

Suggested Further Reading

Arnold, D. *Monteverdi* (London: Dent, Master Musicians, 1963).
Arnold, D. and Fortune, N. (eds.) *The Monteverdi Companion* (London: Faber, 1968).
Drummond, John A. *Opera: A History* (London: Dent, 1979).

5

PART ONE: FRANCE AND ENGLAND IN THE
SEVENTEENTH CENTURY

During the seventeenth century the influence of the musical revolution which
had taken place in Italy was felt first in France and then in England. Opera,
which appeared in Italy from about 1600, was based at first mainly on recitative but as the century progressed was more and more made up of recitative,
arias and choruses. This development of opera was apparent in both France
and England but in both countries it was overlaid with national characteristics
and adapted to the prevailing political conditions. In both countries, moreover, the seventeenth century was dominated by a single composer: in France,
by **Lully** (*c.* 1632–1687); and in England, by **Purcell** (1659–1695).

Lully

Lully was in fact an Italian. He was born in Florence with the name Giovanni
Battista Lulli. We know him as Jean-Baptiste Lully. He died in Paris in 1687.
His origins were humble but he was lucky in that when he was about twelve
he was taken to Paris by a French aristocrat to serve in the kitchens of his
niece's household. He did not remain there long, though, for he was intelligent,
ambitious, sarcastically witty, and an outstanding performer on the violin, the
instrument which was becoming increasingly popular in music for aristocratic
entertainment. All these qualities Lully exploited to the full.

When Lully arrived in France Louis XIV had just begun his reign, in 1643
at the age of five. He reigned for seventy-two years although until 1661 the
country was ruled by the Chief Minister, Cardinal Mazarin. However, absolute power was theoretically vested in the person of the monarch, a fact which
was of great consequence for the course of political and artistic events in
France. Both Louis XIV and Mazarin were interested in the arts and during
the seventeenth century France itself became the leader of Europe in matters
of dress, language, diplomacy, literature, and courtly pomp. The outward
sign of France's ascendancy was the building of Louis's palace at Versailles
from which French influence radiated throughout Europe. It was not for
nothing that Louis became known as the 'Sun King'. Lully was drawn into
this circle.

The Ballet de Cour

Even before the invention of opera in Italy, the French court had a dramatic
musical form of entertainment in the Court Ballet. This was a long-established
and highly developed form of entertainment based on dancing, stage spectacle,
and instrumental music. During the earlier part of the reign of Louis XIV the
ballet became a focal point of court entertainment with the king and the
aristocracy taking part in the dances. The basis of the court orchestra was a
body of twenty-four carefully chosen string players known as The King's

Violins (Les Violons du Roi). The term 'violin' here means members of the violin family, for the players formed a complete string orchestra. The establishment of this orchestra was a very advanced move, for in the mid-seventeenth century the violin was only just displacing the viol as the foremost stringed instrument.

In 1652 Lully entered this courtly and musical establishment. His talents were immediately recognized and he was rewarded by the 14-year-old king by being made a member of the Violons du Roi; within a year he was made an official court composer. In 1656 the king established another string orchestra of sixteen players known as 'Les petits violons', with the express purpose of having them trained and directed by Lully. The results of this were soon apparent. For at the same time as Lully's rise to eminence, Italian opera was becoming increasingly known at the French court. In 1647 a public performance of the opera *Orfeo* by the Roman composer **Luigi Rossi** had been given by Venetian players. The Venetians had a style of instrumental playing which was precise and unemotional and it was this style which Lully adopted for his new orchestra. Added to this, he insisted upon rhythmic accuracy and uniform bowing. His methods had great influence throughout Europe. One of the people who was present at the French court to witness this development in instrumental playing was the exiled King Charles II of England.

From now on Lully began to eclipse all other French composers of the period. His compositions from 1653 to 1672 were mostly for the court ballet. He began to alter this established form by inserting into it music for solo singers and for chorus, in the manner of Italian opera. But he also fixed the form of a number of French dances. These later became part of the instrumental suite. Some of these were: the passepied in $\frac{3}{8}$ time; the bourée; and the rigaudon, usually in $\frac{2}{2}$ time; the loure, with a dotted rhythm usually in $\frac{6}{4}$ time; the gavotte in $\frac{4}{4}$ time; and, most important of all, the minuet in $\frac{3}{4}$ time.

An interesting rhythmic device often found in Lully is the *hemiola* in which two bars of $\frac{3}{4}$ time are accented in such a way as to produce one bar of $\frac{3}{2}$, thus $\frac{3}{4}$ ♩ ♩ ♩ | ♩ ♩ ♩ . Under Lully therefore the court ballet was assimilating more and more elements of Italian opera. The move towards the establishment of French opera, however, was hastened by performances of two operas at the French court by Cavalli in 1660 and 1662. Lully himself supplied ballet music for these two operas in order to make them acceptable to French taste but even so the performances were not a success and French opera eventually stressed its own native elements.

And indeed the operas which Lully came to write between 1673 and his death in 1687 show marked differences from their Italian models. But Lully was not the first to write a French opera. He had in fact originally maintained that the French language was not suitable for such a form of music. However, when the writer Perrin was given permission to found a Parisian operatic institution and when in 1671 Perrin and the composer **Robert Cambert** (1629–1677) produced the first true French opera, *Pomone*, Lully was so annoyed that he carried on a series of intrigues which resulted in the licence being transferred to him. He eventually found himself with a virtual monopoly of operatic production in Paris. This was fortunate, for the Lullian form of opera was to have great influence.

Lully and Opera

The foundation of Lullian opera is the orchestra. Its scoring in five parts
corresponds to the five sorts of instruments making up the twenty-four
Violons du Roi. Because these players were more competent than those found
elsewhere in Europe, the parts have a greater range than in Italian opera. The
importance of the orchestra is heard at the outset of the opera in the *Overture*.
The form of overture developed by Lully is now known as the *French Overture*.
This is in two main sections, both of which are repeated. The first section is
slow and stately in character, usually with a very pronounced double-dotted
rhythm, where the double dot lengthens the crotchet by a quaver plus a semiquaver. However, there is a Baroque convention in which this rhythm was
written down with one dot only; and it is often printed in this way today. The
double dot gives the music a crispness which is a fine example of the rhythmic
vitality favoured by Lully.

The second part of a French overture is quick and often contrapuntal in
texture. A very good example of this type is the overture to Handel's *Messiah*.
The French overture after Lully was developed by the addition of a third
section using one of the dance forms. An example of this is the overture to
Handel's *Samson* which ends with a minuet. After the overture the Lullian
opera is usually in five acts.

Great emphasis is placed on the Chorus and the opera always includes a
Ballet. Because of the exactness with which French composers set their language, Lully paid great attention to the subject of recitative; and at a time
when in Italy recitativo secco was becoming quite distinct from the operatic
aria, Lully raised the importance of recitative so that the difference between it
and aria became less marked. A type of writing which hovers between recitative and aria is known as *arioso*. Lully's recitative contains frequent
changes of time signature in order to maintain the rhythmic precision of the
text. The arias themselves became shorter and less weighty than Italian ones
for at the same time Scarlatti was developing the extensive *da capo aria* as the
central feature of his type of opera. The plots of Lully's operas were taken
from Greek mythology as can be seen from their titles, for example *Alcestis*
(1674), *Theseus* (1675), *Isis* (1677). The plots constantly proclaim a conflict
between love and honour and are acted out by characters flattering to the Sun
King and his court.

French Choral Music of the Seventeenth Century

An area of French music which is quite difficult but worth exploring is that
written by choral composers immediately following Lully. Much of the music
is still not published and that which is available is very expensive to buy or
hire. Some of it has been recorded. Chief of these composers is **Marc-Antoine
Charpentier** (1634–1704) who was a pupil of Carissimi. Slightly later is **Michel
Delalande** (or de Lalande) (1657–1726); and a composer of both opera-ballet
and church music is **André Campra** (1660–1744). The music of these composers
combines the expressiveness of Italy with the grand dignity of the French
court and exemplifies in true measure what we mean when we use the term
Baroque.

Music in England in the Seventeenth Century

The presence of the English King Charles II at the court of Louis XIV during the 1650s is an indication of the difference in political organization between the two countries. In France the monarchy was absolute and everything was done in the king's name. England, meanwhile, was progressing towards a constitutional monarchy. Charles II was in exile. His father, Charles I, had been in conflict with Parliament over their respective powers. A civil war followed, in consequence of which Charles I was beheaded on 30 January 1649. For ten years England became a republic under the title of Commonwealth with Oliver Cromwell as its Lord Protector. Interlocking with this quarrel between the king and Parliament and running parallel with it was a religious problem. Ever since the establishment of the Anglican church under Henry VIII there were people who held that the church reforms had not gone far enough. They said that the church should be purified of anything not authorized by the scriptures; they became known as Puritans.

During the early part of the seventeenth century Puritanism in England gained ground to such an extent that in 1642 all stage plays and all public performances of music were forbidden by Act of Parliament. This ban extended to music in church. Church organs and choir music were therefore not wanted and were destroyed in large quantities. The Chapel Royal choir was disbanded. One of the casualties of these arrangements was the English form of entertainment known as the Masque.

The Masque

The masque is in many ways comparable to the intermezzo in Italy and to the court ballet in France. A masque was an extremely expensive court entertainment which combined music, dancing, elaborate stage machinery, and grotesque costumes. It was given by singers who were professional but was danced by masked members of the nobility. For this reason it was on three dances that a typical masque centred: one dance for the stage entrance of the nobility; one for their stage appearance; and one for their departure. Surrounding this structure was a series of songs and instrumental interludes. Each masque was designed for a single performance and for this reason most of the production details of the masque, including the music, have been lost.

The history of the masque during the seventeenth century may be divided into two periods. The first period dates from 1604 with the masque *The Vision of Twelve Goddesses* by **Samuel Daniel**. In the next year the history of the masque was assured with the beginning of the collaboration between the playwright Ben Jonson and the architect Inigo Jones, whose first masque was *The Masque of Blackness* (1605). By 1633 the rather loose structure of the masque had caused it to fall apart somewhat and a Puritan, Mr Prynne, summed up the prevailing attitude towards it when he decided that it was 'lewd, ungodly, and lust provoking'.

However, it is during this period of the masque that the early influence of the Italian musical revolution may be seen. For in 1617, in the masque called *The Vision of Delight* by Ben Jonson and the musical courtier **Nicholas Lanier**, the introductory speech is to be performed in the 'stylo recitativo'. From this dates the introduction of recitative in English. But the masque never developed into the English form of opera even though Nicholas Lanier spent some time in Rome from 1625 at a time when that city had become the focus of Italian opera. For the activities of the Puritans prevailed. One of the last masques of the first period was Milton's 'Comus' performed in Ludlow Castle in 1634 with music by **Henry Lawes** (1596–1662). The second period belongs to the age of Purcell.

In mid-seventeenth-century England there were no composers of outstanding merit although there are several whose work is remembered. Henry Lawes had been trained by **John Cooper** (*c*. 1570–1627). Cooper had himself been trained in Italy and consequently called himself 'Giovanni Coprario'. Lawes is also remembered as one of the composers of the first English opera, *The Siege of Rhodes*. In 1656 the ban on stage works was lifted and almost immediately *The Siege of Rhodes* was presented. The words were by the poet laureate, William Davenant, and the music was by several composers including Henry Lawes, **Henry Cooke** (*c*. 1615–1672), and **Matthew Locke** (*c*. 1630–1677). Henry Cook served in the army during the Civil War and is known as Captain Cook. Matthew Locke was born at Exeter where his name can be seen carved on one of the cathedral choir stalls. He was aware of Continental developments in music and he defended them in pamphlets of extravagant abuse. His exuberant personality is reflected in his music which is notable for the use of expression marks such as 'lowd' and 'get lowder by degrees' at a time when the use of the *crescendo* was not standard practice.

The Restoration

In 1660 Charles II returned from France and the monarchy in England was restored. With the Restoration came a renewed interest in the arts and in music in particular. The result of this was that the native English music flourished but at the same time there was an influx of Continental ideas. Charles II himself was interested in music. Matthew Locke was appointed court composer and charged with writing the music for the king's coronation. Captain Cook was commissioned to reconstitute the Chapel Royal choir which particularly lacked young voices. One of the boys enrolled for the new choir was **Pelham Humfrey** (1647–74). He was a talented musician and in 1664 was sent, at the age of seventeen, to France by Charles II to study Continental methods of performance and composition. This resulted in the establishment in England of a court orchestra of violins based on the French model, for Charles II is said to have disliked the sound of the viol which was by now in any case becoming obsolete.

Pelham Humfrey returned from France in 1667 and was made master of the choristers of the Chapel Royal. He in his turn was succeeded by **John Blow** (1649–1708). Blow had been one of the boy choristers in the reformed Chapel Royal choir of 1660 and in 1668 became organist of Westminster Abbey. When he succeeded Humfrey at the Chapel Royal in 1674 he combined both posts. Blow wrote much music for the Anglican church, including both services and anthems; but he is also important in the rather tenuous history of early English opera for having written the only court opera of the time, the short *Venus and Adonis* produced in 1684. This work starts with a French overture in the style of Lully but the opera itself is expressive in the Italian manner rather than declamatory in the French style.

At the time of the Restoration the current of music in England was not moving strongly in any particular direction. The opportunity for the establishment of a strongly based national opera seemed to have passed; an important era of instrumental music was only just dawning; as for church music the Anglican service did not readily lend itself to the composition of large-scale works. Moreover, the reaction against Puritanism resulted in a great deal of artificiality both in social manners and in the arts. Against this background, the art of architecture had produced Wren; literature, Dryden; and now in music there arose a composer of the first rank, **Henry Purcell** (1659–1695).

Purcell

Purcell's music is conceived in bold sweeps. He had the ability to sustain a mood of intensity which is lacking in the music of his contemporaries. Moreover his music has a sensuous quality which is rare in English music and which derives from his ability to colour in music the sometimes insipid texts with which he deals. This quality of sensuousness differs from the expressiveness found in Italian opera, and is most effectively seen in his sometimes astonishing *word-painting*. His use of dissonance, too, is a personal one; he both accepts the emergence of tonality and at the same time explores its expressive possibilities with delighted freshness. He combined the pathos of the Italians with the pomp of the French. Purcell founded no school; his influence on English choral music may be seen in the oratorios of Handel, but in a sense he remains inimitable.

Purcell's work may be divided into four areas: music for the English church; works modelled on the Italian cantata and known as *Odes* or *Welcome Songs*; music for the stage; and instrumental music.

Music for the English church

Purcell's musical training was as a choirboy in the Chapel Royal choir, which he joined in 1669. He was taught in turn by Captain Cook, Pelham Humfrey, and John Blow. He succeeded Blow as organist of Westminster Abbey in 1679 and in addition became organist at the Chapel Royal in 1682. In 1683 he was appointed official court composer. Most of his music for the church belongs to the period covered by these events, and his most important single church composition is the Anthem. Purcell's earlier anthems are mostly for choir alone (Full Anthems) of which there are about a dozen. These are accompanied by organ. Following these are about fifty for soloists and choir (Verse Anthems); these are increasingly accompanied by strings as well as organ. These works in general testify to the professionalism of the resuscitated Chapel Royal choir. Great demands are made on the agility of the voice especially in the bass solos, which were written for the extraordinary singer **John Gostling** (1650–1733). His range easily exceeded that of the bass clef, from the D below it to the F above it. Purcell's verse anthems usually start with a French overture, in the second section of which the chorus joins. An excellent example of this type of work is the verse anthem 'They that go down to the sea in ships' for alto and bass solos and SATB (soprano, alto, tenor, and bass) chorus, a setting of part of Psalm 107. The Psalmist describes how the sailors are carried down to the deep and up to the heavens and how they

rejoice when the storm ceases. John Gostling's great range of voice is fully
exploited in the storm music; in the rejoicing Purcell uses a rhythmic figure
which is common to him and very effective and which he often uses to express
joy, praise, triumph, and allelujah. This is a dotted $\frac{3}{4}$ rhythm as follows
♩. ♪ ♩. ♪ ♩. ♪ ♩. As in the Lullian French overture, the dots make the notes
longer in performance than they appear on paper and a crispness is given to
the rhythm if the semiquaver is phrased with the note that follows it rather
than with the one before it. Purcell's anthems overshadow his other music for
the church. The *Ancient and Modern* Hymn Book includes one tune by Purcell,
the splendid 'Westminster Abbey', No. 620.

Odes and Welcome Songs

These works were written for the court. Charles II died in 1685 and was
succeeded by his brother, James II, whose reign was not a success and who
fled in 1689. He was succeeded by William III and Queen Mary who reigned
jointly. The *Welcome Songs* were written for either Charles II or James II.
That of 1689 for James II is the well-known 'Sound the Trumpet'. These
works are written for several soloists, never fewer than five and as many as
eight; chorus; string orchestra; and continuo – and sometimes woodwind as
well. As in the Italian cantata of Carissimi, the works are made up of solos,
duets, choruses, and instrumental sections.

The *Odes* were written either for Queen Mary or to celebrate St Cecilia's
Day (November 22nd), St Cecilia being the patron saint of music. Purcell
seems to have had a particular affection for Queen Mary, for the music he
wrote for her contains passages of supreme mastery while the elegies he wrote
on her death in 1695 contain music of special intensity. Of the four St Cecilia
Odes, that for 1692 is of particular interest for it contains an aria ' 'Tis
Nature's Voice' which was sung by Purcell himself. This song is concerned
with hate, grief, and rejoicing. The chords Purcell uses are at times very astringent and in addition he intended the vocal line to be ornamented by the
singer. The embellishments which Purcell himself used have come down to us
and result in passages of dissonance and expressive harmony.

This Ode also provides another example of the way in which Purcell contrives dissonance quite naturally, in this case by using both the ascending and
the descending forms of the melodic minor scale at the same time: the chorus
'Thou tun'st this World' has the bar shown in Example 5.1 which is a com-

5.1

bination of the ascending scale of G minor in the treble with the descending form in the bass. Purcell's writing for the chorus in his works both for the church and for the stage is much more straightforward than that for the soloists. The individual chorus parts move smoothly and easily whether the music is fugal or chordal in character. This quite often results in an imposing grandeur.

Music for the stage

Purcell wrote music for over fifty stage productions. For some of these he merely provided incidental music; in others the music is so dominant as to result almost in opera. Into this latter category comes a setting of John Dryden's play, *King Arthur*, which contains an interesting passage known as the Frost scene. Here the British turn up to welcome a deity but as it is frosty they are shivering with cold. The music, both for the chorus and orchestra is quite straightforward but it is directed to be performed in a trembling fashion (*tremolo*) with somewhat grotesque results.

Purcell's stage works contain one real opera and the only opera of the period which regularly holds the stage. This is *Dido and Aeneas* (1689), a three-act opera of about one hour's duration. Unlike the church music it was written for amateurs, for a girls' boarding school in Chelsea. In its framework it contains elements of the masque and also shows both an Italian and a French element. The tradition of the masque is seen in the choruses which are set mostly with one word to a note. However the choruses 'Great minds against themselves conspire' and 'With drooping wings' are reminiscent of the Italian madrigal tradition. The Italian influence is seen in the clear division between recitative and aria. Recitative, both secco and accompagnato, is used, the latter being reserved for the most important sections and for the supernatural. A miniature *da capo aria* is seen in 'Pursue thy conquest, love'. The three arias on a ground bass, 'Ah, Belinda', 'Oft she visits', and Dido's Lament derive from both Italian and English practice. Dido's lament 'When I am laid in earth' has rightly become one of Purcell's most celebrated compositions. The five-bar ground bass is played nine times. Over this the voice sings a lament of deceptive simplicity with the melody apparently disregarding the movement of the bass but in fact being closely allied to it. The chromatic notes of the theme's first two bars enable Purcell to produce harmony of exquisite pathos which reaches a pitch of intensity at the final two repeats of the bass after the voice has stopped.

The French influence in Dido and Aeneas is seen largely in the instrumental music which is derived from the methods of Lully whose effect can be seen in the Overture, the Triumph and Echo dances and the music accompanying the sailors and witches. In *Dido and Aeneas* Purcell united the European influences of the mid-Baroque period.

Instrumental music

Purcell's instrumental music is either for harpsichord or for strings. The harpsichord music contains eight suites or *Lessons*. They all start with Preludes, except No. 7; and they each contain an *allemande* in addition to other dance movements. Of the other harpsichord pieces several are adaptations from other works. The string music is of two sorts, depending on whether Purcell was writing in an old-fashioned or an up-to-date way. The old-fashioned group contains a number of *fantasias*, or *fancies*, a type of music written for viols and not supported by a continuo instrument. This group also includes the well-known Chacony in G minor, a work on a ground bass which is not dissimilar to that of Dido's Lament. These works are probably the last of their kind to be written.

The up-to-date group consists of two sets of trio sonatas, published in 1687 and 1697. They are written in a deliberately Italian style. The 5th one of the second set is known as the 'Golden Sonata'. These works are for two violins and a bass instrument (the trio) but must be accompanied by a continuo keyboard instrument which supports and fills out the harmony.

Summary of Purcell's Achievement

A. *Harmony*
   1. Dissonance is an integral part of Purcell's harmonic thinking and does not necessarily spring from his setting of words.
   2. He frequently uses both major and minor scales at the same time.
   3. His suspensions often resolve on to unexpected chords.
   4. He uses the augmented triad (see p. 58) found in the harmonic minor scale.

B. *Vocal Writing*
   1. Purcell was possessed of an apparently unending stream of melody which is often made angular as the result of melodic leaps.
   2. The music tends to illustrate both the literal and the emotional meaning of the words.
   3. The accentuation and rhythm of the words is strictly adhered to.
   4. As he developed, his vocal writing became more decorative. He tended to write out the ornaments in full rather than to use symbols for them.
   5. He often set the same word in the same way: e.g., joy, praise, triumph, allelujah usually have a dotted rhythm; pain and grief are set to a descending 4th or 5th.
   6. He is fond of repeating a word for emphasis.

C. *Phrasing*
   1. Irregular phrase lengths and syncopated rhythms are common.
   2. He often works in units of 5 bars, e.g., Dido's Lament and the Chacony in G minor.
   3. He is fond of the $\frac{3}{2}$ hornpipe rhythm.

D. *Ground Bass.*
   A very common means employed to produce an extended movement. Purcell's treatment of this device is varied and constantly resourceful, e.g., the phrasing of the accompaniment need not coincide with that of the bass. Most of Purcell's grounds are based upon the interval of a descending 4th.

PART TWO

The Chromatic Scale

If we play all the notes (both black and white) from a C to the C an octave above it we get a scale consisting of twelve semitones. This is the *chromatic scale*. Chromatic scales can be formed starting from any note either upwards or downwards. The names of the notes of the chromatic scale can be worked out theoretically from the major or minor scales. The usual practice, however, is to sharpen all the notes going up and flatten them all coming down, as shown in Example 5.2.

5.2

The Metronome

A *metronome* is a mechanical instrument which measures how many beats there are in a minute at any given speed. It was invented by **Maelzel** (an associate of Beethoven) in 1814 since when composers have been able to indicate, if they wish, the exact speed at which they wish their music to be performed. They do this by indicating how many notes of a particular value there are in a minute e.g., ♩ = 60 means that 60 minims take a minute to perform.

Suggested Further Reading

Anthony, J. R. *French Baroque Music* (London: Batsford, 1944).
Blom, E. *Music in England* (London: Penguin, 1947).
Dart, Thurston. *The Interpretation of Music* (London: Hutchinson, 1954).
Tunley, D. *The French Cantata* (London: Dobson, 1974).
Westrup, J. A. *Purcell* (revised, London: Dent, 1979).

6

PART ONE: THE NETHERLANDS AND GERMANY FROM 1550

Music in northern Europe during the early Baroque period is associated with four composers, all of whose names begin with the letter S: **Sweelinck**, **Schein**, **Scheidt**, and **Schütz**. Sweelinck was Dutch; the other three came from Germany. Sweelinck was influenced by musical developments in England and he in his turn influenced Scheidt who was his pupil. At the same time, German musical thinking was being continuously affected by the various phases of early Baroque music in Italy. Another important influence was the music of the Protestant churches of Calvin and Luther, particularly the Chorale. However, all four S's were important composers in their own right.

Praetorius

Before considering them mention must be made of the work of **Michael Praetorius** (1571–1621) clearly a man of immense energy and enormous organizing ability. He lived in Germany and left a huge number of compositions grouped in sets. His most important work, however, is a treatise on music published towards the end of his life under the title of *Syntagma Musicum*. In this work he considers in great detail, and in numerous sections and subsections, all the forms of music available in his day and all the instruments in use – the Greek word 'syntagma' means 'orderly arrangement'. Of these there was a rich variety for which he provides charts, diagrams, dimensions and drawings. Today, when many Baroque instruments have been revived, his work is of outstanding importance.

Sweelinck

Jan Pieterszoon Sweelinck (1562–1621), pronounced 'Svaylink', lived and worked in Amsterdam at a time when the prevailing religion was Calvinism. Calvin believed in the value of hard work and considered that success in this world was evidence of salvation in the next. Coupled with this he had a stern disapproval of sophistication. The only music allowed in his church was that of the hymn book. These facts restricted Sweelinck's output for the church and directed his energies into the composition of organ and harpsichord music, for which he is chiefly remembered. Much of his music for both these instruments is based upon variation technique. In this he was much influenced by the English virginal writers who were active at the beginning of the seventeenth century. He was known to the English keyboard virtuoso John Bull who was born a year after him. Some of Sweelinck's music found its way into the *Fitzwilliam Virginal Book*. The variations which Sweelinck wrote based on music for the church are very complex but they remain interesting as music. His secular variations are simpler.

Another form of keyboard composition employed by Sweelinck was the *toccata*. This time his influence was from Venice. A *toccata* is a piece to be played ('toccare' = touch) as opposed to a piece to be sung, a *cantata*, ('cantare' = sing) and was designed to show off the capabilities of both the instrument and the performer. It is, however, Sweelinck's *Fantasies* which are of greater importance, for they laid the foundations of the *fugue* (see below, 'Fugue' and the 'Fugue before Bach'); Sweelinck is credited with the composition of the first complete fugue. Sweelinck was well known and much respected throughout Europe in his day. His most important pupil was **Samuel Scheidt** (1587–1654).

Scheidt

Scheidt came from Halle, the birthplace of Handel nearly a century later. His importance lies in the way in which he established the German school of organ playing, and in this respect his influence led directly to Bach. Before Scheidt the development of organ music was inhibited by the cumbersome system of writing it down. This was a system of tablature which used letters instead of symbols representing the notes. Scheidt devised the method of writing for the organ using four staves each of five lines. For the instrument itself he wrote a series of variations on church tunes. He follows Sweelinck's method of using complex patterns which become more involved as the variations unfold. He also treats chorale melodies in a form which we would now regard as a fugal exposition. In this departure his music parallels that of **Giovanni Frescobaldi** (1583–1643), organist of St Peter's at Rome and the greatest Italian organist of the time. The work of both Scheidt and Frescobaldi foreshadows the *Chorale Prelude* as composed by Bach. Scheidt's settings of the words of a chorale mark a departure in that he sets each verse in a different way, a method subsequently used in the church cantata of the later seventeenth century.

Schein

Johann Hermann Schein (1586–1630) held the same job at St Thomas's church in Leipzig as Bach was to have over 100 years later. Schein's music unexpectedly unites two styles, that of the German chorale and that of the Venetian early Baroque. The Lutheran chorale was devotional in feeling, deliberately unadorned and intended to be sung by a non-literate congregation. Early Baroque music for voices is florid, essentially dramatic and very expressive of emotion. It was these latter characteristics which Schein imposed upon the chorale. In his settings he deliberately sought to express the words in music. In order to do this he distorted the chorale tunes, he broke them up into short phrases, he transformed the rhythm of them and ornamented them with such additions as chromatic passing notes. Instead of using a four-part choir, he often then set the chorale, thus altered, for either two sopranos or for a solo voice. This type of writing led the way to the *solo cantata* later in the seventeenth century.

Schütz

Heinrich Schütz (1585–1672) is the most important of the quartet of S's. His outlook is quite the opposite of Schein's. Very little of his work is based on the German chorale; and although he was more directly concerned with Italy than the other Northern composers, he remained aloof from its excesses.

Indeed, he viewed with distaste what he thought was happening to German music through Italian influences. He was trained in Venice between 1609 and 1611 under Giovanni Gabrieli. He visited Italy again in 1628 after the death of his wife, in order to immerse himself in a study of the work of Monteverdi. For fifty-five years (1617–1672) he was officially employed at the court of Dresden, a city later associated with Weber and Wagner. However, he suffered from the general disruption caused to artistic life during the Thirty Years War (1618–1648), and spent much time at Copenhagen.

Schütz's first publication was a set of Italian madrigals composed in 1611 during his first Italian visit. They follow the practice of Monteverdi in using sudden contrasts of emotion and in the pictorial handling of the words. In 1619, still under the influence of his teacher Gabrieli, he issued settings of the Psalms in the grand Venetian manner for as many as four separate choirs and instrumental accompaniment. In the preface to these Schütz uses the term 'stilo recitativo'. This was one of the earliest uses of this phrase in Germany, two years after its introduction into England (see p. 45). In 1625 Schütz issued forty-one pieces for four-part choir under the name of 'Cantiones Sacrae' (sacred songs) which are good examples of his unadorned style and the way in which he uses discord to underline the austerity of his thought. These works were followed by three sets of 'Symphoniae Sacrae', containing nearly sixty pieces to the words of the Bible. The style of these is of sophisticated simplicity.

This music is for bass voice and four trombones. The sonorousness is heightened by the chord structure implied in the thirds, both major and minor. In 1627 an event of great historical importance for music in Germany was the production of Schütz's opera *Dafne*, the first German opera, the music for which is now lost. Of equal importance are his compositions in the oratorio style. These include the 'Seven Words from the Cross' and three settings of the Passion story, those of Matthew, Luke, and John. The 'Seven Words from the Cross' is a complex work containing recitative, and movements for instrumental and choral groups. Schütz uses the device of accompanying the words of Christ with strings scored in such a way as to surround the voice giving the effect of the halo, a device later used by Bach in the St Matthew Passion.

Schütz's Passion music is the product of his old age and carries his austere method of writing to its limits. The Passions are scored for unaccompanied voices. The story is told in a brand of plainsong recitative, but such is Schütz's control of his material that this stringency results in deeply expressive music.

All Schütz's music includes the human voice. He is the foremost example of how the Italian style can be made to suit a musical tradition apparently alien to it.

Fugue

The term *fugue* is used to denote:

1. a specific form of music;
2. a method of writing music, i.e., its texture.

The following is an outline of the first of these definitions. A fugue is a piece of music, necessarily contrapuntal in texture, based on a single theme

called the *subject*. The separate contrapuntal strands are called *voices*; fugues
are said to be in as many parts as there are voices. Fugues may be in two or
more parts; fugues in three, four, or five parts are both comfortable to work
in and produce a texture which is not too dense to follow. The structure of a
fugue is perhaps more variable than that of any other musical form. There is,
however, general agreement as to what it is that composers more often than
not depart from.

A fugue is in three sections called Exposition, Middle Section, Final
Section.

Exposition

The purpose of the Exposition is to present the subject in each voice in turn.
This is done alternately on the tonic and dominant parts of key. A dominant-
based entry is called an *answer*. An answer may be an exact repetition of the
subject a 5th higher (or a 4th lower): in this case it is called a *real answer*.
However, often the theme does not sound right, literally transposed, and has
to be adapted to suit its altered place in the scale. If so adapted it is called a
tonal answer.

The voice which has just given up the subject, or the answer, to another
voice then proceeds independently, perhaps to a countertheme. If all voices
proceed to the same countertheme this then becomes the *countersubject*. A
countersubject has to be devised in such a way that it will fit either above or
below the subject. This process is known as *invertible counterpoint* or *double
counterpoint*. A voice which is engaged upon neither the subject nor the
countersubject is said to have a *free part*. If all voices have free parts together
(e.g. between entries of the subject) this is known as a *codetta*; the term
'codetta' is used only for free writing in the exposition. When each voice has
entered with the subject or answer, the exposition is complete.

But the completion of the exposition may be delayed by:

1. an extra entry of the subject in the original voice. This is known as a
   redundant entry. Since the first voice started by itself it has not been
   heard with the countersubject. A redundant entry allows this to
   happen.
2. a *counterexposition*. Here the subject is presented again in all the voices
   but this time the parts which previously had the subject now have the
   answer and those which previously had the answer now have the subject.

Middle Section

Here the composer works out the implications of his subject in keys other
than the original one. An appearance of the subject in the middle section is
known as a *middle entry*. Middle entries are separated by passages of free
counterpoint, often modulatory, known as *episodes*. An episode may be based
on the subject or countersubject.

Final Section

It is here that the fugue reaches its climax and it is here that the composer
takes the opportunity of displaying his contrapuntal skill at its most extended.
This section starts with the subject in the original key. This is the only fixed

feature of the final section for the composer may introduce the subject in as many or as few voices as he wishes. If the music continues after the subject has finished for the last time this music forms a *coda*.

Various contrapuntal devices are available to the writer of a fugue. These include:

Augmentation where a theme is presented in notes longer than those of its original form, as in Example 6.1.

6.1

Diminution where a theme is presented in notes shorter than those of its original form – see Example 6.2.

6.2

Stretto where a voice enters with the subject before another voice has finished it, shown in Example 6.3.

6.3

Inversion where the subject is presented upside-down.

Pedal where one note is sustained in the bass, usually the tonic or the dominant, while the other parts continue to move irrespective of it; a means of creating tension in the music.

Of the three sections of a fugue the Exposition is the most predictable. Below is a diagram of a possible exposition of a three-part fugue. Notice that the redundant entry allows the countersubject to appear with the subject in the original voice, and that the countersubject therefore has to be able to fit either above or below the subject.

VOICE 1		SUBJECT	FREE PART	COUNTER SUBJECT
VOICE 2	ANSWER	COUNTER SUBJECT	FREE PART	FREE PART
VOICE 3	SUBJECT	COUNTER SUBJECT	FREE PART	FREE PART	SUBJECT
			Codetta	Redundant Entry

The Fugue before Bach

As a form the Fugue is rightly associated with Bach in particular; its development before Bach may be summarized as follows:

1. The *Fantasia* or *Fancy*: an instrumental form favoured for instance by Byrd and Gibbons. It is based on a single musical idea, and each voice enters in turn.
2. *Contrapuntal devices* such as stretto, inversion, augmentation, diminution, were all practised by seventeenth-century composers.
3. The fantasias of Sweelinck are constructed in three sections corresponding to those of a fugue.
4. The form known as *Ricercar*, which was used by Frescobaldi, consisted of several sections each with its own subject treated contrapuntally.
5. **Froberger** (1616–1667), a pupil of Frescobaldi, unified the various sections of the *Ricercar* and *Canzona* by giving them the same theme.
6. **Johann Kaspar Kerll** (1627–1693) was a writer of fugues notable for their use of stretto. Handel used one of his fugues in the oratorio *Israel in Egypt*, setting it to the words 'Israel was glad when they departed'. A Canzona in C major by Kerll is a combination of binary form and fugue, since the exposition has a repeat indicated.
7. **Johann Pachelbel** (1653–1706) was a pupil of Kerll in Vienna. He wrote many fugues, using a smoothly flowing counterpoint. He tends not to use his countersubjects after the exposition and introduces fresh material in the coda.
8. **Dietrich Buxtehude** (1637–1707) was probably the most important writer of fugue before Bach. His fugues have strength and dignity but are devoid of episodes. This results in a constant repetition of the subject which may become monotonous.

PART TWO: HARMONY

The preceding chapters have been concerned with the emergence, in the seventeenth century, of *tonality* based on the major and minor scales. The *tonal period* of music lasted from about 1650 to about 1900.

The sounding together of two or more notes of the major or minor scales results in a *chord*. Harmony is concerned with the way in which chords are formed and the way in which they are used one after another to make musical sense.

Harmony was the basis of composition, whether in one part or more, during the tonal period. A composition may be in as many parts as a composer wishes to write; e.g., *Metamorphosen*, a composition for strings by Richard Strauss, is scored for twenty-three independent parts. In practice students are asked to write in either one part (a melody), two parts, three parts, or four parts.

The music of the tonal era is based upon a number of harmonic procedures. *These procedures are well established, clearly defined, and can be learnt.*

Triads

The basic building block of harmonic writing is the *triad*.

A triad is a three-note chord and consists of a *note*, plus a *3rd* above the note, plus a *5th* above the note: e.g., C E G forms a triad. (See Example 6.4.)

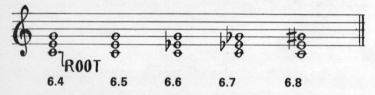

ROOT

6.4   6.5   6.6   6.7   6.8

The basic note of a triad is called the *Root*.

Triads are of four kinds depending upon whether the 3rd is major or minor and whether the 5th is perfect, augmented, or diminished.

1. A *major triad* consists of a root, a major 3rd and a perfect 5th, e.g., C E G (see Example 6.5).

2. A *minor triad* consists of a root, a minor 3rd and a perfect 5th, e.g., C E♭ G (see Example 6.6).

3. A *diminished triad* consists of a root, a minor 3rd and a diminished 5th, e.g., C E♭ G♭ (see Example 6.7).

4. An *augmented triad* consists of a root, a major 3rd and an augmented 5th, e.g., C E G♯ (see Example 6.8).

By far the greater number of triads in common use are major and minor ones. Triads may be formed on any degree of the scale and are numbered, using Roman numerals, as shown below in Example 6.9, where the key is C major. Triads I, IV, and V (tonic, subdominant, and dominant) are *major* (i.e. formed

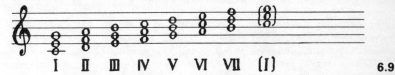

I   II   III   IV   V   VI   VII   (I)   6.9

of a major 3rd and perfect 5th), and are called *primary triads*: Triads II, III, and VI (supertonic, mediant, and submediant) are minor (i.e., formed of a minor 3rd and perfect 5th). They are called *secondary triads*.

Triad VII (leading note) is diminished.

Exercises

1. Identify the triads in Example 6.10 as major or minor, and their keys.

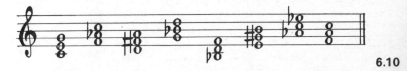

6.10

2. Form both a major and a minor triad in the treble clef using the following notes as the root: (a) C; (b); D; (c); E; (d); F; (e); G; (f); A.

The Forming of Chords

A four-part chord is formed when one of the notes of a triad is doubled. Example 6.11 is a chord of C major with the root doubled.

ROOT

ROOT   6.11

Doubling of notes in a chord

In all chords, major and minor, the best note to double is the root. In a major chord the 5th may be doubled to good effect; it is best not to double the major 3rd if it can be avoided. (But see Chapter 23, p. 252.)

In a minor chord both the 5th and the 3rd may be doubled to good effect.

It is possible to leave out the 5th of a chord without destroying its character. Without the 3rd a chord sounds hollow and without its root it is liable to be mistaken for something else.

Arranging a chord on two staves

The simplest method of arranging a chord is on two staves as if for four voices, soprano, alto, tenor, and bass. The soprano and alto parts are placed on the treble stave, the tenor and bass on the bass stave, as follows. Notice the way the tails of the notes go in Example 6.12. This arrangement is known as writing in *short score*.

6.12

When writing in four parts as above it is assumed that you are writing for voices unless otherwise stated. It is necessary therefore to be aware of the ranges of the four voices which are shown in Example 6.13. It is best to write for the tenor voice in the upper part of its range. You will see that this means using frequent ledger lines. Music for part singing is often written with each voice on a separate stave. This is called writing in *open score*. In open score the tenor part is written an octave higher than it sounds, in the treble clef, in order to avoid the frequent use of ledger lines.

6.13

Inversion of chords

A chord may have as the bass note its root, 3rd or 5th. When the root is in the bass the chord is said to be in *root position*.

Example 6.14 shows chord of C major in root position.

When the 3rd is in the bass the chord is said to be in its *first inversion*, as in Example 6.15. Chords in their first inversion have a rich, arresting sound.

6.14   **6.15**   **6.16**

When the 5th is in the bass the chord is said to be in its *second inversion*, as in Example 6.16. Chords in their second inversion sound incomplete and restless. In writing harmony their use is limited and clearly defined.

The small letters 'a', 'b', and 'c' are used to refer to chords in their root position, in their first inversion and in their second inversion, thus:

> Ia is the tonic chord in its root position, IIb is the supertonic chord in its first inversion, IIIc is the mediant chord in its second inversion.

Quite often the 'a' is omitted when referring to chords in their root position: e.g., V implies the root position of the dominant chord. There are some chords which have a third inversion, for which the letter 'd' is used.

Spacing of chords

When the bass note of a chord has been fixed (i.e., whether the chord is in root position, first or second inversion) the remaining notes may be placed anywhere above it and in any order. When writing harmony it is best if possible to have the biggest gap in the chord between the bass note and the tenor part next above it. Example 6.17 shows four-part chords set out on two staves.

6.17

Note: because the root of a chord need not be the lowest note it is necessary to distinguish quite clearly between the *root* of a chord and its *bass note*.

How to Write Down a Four-Part Chord

In writing harmony, particularly for examinations there is rarely a shortage of time. The following method of writing down chords may seem somewhat laborious but if you follow it you will write sense. To write down a chord of, for example, C major:

1. write down the letters of the triad on a piece of scrap paper: C E G;
2. cross off each letter as you put its note on the stave. (See Example 6.18.)

6.18

If you do this with every chord you write you will be prevented from leaving out one of the notes of the chord and you can see exactly which note you have doubled. If you space the chord nicely you can be sure that what you have written is sensible and acceptable.

Revision

Example 6.19 is a chord of D major placed on the stave as if it is the beginning of a piece of music in $\frac{3}{4}$ time. From it you can study some of the elements of music we have discussed in previous chapters.

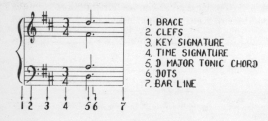

1. BRACE
2. CLEFS
3. KEY SIGNATURE
4. TIME SIGNATURE
5. D MAJOR TONIC CHORD
6. DOTS
7. BAR LINE

6.19

Suggested Further Reading

Bukofzer, Manfred F. *Music in the Baroque Era* (London: Dent, 1947).
Harman, A. and Milner, A. *Man and His Music Part Two* (London: Barrie & Jenkins, 1973).
Palisca, C. V. *Baroque Music* (New Jersey: Prentice-Hall, 1968).

PART ONE: LATE BAROQUE MUSIC IN ITALY AND FRANCE

The long period of Baroque music (1600–1750) entered its final phase with the dominant position of Italian opera finally weakened. This was not because operatic activity had lessened; on the contrary, opera from 1600 to the present day forms a continuous and important aspect of western music. But it was the spectacular arrival of the *violin* at the end of the seventeenth century which mainly caught the attention of composers and released a spate of purely orchestral music of the highest quality. Moreover music for a great variety of instruments, either singly or in small groups, was written in great abundance. And the quality of music written for the Protestant churches, particularly that of Handel and Bach, reached a standard which subsequent composers have found difficult to equal. The functioning of tonal harmony, as outlined in this and subsequent chapters, was finally understood during the late Baroque and used with great assurance. As a consequence late Baroque music is written in a coherent style and has an arresting sound.

Alessandro Scarlatti

The course of opera was influenced greatly by the work of **Alessandro Scarlatti** (1660–1725). He was born at Palermo in Sicily and worked in Naples for a period of eighteen years (1684–1702). He died at Naples. He therefore brought into his music some of the idioms of southern Italy:

1. He was fond of the rhythm known as *siciliano*, that is $\frac{6}{8}$ with a dot in it, as in Example 7.1.

7.1

2. He made use of the chord known as the Neapolitan 6th. This is a juicy chord formed on the flattened supertonic (in C major = D♭) and used in its 1st inversion.
3. His operas start with a Neapolitan or *Italian Overture*: this consists of three sections fast–slow–fast and is therefore quite distinct from the French Overture of Lully (p. 44). The Italian Overture is one of the direct forerunners of the symphony.
4. He introduced comic (*buffo* in Italian) characters into otherwise serious operas.

Scarlatti wrote about seventy operas. They are *aria-based*. Early Italian operas were recitative-based, with the flow of recitative highlighted but not interrupted by songlike sections (arioso). In Scarlatti it is the aria which is predominant – and in particular the form known as the da capo aria which he himself perfected. A da capo aria is in the form ABA. Section B is contrasted with section A by means of its key and speed but is recognizably part of the same piece of music because it uses the same material. The singer performs section A and proceeds to section B, at the end of which he is directed to go back to the beginning (da capo) of the whole aria. Section A is therefore performed again, this time with vocal embellishments in order to avoid monotony. At the end of section A appears the word *fine* ('end') which the singer had disregarded the first time round. It can easily be seen that a da capo aria tends to hold up the action of a drama rather than to advance it: Scarlatti's operas therefore become a series of set solo pieces. This effect is heightened by his scarce use of the chorus. He did, however, pay great attention to the recitative which precedes the arias, using both secco and stromentato forms (see Chapter 4, p. 35). He established the standard recitative ending, whereby the singer's part falls a 4th and is immediately capped by an instrumental perfect cadence. Alessandro Scarlatti's name is far better known than his music; the works of his son Domenico are more accessible.

Domenico Scarlatti

Domenico Scarlatti (1685–1757) was born in the same year as Handel and Bach. He was a virtuoso harpsichord player and is mainly remembered for his sonatas for that instrument. There are about 555 of them. They are now identified with the letter K. before the number, according to the classification of Ralph Kirkpatrick, though older editions may use an L. (Longo) numbering. The word *sonata* had a variable meaning during the Baroque period but it has always been applied to Scarlatti's works; he himself modestly called them 'exercises' (*essercizi*). This name is not irrelevant for they are each in one movement; and for the most part each is based upon a single technical device such as trills; arpeggios; wide leaps; crossing the hands; scales; or repeated notes. Scarlatti's inventiveness with these devices is seemingly endless and gives the sonatas their charm.

The form of a Scarlatti sonata is practically invariable. He uses *binary form* which was much used during the Baroque period for shorter movements. The structure is basically simple; it consists of two sections, each of which is played twice. The sections are held together as a result of being based on the same material. This gives the scheme AB. Section A ends in the dominant or relative major; section B starts in this key and passes through further keys eventually returning to the tonic. Section B is usually longer than section A. The combination of the formal structure with the key structure produces an interesting result – the formal pattern is of two parts, AB; the tonal pattern is of three parts, tonic – other keys – tonic and is thus *ternary* in structure.

The combination of these two patterns in a single movement was of great importance for the development of sonata form later in the eighteenth century.

Couperin

Harpsichord playing flourished also in France during the early part of the eighteenth century. A group of player/composers known as the Clavecin School (*clavecin* = harpsichord) was headed by **François Couperin** (1668–1733), known as 'le grand'. Couperin's harpsichord music is arranged in four volumes, each containing a number of works called *ordres*. A Couperin harp-sichord ordre is a collection of short pieces which may number as few as four or as many as twenty-two. The pieces within any ordre vary in speed and mood but are unified by being in the same key. Most of the pieces are given fanciful titles, though they do in fact use the forms and rhythms of music for dancing. The most extended form, and a favourite with Couperin, is the *ron-deau*. A rondeau, or *rondo*, consists of a main, recurring section of music which is interspaced with contrasting sections. Its standard form is ABACA. Later in the eighteenth century the rondo became an extended piece of music where the sections flow into one another. In Couperin's music, the sections are detached and correspond to the patterns of a formal dance; the contrasting episodes are known as *couplets*.

Couperin's music is heavily ornamented. This results partly from the nature of the harpsichord, which is unable to sustain the sound of a note once it has been struck, and partly from Couperin's own style of writing and playing: Couperin revolutionized the system of fingering the harpsichord. His method of playing and a key to the signs he used denoting ornaments are contained in his book *The Art of Harpsichord Playing* (1716) (*l'Art de Toucher le Clavecin*).

Rameau

One of the members of the French Clavecin School was **Jean Philippe Rameau** (1683–1764). His importance, however, lies in two other directions. Firstly, he was the successor to Lully in directing the course of French opera; and secondly, he codified the tonal system of writing harmony.

In the generation after Lully, French opera had leaned heavily on his methods without producing any work of importance. Rameau belonged to the generation after that, and it was not until he himself was fifty that he produced an opera, *Hippolyte et Aricie* (1733), which was comparable in stature to those of his predecessor. In this and in subsequent works Rameau follows Lully's practice of writing the music in a continuous narrative style, interspersed with ballets, light songs, and dances. He brought to these various elements a dignity and pathos which had eluded other French composers. To achieve this he made much use of the orchestra, giving the woodwind section much prominence: the flutes, oboes, clarinets (here at the beginning of their career), and bassoons.

The intensity of Rameau's music derives largely from his use of harmony. In 1722 he had published a *Treatise on Harmony* (*Traité de l'Harmonie*) in which he showed how chords were based upon triads (*see* Chapter 6) and how important was the tonic triad as the basis of the key structure. He felt that chords other than the tonic should have discordant elements in them. In his music he therefore added extra notes, the 6th or 7th, to the 3rd and 5th of the basic triad. He showed that chord progressions were being used in a standard-ized way by contemporary composers; in particular he studied the works of Corelli. He invented the terms tonic, supertonic, mediant, etc., for the degrees of the scale and showed that chords had a *function* in the tonal scheme quite apart from their pitch.

The Figured Bass

During the whole of the Baroque era and beyond, the performance of music was directed from a keyboard instrument, normally a harpsichord. The keyboard player was supplied with the bass part of the music, and perhaps the main melodic parts. Beneath the notes of the bass part were figures. The figures indicated the intervals of the notes above the bass which were to be played. As is shown in the second part of this chapter, the figures did largely indicate chords, but there was no indication of the spacing of the chord's notes, or of how the chord was to be interpreted to suit the mood of the music. *Extemporization* was part of the standard equipment of the Baroque practising musician. Subsequently the art tended to die away, particularly during the nineteenth century, but it is again very much a part of twentieth-century musical practice in such areas as jazz and aleatory music.

The Italian term for Figured Bass is *basso continuo* and consequently such a bass part is known as the *continuo* part; sometimes the term *thoroughbass* is used. The player is known as a *continuo player* and is often accompanied by a cello player reinforcing the given bass line. When the continuo part is performed or if the chords of the bass are fully written out, the part is said to be *realized*.

The Baroque Sonata

The term *sonata* used in connection with Baroque music has a much less definite meaning than it was to acquire later in the eighteenth century. However, it always indicates music for instruments rather than for voices. Beyond this definition lies confusion, since the situation regarding the term during the Baroque period *was* confused. Mention has already been made of the keyboard sonatas of Scarlatti. Three other uses of the word may be considered: the *trio sonata,* which embraced both the *church sonata* (*sonata da chiesa*) and the *chamber sonata* (*sonata da camera*).

The term trio sonata is a general one; it does not denote a piece of music in any specific form. 'Trio' refers to the number of parts, i.e., three, in which the music is written; it does not refer to the number of people required to play it. Because of the figured bass system a typical trio sonata for two violins and cello would require a fourth person to play the continuo part; and Bach wrote organ trios to be played by one person. Both the church sonata and the chamber sonata may use trio sonata scoring.

A church sonata is a work of polyphonic texture often in four or five movements. It was intended to be played in church during the silent parts of the Mass. The movements are headed with tempo markings, e.g., allegro, and not with names of dances. The basic scheme of the movements is fast–slow–fast, all of which may be preceded by a slow (grave) section in the dotted style of Lully. The slow movement may itself be divided into slow–fast–slow.

The texture of a chamber sonata is that of violin music. The work is usually in four or more movements corresponding to those of the Baroque Suite, most commonly Allemande, Courante, Sarabande, and Gigue. The form of the movements is binary (see the form of Scarlatti's keyboard sonatas above).

The Violin

The violin is the outstanding instrument of the Baroque era. Its arrival in northern Italy about 1520 was an event of the utmost importance for subsequent music. The three standard members of the family are the violin, viola, and cello whose full spelling is violoncello. The double bass is less standardized than the other three instruments; it has four strings tuned in fourths whereas the other members of the family are tuned in fifths. Its music is written an octave higher than it sounds to avoid the continual use of ledger lines. The tuning of all four instruments is shown in Example 7.2. See also Instrumental Ranges, Chapter Ten.

7.2

The fingerboard of the violin is not fretted and the bow is held with an overhand grip, although underhand bows are also in use for the double bass. The resultant tone is clean and loud with sharp attack and emphatic rhythmic possibilities. The violin is capable of being played in a great variety of ways: it can sustain a smooth line indefinitely; it can execute rapid scales and wide leaps; it is capable of a wide range of figurations; it can be played with the bow on the string or bouncing off the string (*spiccato*); it can be played by being plucked (*pizzicato*), muted or on more than one string at a time; it has developed its own vocabulary of musical terms a list of which appears in Appendix II. During the second half of the seventeenth century there arose in northern Italy, particularly in Cremona, several families of violin makers whose instruments have not been surpassed. The most famous maker is **Antonio Stradivari** (1644–1737) – 'Stradivarius' is the Latinized form of his name. Instruments from his workshops and from those of the Guarneri and Amati families gave an impetus to late Baroque performer/composers which resulted in music of the greatest importance. Two forms in particular stand out: the *concerto grosso* and the *solo concerto*.

The Concerto Grosso (plural: concerti grossi)

This form is an extension of the principal of the trio sonata and has much in common with the church sonata. It is a work where a small group of players (the *concertino*) are contrasted with a string orchestra (the *ripieno* or concerto grosso) in four parts: violin 1, violin 2, viola, cello/bass. When both groups play together the term *tutti* (everybody) is used. The movements are usually headed with tempo markings, i.e., they are not related to the dance. The form was established by **Arcangelo Corelli** (1653–1713), a mild man, somewhat mean, who liked collecting pictures and dressing in black. He was a first-class violinist and a careful composer. His method of writing for strings laid the foundations for subsequent composers. His total published work consists of four sets of trio sonatas, one of solo violin sonatas, and one of concerti grossi, all in dozens. The concerti grossi were published as Opus 6 in 1714, after his death. They are scored for a total of seven parts: two violins and cello (concertino), two violins, viola and bass (ripieno or concerto grosso). They require nine players each, since each group has its own continuo player. In the preface to the works, Corelli admits the possibility of doubling the number of ripieno players. The most famous of the set is No. 8 which has become known as the Christmas Concerto.

Also important in defining the form of the Concerto Grosso is **Giuseppe Torelli** (1658–1709). He was a virtuoso violinist who led the cathedral orchestra at Bologna. His concerti grossi have much in common with church sonatas, although they have the string texture of the chamber sonata. They have the fast–slow–fast pattern of movements with perhaps a slow one to start with. The middle slow movement may be subdivided into largo–allegro–largo.

The form of an individual fast movement most often used is *ritornello*. This is the most common form in extended instrumental movements of the late Baroque period. Ritornello is based on a passage of music which is heard in full and in the tonic key at the beginning of the movement. As the movement progresses there are reappearances (ritornelli) of the basic theme either in whole or in part. These are worked into a continuous texture as the music moves from key to key. Eventually the original passage is heard again in full and in the tonic key. This procedure allows a composer considerable freedom in working out the course of a movement. A frequently heard example of this form is the first movement of Bach's *Brandenburg Concerto No. 3*.

The Solo Concerto and Vivaldi

The standard definition of a solo concerto is of a work in three movements fast–slow–fast. This is a direct result of the concerti written by **Antonio Vivaldi** (*c*. 1670–1741) who worked for a great deal of his time as violinist/composer/teacher/priest at a musical convent for girls in Venice. His nickname of 'the red priest' refers to the colour of his hair. Vivaldi wrote over 450 concerti, mostly for solo violin and string orchestra. He published his work in sets to which he gave fanciful titles. His best known violin concerti are nowadays known as the *Four Seasons* – one each for spring, summer, autumn, and winter. These works have delightful freshness which comes from the deceptive simplicity of his themes; their direct appeal is enhanced by the fact that the composer has provided a detailed programme of the events depicted by the music. However, in spite of storms, drunkenness, and skating on the ice the music can be listened to purely on its own terms.

The Late Baroque Style

Late Baroque music has a very distinctive sound. This arises from an understanding and an assured handling of the capabilities of the violin and from the use of sequence, both harmonic and melodic. In particular, composers were fond of moving through what is called the 'Circle of Fifths'. This is a harmonic device in which the music moves continuously through a series of chords based upon roots differing by the interval of a 5th (see Chapter 23). Technically, the bass keeps moving up a 4th and down a 5th while the chords which it supports always include a 7th; the 7th of one chord then becomes the 3rd of the next, as shown in Example 7.3.

The beauty of this sequence is that it allows the composer to stop off whenever he wishes. Numerous twentieth-century popular tunes are built on this

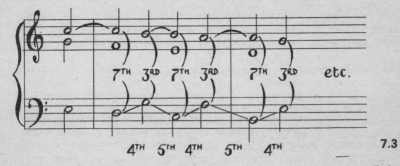

7.3

principal, e.g., the theme from the film *Love Story*, *Autumn Leaves*, *All the things you are*.

Another well-used Baroque harmonic sequence consists of a descending series of chords in their 1st inversion. Example 7.4 shows a passage from Corelli's violin sonata Opus 5 no. 7 which illustrates this.

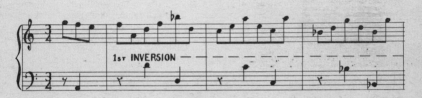

7.4

Late Baroque music is also distinguished by the continuity of mood found in each separate movement, known as the Baroque doctrine of the 'affections'; and by the principle of making the music get louder or softer suddenly rather than gradually, a procedure now known as 'terraced dynamics'. Perhaps mention should also be made of the *Alberti bass*, a means of lightening a keyboard texture by splitting up chords in the bass as shown in Example 7.5. The richness and diversity of Baroque music may be gathered from the fact that it could accommodate at the same time such outstanding figures as Handel and Bach, whose music overlaps at very few points. These men were both born in the same year, 1685. However, their careers, style of writing, and musical outlooks were very different. Handel lived on until 1759, well into the Pre-classical era; with the death of Bach in 1750 the Baroque era traditionally ends.

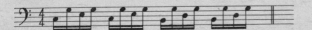

7.5

PART TWO: HARMONY

Exercises

1. Example 7.6 contains four-part chords each with one note missing. All the keys are major ones; all the chords are in root position; in all cases it is the root which is doubled; all the chords are major ones. In order to fill in the missing notes adopt the following procedure:

    (a) Identify the key.
    (b) Refer to the triads for that key (see Table on p. 74).
    (c) Starting with the first chord identify its triad.
    (d) Write out the notes of that triad.
    (e) Cross off the notes of the chord already given.
    (f) Place the remaining notes in position on the staves and cross them off as you do so.

7.6

2. The chords in Example 7.7 are all in their 1st inversions, i.e., the bass note is the 3rd of the chord: for example, in the key of C major if the bass note is B then the triad is G*B*D, that is, the dominant chord V. Fill in the missing notes using the same procedure as above.

7.7

3. Each of the bass notes in Example 7.8 is the root of a chord. Form a four-part chord above each of these notes; for the purpose of this exercise when you double the root put it as the soprano (top) part.

7.8

4. Each of the bass notes in Example 7.9 is the 3rd of a chord. Form a four-part chord above each of these notes; these chords will automatically be in their 1st inversion. Put the root of the chord in the soprano (top) part. Insert Roman numerals indicating the chords below the completed exercise. Use the same procedure as in 1. above.

7.9

Figuring of Chords

The Baroque Figured Bass system is outlined earlier in this chapter on pp. 65–6. In practice the system works as follows:

1. In a root position triad the notes above the bass note are a 3rd and a 5th (see Example 7.10).

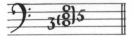

7.10

The chord may therefore be deduced from the bass note and its figures as in Example 7.11:

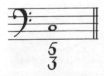

7.11

2. In a 1st inversion triad the notes above the bass note are 6th and a 3rd (see Example 7.12).

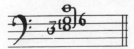

7.12

The chord may therefore be deduced from the bass note and its figure as in Example 7.13:

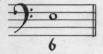

6

7.13

A 1st inversion is therefore known as a *six-three chord* or simply as a *chord of the sixth*.
3. In a 2nd inversion triad the notes above the bass are a 6th and a 4th (see Example 7.14).

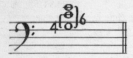

7.14

The chord may therefore be deduced from the bass note and its figures as in Example 7.15:

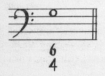

6
4

7.15

A 2nd inversion chord is therefore known as a *six-four chord*.

In this way it is possible to figure any chord.

In practice the figured bass system as this method is called, became refined as follows.

(a) Root position chords were not figured at all. This was eminently sensible and makes a continuo part far less cluttered with figures than it otherwise would be.

(b) Since it is assumed that every chord contains a 3rd the figure 3 is usually omitted. This is why a 1st inversion is known merely as a chord of the sixth.

The three chords of C major given above (in Examples 7.10, 7.12 and 7.14: root position, 1st inversion and 2nd inversion) would therefore appear to a continuo (figured bass) player as in Example 7.16. There are, therefore, two parallel methods of identifying chords, one using Roman numerals (I, IV, V, etc.) and one using Arabic numerals ($\frac{5}{3}$ $\frac{6}{3}$ $\frac{6}{4}$). They are never used together. Both are useful and in practice avoid confusion.

Perfect Cadences

A *cadence* is the means by which a piece of music is brought to a halt, either

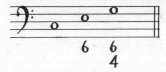

6 6
4

7.16

permanently or temporarily. Most pieces of music in the eighteenth century
end with the dominant chord followed by the tonic – V – I. In fact this
sequence is identified by Rameau in his Treatise (see p. 65) as the basis of all
chordal movement. The progression V I is known as a *Perfect Cadence.*
Example 7.17 is a perfect cadence in C major. We now have two chords in
progression rather than in isolation.

7.17

1. Notice that the note G is common to both V and I and that the G of
   both chords is placed in the same (alto) part. This is something to be
   aimed at rather than to be avoided: it makes for a smooth transition
   from one chord to the next.
2. Notice the ledger lines of the tenor part causing a large gap between the
   two lower parts. Tenors are happiest working from the F below middle
   C to the G above it.
3. If the tenor were given the E a 3rd above the bass part the two successive
   combinations of tenor and bass would be in different pitch ranges. This
   is called *overlapping* and is not a good thing.
   Keep the tenor part up

Example 7.18 is a perfect cadence in B♭ major with only the soprano and
bass parts given. To fill in the other parts follow the procedure on p. 70.

7.18

Music

1. The chords are V I: the notes of the triads are FAC B♭DF. Write these out.
2. In chord V the given notes are F and C. Cross them off: F̶A̶C̶.
3. Fill in the A in the tenor. Cross it off F̶A̶C̶.
4. Fill in the F in the alto. Cross it off F̶A̶C̶.
5. Do the same with chord I keeping the F in the alto part. The tenor then has B♭.

Table of Triads belonging to the most commonly used major keys

		C	D	E♭	E
I	Tonic	I CEG	I DF#A	I E♭GB♭	I EG#B
II	Supertonic	II DFA	II EGB	II FA♭C	II F#AC#
III	Mediant	III EGB	III F#AC#	III GB♭D	III G#BD#
IV	Subdominant	IV FAC	IV GBD	IV A♭CE♭	IV AC#E
V	Dominant	V GBD	V AC#E	V B♭DF	V BD#F#
VI	Submediant	VI ACE	VI BDF#	VI CE♭G	VI C#EG#
VII	Leading Note	VII BDF	VII C#EG	VII DFA♭	VII D#F#A

F	G	A♭	A	B♭
I FAC	I GBD	I A♭CE♭	I AC#E	I B♭DF
II GB♭D	II ACE	II B♭D♭F	II BDF#	II CE♭G
III ACE	III BDF#	III CE♭G	III C#EG#	III DFA
IV B♭DF	IV CEG	IV D♭FA♭	IV DF#A	IV E♭GB♭
V CEG	V DF#A	V E♭GB♭	V EG#B	V FAC
VI DFA	VI EGB	VI FA♭C	VI F#AC#	VI GB♭D
VII EGB♭	VII F#AC	VII GB♭D♭	VII G#BD	VII ACE♭

Suggested Further Reading

Baines, Anthony, ed. *Musical Instruments through the Ages* (London: Penguin, 1961).
Hogwood, C. *The Trio Sonata* (London: BBC Publications, 1979).
Hutchings, A. *The Baroque Concerto* (London: Faber, 1978).
Kolneder, W. *Antonio Vivaldi, His Life and Work* (London: Faber, 1970).
Rameau, J.-P. *Treatise on Harmony* trans. Philip Gosset (Dover, 1971).
Talbot, Michael. *Vivaldi* (London: BBC Music Guides).

8

PART ONE: HANDEL AND MUSIC IN ENGLAND IN THE EIGHTEENTH CENTURY

Foreign Musicians in England

After the death of Purcell in 1695 English native musical talent settled down to a lengthy period of inactivity. Throughout the whole of the eighteenth and for much of the nineteenth centuries very little English music of consequence was written. During the eighteenth century, however, the vacuum thus created was amply and richly filled by a vigorous musical activity from abroad. London became an accurate reflection of every type of music on the continent. The court was actively engaged in promoting both composition and performance, at least during the reigns of the first two Georges (1715–1760). Teachers, performers, and composers came either to visit or to live. A constant supply of singers of the highest quality and of uncertain temperament made London their headquarters; they were either Italian or gave themselves Italian names. An outstanding Italian violinist/composer was **Francesco Geminiani** (1687–1762). He arrived in London in 1714 and stayed for the rest of his life. He was a pupil of Corelli whose teaching he embodied in a work *The Art of Playing on the Violin* which was published in London and had great influence on subsequent string technique. Among others who later came were the youngest son of **Bach, Johann Christian** – the 'London' Bach – (1735–1782) and the viola da gamba player Carl Friedrich Abel (1723–1787). Those who visited for a season or more included **Gluck**, **Mozart**, and **Haydn**. There was, then, nothing unusual in the fact that Handel made London his home for nearly half a century and that, as far as was possible, he became a British citizen. But his presence during that time dominated the musical scene and affected the course of music in England in a way whose influence can still be seen today.

As a man Handel was intelligent and shrewd, hot-tempered, generous and compassionate, cosmopolitan in his outlook, equally at home with members of the artistic and literary worlds as with members of the business community. His music is based on a superb gift for strong melody couched in a style of simple grandeur; it is music of inspired obviousness. He appeals equally to the scholar and to the ordinary music lover. His career falls into three phases of which the last is the most extended: his early years, to 1706 in Germany; 1706–1710 in Italy; and from 1710 until his death, in England.

Handel: the Early Years

George Frederick Handel (1685–1759) was born in Halle, a small town in central Germany. He was in his youth the victim of a wide generation gap. His father, 63 years older than he was, was disappointed to find his son turning into a musician instead of a lawyer. Handel was lucky to find locally a teacher, a professional composer and organist of some standing, in **Friedrich**

Wilhelm Zachau (1663–1712). From him Handel learned both advanced composition and performance, playing the oboe and violin as well as the keyboard instruments. He was made cathedral organist at seventeen but outgrew the facilities which his home town offered. In 1703 he left for Hamburg which was the German operatic centre. He established himself there and at nineteen had composed his first opera, *Almira*. This was performed at Hamburg in 1705 with some success. He left Hamburg the next year and wandered about Italy for the four years from 1706–1710.

These years were extremely important for the development of his career and produced some splendid music from him. He visited all the major centres of music and met both Alessandro and Domenico Scarlatti and Corelli. Italian music, both instrumental and operatic, was in a flourishing condition. Handel wrote with youthful zest and complete assurance in the prevailing style; his music at that time was much more complex and florid than it was later to become. His importance as a composer of the first rank was recognized. Although he was a Lutheran he handled Catholic texts with complete conviction; his setting of Psalm 110, *Dixit Dominus*, for five-part choir is a splendidly virile piece of music and presents choral difficulties which his later music does not. His greatest success of this period was the opera *Agrippina*, written for Venice in 1709. What attracted the audiences was the freshness of his melody and the spaciousness with which the music expands far beyond the point at which it might have ended. In 1710 he left Italy to become the Director of Music at the court of the Elector of Hanover. Almost immediately he was given permission to go to England.

Handel in London

In the London season of 1710–1711 Handel's opera *Rinaldo* took the capital by storm. Rinaldo was the first of more than forty operas which Handel wrote for the London stage over the next thirty years. He returned to Hanover and in 1712 was given permission to visit London a second time. This time he stayed. He was given a pension by Queen Anne who died in 1714 with none of her fourteen children alive to succeed her. In the confusion surrounding the Stuart succession it is perhaps possible that Handel could have foreseen that George Elector of Hanover would become George I of England; his great-grandfather had been James I. However, the accession was a cause of some embarrassment to Handel. The legend exists that the composer was restored to favour after having composed and conducted a suite of pieces for wind instruments during a royal boating party on the Thames. But the story is now generally discredited. Certainly *The Water Music* suite was published some twenty-five years later, in 1740. Between 1716 and 1720 Handel wrote no opera. Instead he worked for the Duke of Chandos at his estate at Cannons near Edgware. The most important works of this period are the *Chandos Anthems*. In these Handel showed that he had fully mastered and absorbed the Anglican choral style; his career as a writer of oratorio had already begun. He left Cannons in 1720 and continued on the course of opera writing which was to keep him working for 21 years. The best of these operas are *Ottone* (1723), *Giulio Cesare* (1724), *Admeto* (1727), *Alcina* (1735), *Serse* (1738), and *Deidamia* (1741). These are all serious operas except for the last two which incorporate comic scenes. *Serse* has achieved unwitting fame from its opening number which has become known as 'Handel's Largo'. This tune is an excellent example of the fullness of a Handelian melody; today it is usually played much more slowly than the composer intended.

Handel's Operas

Handel's operatic career was not without its troubles. In 1720 a group of businessmen founded a Royal Academy of Music which lasted until 1728. Both Handel and **Giovanni Bononcini** (1670–1747) were engaged to write for the Academy. Professional rivalry between the two composers caused much unpleasantness. Handel also had trouble with his singers. Whether it is mechanically possible actually to hold a lady out of a window until she agrees to sing what was wanted is doubtful; but certainly there are reports of catcalls and hissing on stage between the actresses Cuzzoni and Faustina. In 1727 George II came to the throne. He and his son, Frederick Prince of Wales, took sides in the operatic war, each backing a different organization, both of which were bankrupt by 1737. But the new king had doubled Handel's pension to £400 a year. For the coronation Handel had composed four anthems the first of which, *Zadok the Priest*, has been performed at British coronations ever since.

Further damage to the progress of Italian opera was caused in 1728 by the production of *The Beggar's Opera*. This was promoted by John Rich with words by John Gay and music arranged from popular tunes by **Johann Pepusch** (1667–1752). It was a *ballad opera*, and is a forerunner of musical comedy. It satirized Italian opera and was immensely successful. *The Beggar's Opera* was modernized, again with great success, by Kurt Weill in 1928 with the title of *The Threepenny Opera* (*Die Dreigroschenoper*).

After the collapse of The Royal Academy Handel and a colleague ran the King's Theatre themselves as a commercial venture for the promotion of opera. In 1737 Handel's health gave way and he went abroad to recuperate. Social pressures were bringing Italian opera in London to an end; but by that time Handel had already turned his attention to the composition of oratorio.

Handel's operas are composed according to the traditional methods of *opera seria*. They usually start with a French overture and are made up of recitative, both secco and accompagnato, arias and arioso passages, duets, and choral ensembles for the soloists combined. The number of arias and their different types were dictated by the demands of the solo singers; of these there were six, three women and three men; the first woman was a high soprano, the second a contralto and the third usually took a man's part. Of the men two were castrati, one a soprano and the other an alto; the third man was a tenor. Exceptionally the cast included a fourth man, a bass. There were five types of aria which were given to the singers strictly according to convention. The most important person on the stage was the first castrato. In particular the main characters (prima donna, primo uomo) had to be given a definite number of *exit arias* at the end of which they could sweep off the stage amid much applause. To these conventional ingredients Handel added another, essentially dramatic, one in the form of a complete musical scene (*scena*). The scena was reserved for the principal characters and allows the drama to develop unhindered by the demands of the da capo aria.

Handel's operas may be divided according to subjects: historical, e.g., *Giulio Cesare* (1724); classical, e.g., *Arianna* (1734); and romantic, e.g., *Alcina* (1735).

Most of the operas contain music in siciliano rhythm (p. 63). Great care is given to the orchestral writing which is used not merely to support the voice. In particular the writing for strings uses all the resources of the time. Handel's operas contain some of his most forceful music, for the da capo aria did not prevent him from presenting his characters with profound human insight. The recitatives move swiftly and surely; in both recitative and aria the thoughts, hopes, and passions of the characters succeed each other in music of great variety and dazzling brilliance.

The Oratorios

Handel's decision to concentrate on the writing of oratorio after 1737 was the result of a shrewd calculation of the artistic possibilities of the medium and of the social acceptability of music for the concert hall rather than for the theatre. Lacking the support of the nobility he started writing for the increasingly prosperous and artistically aware middle class. In doing so he combined the English choral tradition, stemming from Byrd through Purcell, with the form of oratorio developed by Carissimi. He transmuted these elements and perfected a form whose success was immediate and which shows no sign of waning today. Even before the end of the eighteenth century, massive performances of Handel's oratorios were being given in Westminster Abbey. Handel's choral works set to English words start as far back as 1713 with the *Te Deum* and *Jubilate* written to celebrate the Peace of Utrecht. A few years later, at Cannons, came the delightful work *Acis and Galatea*, a serenata, which paints an idyllic picture of rural peace that the presence of the one-eyed monster Polyphemus among the characters does little to dispel. The work included such well-known numbers as 'Love in her eyes sits playing' and 'O ruddier than the cherry'. But it was with *Saul* and *Israel in Egypt* of 1739 that the Handelian oratorio took its definitive shape.

Handel's oratorios contain much the same ingredients as his operas but the mixture is different. The oratorio usually starts with a French overture, sometimes with a dance movement added to the strict Lullian formula as in *Samson* (1743), and continues with a succession of recitatives, arias, duets, and choruses. The words are in English. Performances are intended for the concert hall, not the opera house or the church, for not all of them are on sacred subjects. Of the secular oratorios *Semele* (1744) and *Alexander's Feast* (1736) are both outstanding works, rarely heard. The texts of the sacred oratorios are drawn particularly from the Old Testament. In this respect they were aimed at the middle class whose education stemmed from the Bible. The texts often have relevance to national causes of rejoicing, for example *Judas Maccabaeus* (1747) celebrates the battle of Culloden. But the most important aspect of a Handel oratorio is the use of the chorus. The chorus is central to both Handel's dramatic and to his musical purpose; it bears the weight of the work; in this respect it usurps the function of the aria in opera. This method of working is ideally suited to Handel's ability to create grandiose effects by the most direct means.

Messiah (1742) is by far the most universally popular of all Handel's work. It is a somewhat unrepresentative oratorio in that it does not tell a story; rather the life of Christ is inferred from the text. The fact of the Crucifixion, for example, is embodied in the five bars of recitative of number

31. *The Messiah* is, however, a true example of Handel's pictorial method and of his splendid use of the chorus. For example, the music of 'All we like sheep' goes in two directions at 'have gone astray'; it twists upon itself at 'we have turned'; it stubbornly insists on one note at 'every one to his own way'. The Hallelujah chorus presents a favourite structural device of Handel's. One idea is presented (Hallelujah), shortly followed by another (For the Lord God omnipotent). These two ideas are then combined and together lead on to greater things. (The custom of English audiences standing during the singing of this chorus started with George II at the first London performance; the king was affected by the music, and stood up, causing everybody else to do the same.) *The Messiah* was composed in three weeks, between 22 August and 12 September 1741.

Instrumental Music

By far the greater part of Handel's music contains voices, although he left a large amount of music for instruments. The set of Harpsichord Suites of 1720 contains examples of most of the keyboard forms of the time. No. 5 in E contains variations upon the tune known as 'The Harmonious Blacksmith'. There are two sets of organ concerti, published as op. 4 and op. 7; this type of work seems to have been an invention of Handel's; in it he combined the forms of organ solo and concerto grosso. His purely orchestral works include the *Water Music* and the *Fireworks Music*, the latter being written to celebrate the Peace of Aix-la-Chapelle in 1748 and causing a fire in Green Park.

The concerti grossi represent Handel's main contribution to orchestral music. There are two sets, op. 3 containing six works for wind and strings and op. 6 containing twelve works for strings alone. The op. 3 set are often known as the oboe concertos. It is possible to regard Handel's op. 6 as the culmination of all concerto grosso writing. It is supposed that they were put together some time in September 1739 each one taking a day in its composition. They are not all concerti grossi in the strict Corellian sense; some are suites for strings (sonata da chiesa); some movements resemble the solo violin concerto. Today they are usually recorded on three discs; the placing of the stylus practically anywhere produces superb music. The first movement (Larghetto) of No. 4, the Musette of No. 6, the first Allegro of No. 9 or the Larghetto of No. 12 are all superb examples of Handel's style.

Handel became blind later in life. Tradition has it that he was operated on by the same surgeon who attended on Bach and with equal lack of success. When he died he was buried in Westminster Abbey where there is a monument to him. He did not marry and no scandal attaches to his name. He left a large fortune. Handel was an inveterate borrower of his own and other people's music, especially when ill or pushed for time; using other people's music in your own compositions was a common Baroque practice. The problem of which passages in a Handel work are not original to it has become important in relation to the importance of Handel himself.

Arne and Boyce

Although it was to Handel that the nation turned to celebrate its coronations, victories or acts of peace two at least of his English contemporaries deserve notice, Arne and Boyce.

Thomas Augustine Arne (1710–1778) was a prolific writer of music for the
stage. His works vary from incidental music for productions of Shakespeare
at Drury Lane to a full-scale Baroque Italian opera, *Artaxerxes* (1762). His
music is simply expressed and technically competent. He is the composer of
'Rule, Britannia', which forms the finale of the masque, *Alfred*, performed in
1740. There exists a pleasing arrangement of the National Anthem by Arne.
He was oppressed by the overwhelming presence of Handel.

William Boyce (1710–1779) was steeped in the Anglican tradition. He
became composer to the Chapel Royal producing anthems and services some
of which are still performed. His main work was the collection in three
volumes of what he considered the most important cathedral music written
during the previous two centuries. Like Arne he was responsible for stage
works at Drury Lane. He wrote 'Heart of Oak'. Of Handel's borrowings he
said, 'He takes pebbles and converts them to diamonds.'

PART TWO: HARMONY

Cadential Formulae

The progression II–V–I

The standard way of ending a piece of music in the eighteenth century was with a perfect cadence (V–I). There are various conventional ways of leading up to this cadence. One of the commonest is by using chord II. This produces the formula II–V–I (see Example 8.1). The melody here consists of DDC. If

II   V   I

8.1

you look at the triads of II, V, and I in C major you will see that they do harmonize these melody notes: II = DFA V = GBD I = CEG. Example 8.2 shows the end of a melody in Bb major. The notes are CABb. We can test the

8.2

II–V–I formula here as follows: in Bb major II = CEbG V = FAC I = BbDF. The notes CABb may therefore be harmonized as shown in Example 8.3.

II   V   I

8.3

Exercise

1. Fill in the alto and tenor of the melodies in Example 8.4. Do not forget to

8.4

write out each of the triads as you use them. You will notice that in all
these progressions the bass line jumps about. It becomes smoother if instead
of chord II in its root position we use IIb (1st inversion). For instance the
bass line of the first example above becomes as shown in Example 8.5: IIb–

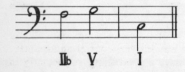

8.5

IIb–V–I is therefore a little more sophisticated than II–V–I. Example 8.2 in Bb
can be completed using IIb–V–I as shown in Example 8.6.

8.6

2. Now try the exercises in Example 8.7 using IIb–V–I.

8.7

Consecutive 5ths and Octaves

If when writing harmony you find that any two parts in successive chords are moving in the same direction a 5th or an octave apart, you must rewrite one or both of the chords. They are known as consecutive 5ths and octaves. For nearly 500 years they were unacceptable in part-writing. Example 8.8 shows

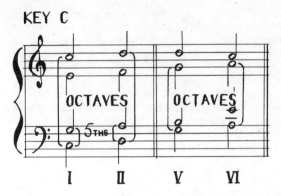

8.8

them. Consecutive 5ths and octaves are most insidious things. Corelli, an otherwise courteous man, tried to bluff his way for years out of an argument over the passage in Example 8.9. It is always a good thing, particularly in examination harmony, to go through each exercise with the express intention of spotting consecutives. If they are there the examiner will be sure to find them!

8.9

The Cadential Six-Four

It is comparatively easy to deal with 2nd inversion ($\frac{6}{4}$ or 'six-four' or 'c') chords. Their uses are limited and clearly defined. One of the four ways in which they may be used is in connection with the perfect cadence. They may be incorporated into the IIb–V–I scheme by using the 2nd inversion of the tonic before the cadence, producing IIb–*Ic*–V–I. This formula can harmonize all the many pieces of music which come to rest as shown in Example 8.10.

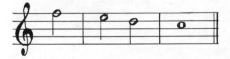

8.10

The rules for using Ic in a cadence include V as well. Take them together, Ic–V, and work as shown in Examples 8.11 and 8.13.

    (IIb)   Ic   V   (I)

8.11

1. Double the bass note in both Ic and V, keeping the doubled note in the same part (see Example 8.12).

    (IIb)   Ic   V   (I)

8.12

    (IIb)   Ic   Y   (I)

    Ic   V   I

8.13

2. The remaining two notes of each chord will then move to the next note down the scale. You will find that they are either a 6th apart or a 3rd apart depending on which notes of the chords are at the top (see Example 8.13).

Exercise
At this point it is worth pausing until you can say the above two rules by heart. Then try filling in the alto and tenor in Example 8.14.

3.

8.14

VI IIb Ic V I

To recapitulate: the perfect cadence V–I is often led up to by IIb or II, making IIb (II)–V–I. This may be filled out with a cadential six-four, making IIb–Ic–V–I. This formula can be (and often was) led up to by chord VI, making a grand flourish of VI–IIb–Ic–V–I. It is shown in Example 8.15, and is very useful and well worth remembering.

8.15

Suggested Further Reading

Abrahams, G. (ed.) *Handel: A Symposium* (Oxford: OUP, 1954).
Blom, E. *Music in England* (London: Pelican, 1942).
Sadie, S. *Handel* (London: Cabler, 1962).
Walker, E. *The History of Music in England* (Da Capo, 1978).

9

PART ONE: BACH

Bach occupies a central and dominant position in the history of western music. During his lifetime the Baroque contrapuntal method of writing had begun to give way to a system which was largely chordal. Counterpoint is horizontal; harmony is vertical. In Bach's music these two aspects of composition appear in balance. Bach moreover was a composer of supreme technical ability whose music reflects the deepest of human emotions. His music, therefore, appears to stand outside of time; he himself dedicated all his mature works to God; and although symbolism plays a great part in his work he conceived of music as an abstract art. It is music written for an idealized performance. In our own day we have seen how Bach's music can be interpreted either electronically or with wordless vocalizing or arranged for various combinations of instruments; we have seen how his long melodies can be adapted to the popular idiom; and still his musical thought survives intact. Every branch of music that he touched he ennobled and brought to perfection. With the death of Bach in 1750 the Baroque period is said to end.

Life

Johann Sebastian Bach (1685–1750, J. S. Bach) was born at Eisenach, a small town in central Germany. He came from a family which from the sixteenth to eighteenth centuries produced dozens of well-known musicians. His life, compared with that of Handel, was quite uneventful and was lived entirely in northern and central Germany. His parents died before he was ten and he was brought up by one of his brothers. He was a good violinist but the organ was his main instrument and it was chiefly as an organist that he was known during his lifetime. He was given a musical education by members of his family. He also derived great benefit from the laborious but rewarding process of copying out or arranging the music of other people; this practice stayed with him throughout his life. In this way he came to appreciate all the main European styles of writing. He left home at fifteen and for a time stayed at Lüneberg near Hamburg where he earned enough to pay for his further education. He travelled, often on foot, to hear famous organist/composers such as Reinken and Buxtehude. Until 1708 he held various posts in northern and central Germany; and 1707 he married his cousin Maria, who died in 1720. Bach soon married for a second time. His two wives bore him a total of twenty-two children, several of whom became well-known musicians. Bach was devoted to his family; but his relations with his employers were never very cordial. At the end of his life the close work of copying and writing music took its toll and he became blind.

Throughout his life Bach was a devout Lutheran, a fact which had a great effect upon his music. His contemporaries saw him as a working composer and an excellent organist. When he died his grave in a Leipzig churchyard was not specially marked.

Bach's main working life falls into three periods corresponding to the three main posts which he held. These posts determined the sort of music which he wrote: from 1708–1717 he worked as a violinist and organist at the court of the republic of Weimar; from 1717–1723 he was Director of Music at the court of Cöthen, but here his duties did not include those of an organist; and from 1723 until his death he was employed by the city council at Leipzig. His appointment was as Director of Music (Cantor) and teacher of Latin at St Thomas's boys' school but his duties also included providing music for the city, for the university and for two of the city's five churches. It was one of the most important and highly prized jobs in the Lutheran world; and Bach was not the city council's first choice but the other candidates were unable or unwilling to take up the appointment. One of the councillors apparently remarked that as the best musicians were not available an average one would have to do!

In these three posts Bach composed in practically every form available to the late Baroque composer with the important exception of opera. In this respect he differs greatly from Handel. Bach's music may be considered under the following headings: that for the organ, for the other keyboard instruments (clavier); for chamber groups and orchestra; and for voices.

Organ Works – The Pipe Organ

Together, Bach's works for the organ form the most important body of compositions written for the instrument. They were written throughout Bach's career but a great many of them naturally stem from the Weimar period. Bach was the inheritor both of the Italian school of composition, through **Froberger** (1606–1667) who was a pupil of Frescobaldi, and of the German school, whose tradition rested with **Reinken** (1623–1722), **Buxtehude** and his contemporary, **Telemann** (1681–1767).

The *pipe organ*, for which Bach wrote, consists of a keyboard (manual) or keyboards, a pedal board and pipes arranged in sets (ranks). Each pipe produces only one note. In general each rank of pipes consists of the same number of notes as either the manuals or the pedal board. Each rank of pipes produces its own quality of sound and its own range of pitch. Ranks of pipes are attached to a specific manual or to the pedal board. The manuals and pedal may be coupled together in various combinations in order to link together separate ranks of pipes. The ranks of pipes to be brought into play at any one time are controlled by movable plugs called *stops*. A pipe organ contains also a collapsible box (*wind chest*) which can be inflated by pumping air into it. When the player engages a rank of pipes by means of a stop, that rank is supplied with air from the wind chest. As the player depresses a key or pedal so air is allowed to enter the appropriate pipe causing it to sound its note. The structure which houses the complete organ is known as the *case work*. Organ builders may supply instruments ready-made to a pattern but instruments are also commonly built individually as a result of consultation between the makers and the purchaser. The complete range of stops which any instrument possesses is known as its *specification*.

Of Bach's organ works by far the most numerous single type is the *Chorale Prelude*. A chorale prelude, as its name implies, is a short organ introduction to the singing of a hymn, as a modern organist might play the first line before the singing starts. However, Bach's chorale preludes are important musical compositions in their own right, for in them the whole hymn tune is played against a variety of different treatments. The earlier preludes average from 16–24 bars in length; some of the later ones are extended compositions.

The Lutheran morning service lasted from 7.00 until about 11.00 and included several congregational hymns. Bach left about 140 chorale preludes, grouped into six collections. The first of these is *The Little Organ Book* (*Orgelbüchlein*) and contains forty-six compositions. This collection was made at Weimar, dedicated to God, and intended to show the beginner at the organ the way to go about dealing with a chorale tune. The other collections are: seventeen Catechism Preludes; twenty-five collected by Kirnberger; six collected by Schübler; twenty-eight miscellaneous; and a set known merely as 'Eighteen Preludes'.

Among the most important of Bach's organ works is a series of fugues. Some of these are prefixed by a conventional Prelude or by a more showy Fantasia or Toccata; some stand alone. There are forty-one such compositions, twenty-three of them dating from the Weimar period. Contrary to Bach's usual practice of designing or publishing his works in systematic collections, these appear as gigantic feats of composition scattered through his total output. The most well known of them is the Toccata and Fugue in D minor; the fugue is interesting because its course is interrupted by passages of free writing in the manner of Buxtehude.

Six of these works in particular display Bach's art at its highest level and are normally labelled 'the great', although this is done in part to distinguish them from other works in the same key.

In all of these works Bach brought to the fugue supreme technical perfection conveying music of the height of expressiveness. Each fugue derives a particular character from its fugue subject; Bach's fugue subjects are always clearly defined both melodically and rhythmically and differ markedly from one another in length, shape and pattern. Equally important but less spectacular than the above fugues are six trio sonatas for organ which Bach wrote at Leipzig. They consist of three independent contrapuntal parts, one for each of two manuals and one for pedals; they contain music of great beauty.

Other Keyboard Works

No less outstanding in their variety of structure and in their musical significance are the works which Bach wrote for harpsichord, with or without pedals, and for clavichord, most of which are from his period at Cöthen. The best-known of them are two sets each of twenty-four Preludes and Fugues. Each set of twenty-four is made up of a Prelude and a Fugue in each of the twelve major and minor keys, i.e., with key signatures up to seven sharps or flats. Baroque composers rarely wrote in more than four sharps or flats because of the way in which keyboard instruments were tuned. Bach showed that by using a system of equal tuning (temperament) it was possible to write in any key. The title of the sets is *The Well-Tempered Clavier* (*Das Wohltemperierte Clavier*). Since they were written the '48' have proved to be an inexhaustible source of delight for both the keyboard player and for the student of contrapuntal writing.

More accessible for the average player, for whom Bach wrote them, and equally rewarding are the Two and Three Part Inventions. These are contrapuntal works and show clearly the art of fitting together different lines of music using the same basic material. Both sets are arranged in ascending order of key, both major and minor, but Bach does not write in more than four sharps or flats. This gives fifteen works in each set.

Finally there are the keyboard suites. These too represent the ultimate in this form of writing. There are three sets of six of them; consisting of one set of Partitas (another word for suite) and one set each of French and English suites. The latter two all contain the standard four suite movements – Allemande, Sarabande, Courante, and Gigue; the English suites all open with a Prelude.

Between 1726 and 1743 Bach issued his collected organ and clavier works in four sets with the title of 'Keyboard Diversions' (*Clavier Übung*) Parts I–IV. Parts I–III contain most of the works discussed above; Part IV consists of one work, known as *The Goldberg Variations*, written in 1742. These were written to be played by Johann Goldberg in the middle of the night in order to amuse his employer, at the court of Dresden, when he was unable to sleep. The work consists of a theme and thirty variations and provides a profound contribution to the literature of the form. In particular Bach exploits to the full the compositional device known as *Canon*, where the music moves in two (or more) identical parts but the second one begins after the first one has started. The second part may be at the same pitch as the first or at a different pitch. Canons at certain intervals – e.g., the 7th – present great difficulty in their composition. The Goldberg Variations contain canons at intervals from the unison to the ninth, each Variation moving with complete inevitability.

Orchestral Music

A considerable part of Bach's instrumental and orchestral music was written during his stay at Cöthen (1717–1723), for here he was writing for the court rather than for the Church. To this period belong the Brandenburg Concerti, four orchestral suites, six sonatas for solo cello, six sonatas (partitas) for solo violin, and several concerti for violin and from one to four harpsichords.

The six *Brandenburg Concerti* of 1721 may be regarded as concerti grossi in the same way as Handel's opus 6 set, although two of the Brandenburgs, numbers 3 and 6, have no solo instruments. They were commissioned by the ruler of Brandenburg, who was dignified by the title of Margrave. They each have three movements and follow the fast–slow–fast pattern of the Vivaldi type of solo concerto. The best-known of the Brandenburg concerti is No. 3 in G which is scored for nine stringed instruments with continuo.

The four Orchestral Suites (Bach called them Overtures) are all for strings, wind, and continuo and contain some of Bach's most exuberant music. Their movements are not those of the standard suite (Allemande, Courante, Sarabande, and Gigue). Instead they all start with a Largo: Allegro movement, followed by a series of dance movements. The only dance movement common to them all is the Bourrée. Two of the suites are more popular than the others: No. 2, in B minor, is for flute, strings, and continuo. The flute is used very much in a solo capacity. The suite's final movement is marked Badinerie (a fun piece) and is a most exacting movement for the flute, presenting the player with great problems of breath control. Suite No. 3 in D is ceremonious in character, with trumpet and drums. Its slow movement, popularly known as the 'Air on a G String', is an excellent example of Bach's ability to sustain a long, flowing melody.

In the sonatas for solo cello and solo violin Bach presents the player with a technical, intellectual, and interpretative challenge of the highest order, for the composer contrives to create the impression of both a harmonic and a contrapuntal texture from an essentially single-line instrument. An excellent example is the Chaconne of the solo violin Partita in D minor, a movement which is also one of the best-known in this form.

Of the solo concerti, several are transcriptions of other works by Bach or by Vivaldi. The most celebrated of the original works is the Concerto for Two Violins in D Minor, whose slow movement forms a dialogue of great intensity between the two instruments.

Church Cantatas

The four-hour Lutheran morning service contained a sermon lasting about an hour. Before that came the Creed, and before that there was a substantial musical work for soloists, choir, orchestra, and organ lasting up to three-quarters of an hour. This was the *Church Cantata* and was formed of chorales, choruses, recitatives, arias, and duets. It was the duty of the resident musician to compile or compose a different cantata for each Sunday of the church's year. Bach composed about 300 such works, at Weimar and at Leipzig. Of these about 200 have survived. Their musical importance can be seen from the fact that choral societies are formed today with the express purpose of performing them. For Bach's cantatas are infinitely varied in their structure; they contain much music of superb quality and great beauty and again are examples of Bach's complete technical mastery. Because of their great range they show the various facets of Bach's art more clearly than perhaps any other single type of composition. One of the most famous is No. 140, 'Sleepers Wake' (*Wachet auf*) which illustrates several features of Bach's compositional technique. The basis of the work is a hymn of three verses set to a traditional chorale tune. Bach uses these three verses to present a balanced work of seven sections with a verse of the hymn forming the basis of sections 1, 4, and 7. Sections 2,3 and 5,6 are both recitatives and duets. The first section is an extended setting of the chorale tune forming a grand ritornello movement. In section 4 (the second verse of the chorale) the tune is set against a long, flowing melody (which has been effectively used in our own day as a pop tune). The third verse, section 7, is a straightforward four-part setting of the hymn intended for congregational use. In addition to a balanced overall structure, *Wachet auf* has a careful key structure, as is common in Bach. The basic key is E♭ which is the key of the three verses of the chorale melody; the keys of the intervening sections carefully balance the main key. Six of Bach's cantatas were collected together in 1734 to form the *Christmas Oratorio*. Much of this music was drawn from Bach's secular output; no difference of style is apparent between these sections and those originally intended for church use.

The church cantata formed the main musical part of the Lutheran morning service. On special occasions the whole service could be introduced with an extended piece for choir, lasting about half an hour in the form of a motet.

Instruments doubled the singers in their music. Six of Bach's motets have come down to us, four of which are for eight-part choir.

Although Bach was a Lutheran two of his church works have Latin words, both of them dating from the Leipzig period. They are the *Magnificat* and the *Mass in B minor*. The *Magnificat* formed part of the afternoon service at Christmas time. Bach's setting for five-part choir, soloists and orchestra is splendidly melodious and to the point, for after another hour-long sermon it was necessary to finish the service before the daylight faded.

The Mass in B Minor and Passion Music

The Mass in B minor is a much more spacious work than the *Magnificat*. Of its twenty-four numbers, fifteen are choruses. The first half was written by 1733 but the rest was not put together until near the end of Bach's life. The very first chord of this work is astonishing in performance; the Mass starts with a loud chord of B minor by both chorus and orchestra, and the singers have to pitch their notes without apparently having first heard what they sound like. The work contains some very fine moments; the Crucifixus is an outstanding example of the use of an ostinato bass. The technique is similar to that used by Purcell in Dido's Lament but with startlingly dissimilar results.

The main music of the Lutheran church at Easter was a setting of the events leading up to and including the Crucifixion. From the time of the Reformation this setting had consisted of a mixture of recitatives and chorales. But in the early eighteenth century in Germany it became the custom to set the Passion story in an operatic style, with recitatives, arias, choruses, and chorales. Two of Bach's works in this style have survived: they are the *St John Passion* and the *St Matthew Passion*. The St John Passion dates from Bach's appointment to Leipzig in 1723. It is a dramatic and swiftly moving work scored for four-part chorus, four soloists, orchestra and both organ and harpsichord continuo.

The *St Matthew Passion* is one of the most important works of Western music. It is conceived on a grand scale, with regard both to the musical forces employed and to Bach's conception of the music itself. It is scored for two four-part choirs (plus a third one in the opening number), two orchestras, two organs and two continuo parts in addition to solo parts for a number of voices. Of these solos the part of the narrator (The Evangelist, i.e., St Matthew) is the most prominent and is written for a high tenor who sings entirely in a very expressive recitative, in accordance with tradition. The part of Jesus, also conforming to tradition, is a bass. Throughout the work Bach embeds this voice in a texture of string sound representing a halo. The halo disappears once, at the words 'My God, why has thou forsaken me'. The hymn tune known as the Passion Chorale appears five times; Bach alters the harmony of the tune in accordance with the point of the drama with which he is dealing.

One of the facets of Bach's agile and all-embracing intellect is his ability to make the music symbolize whatever mood or thoughts it is expressing. This is true of all Bach's music, but in the St. Matthew Passion there is scarcely a phrase which does not reflect some pictorial effect couched in dignified and controlled music of the highest quality. Bach dedicated all his mature music to God in recognition of his great gifts. In consequence the two bars of music to the words 'Truly this was the Son of God' have, in their context, an impact which is scarcely to be found elsewhere.

Late Works

Towards the end of his life Bach was received at Potsdam by King Frederick of Prussia who was a competent flute player. The king presented Bach with a theme of his own composition to use as the basis for some improvisation. This resulted in a work known as the *Musical Offering*. It is seven sections, four of which form a trio sonata for flute, violin, and continuo. Bach crowned his life's work with a composition which systematically demonstrates all the possible types of fugal writing. It is known as *The Art of Fugue*, and consists of eighteen sections, all based on the same fugue subject, which start simply and become gradually more complex. Bach handles the most difficult contrapuntal devices with an ease and inevitability which has always excited the wonder of succeeding generations of musicians.

After Bach's death his music was known only to a few people for nearly half a century. But in 1802 his first biography, by J. N. Forkel (1749–1818), appeared. The seal was set on the increasing interest in Bach and his music with a performance by Mendelssohn of the St. Matthew Passion in 1829. In 1850 the Bach Society was formed (Bachgesellschaft) which by 1900 had published all Bach's works. In our own century his technical mastery, the scope of his imagination, his co-ordinated control of vast musical projects and the expressive intensity of his music have given rise to the judgement with which this chapter starts.

PART TWO: HARMONY

In the last two chapters we saw that many pieces of music, particularly in the eighteenth century, ended with a Perfect Cadence V–I. These chords could be approached and amplified into a cadential formula forming the sequence VI–IIb–Ic–V–I.

Starting a Piece of Music

The aim is to fix the key in the hearer's mind at the beginning of the piece. The most effective way of doing this is to use the tonic chord on the first beat of the bar, but many pieces of music start with an upbeat before the first bar. The upbeat note is quite often the dominant, leading to the tonic (see Example 9.1). This upbeat is called an *anacrusis*, and there are two ways of harmonizing an anacrusis:

9.1

1. because the melody notes are dominant-tonic the natural chord sequence is V–I, as shown in Example 9.2.

V   I

9.2

2. but since we are aiming to establish the key both notes may be harmonized by the tonic. This method is usual in Bach (see p. 252). Variety can be

achieved by placing the second tonic chord in its first inversion, as in Example 9.3.

9.3

Numbering of Bars

An anacrusis starts at the end of a bar; the bars of a piece of music are numbered starting from the first *complete* bar. Orchestral scores and instrumental parts are often numbered every ten bars, the number being placed at the beginning of the bar to which it refers; letters may also be used. Such numbers or letters are necessary when orchestral or chamber music is being rehearsed so that if the playing stops everyone can identify where they are. An anacrusis is accounted for by having its value taken from the last bar of the piece, as shown in Example 9.4.

9.4

The Imperfect Cadence

Music breathes by means of phrases, shown by a curved line above the music. The end of a phrase may be marked by a cadence. This cadence can be a perfect one, in which case its effect is very final; but the sense of finality disappears if the last chord of the cadence, i.e., the tonic, is simply left out. The phrase now ends Ic V (I). A Perfect cadence without its last chord is known as an *Imperfect cadence*.

Example 9.5 shows two instances of Imperfect cadences.

Exercise

1. Fill in the alto and tenor parts of the Imperfect cadences in Example 9.6.

Example 9.7 shows a melody in two phrases, each starting with an anacrusis.

9.5

9.6

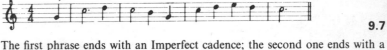

9.7

The first phrase ends with an Imperfect cadence; the second one ends with a
Perfect cadence. It is possible to harmonize this melody completely by using
the following steps:

1. Identify the key.
2. Refer to the triads for that key.
3. Test the final cadence for VI–IIb–Ic–V–I. These are the chords for the
   last two bars.
4. Taking each of these chords separately fill in the bass, then the alto and
   tenor. Remember to write out the notes of the triad belonging to each
   chord as you work at it; cross off the letters as you put the notes on the
   stave.
5. Look at the end of the first phrase. Do the last two notes fit an Imperfect
   cadence (I V or Ic V)? Fill in the notes of this cadence using the procedure
   in 4 above.
6. Look at the note before the Imperfect cadence. Is it part of the traditional

approach chord to a Perfect/Imperfect cadence? Fill in the notes of this
chord.

7. Now look at the anacrusis and the first chord of the first phrase. You
may harmonize them by V–I or I–Ib, as above.

8. Now fill in the anacrusis of the second phrase – either I or V. See
Example 9.8.

V   I   IIb   Ic V   V   VI   IIb   Ic V   I   **9.8**

Let us look at the harmonization of the last two chords (V–I) shown in
Example 9.9. The note B in chord V is the leading note of C major. Because it
is a *leading* note it feels as if it ought to *rise* to the tonic, and most composers
let it do this. This can result in the chord consisting of three tonic notes (= C)
and one third (= E) with the fifth left out, which is quite acceptable. But Bach
generally allows the leading note to fall to the dominant, so you may also do
this on very good authority (see Example 9.9(b)).

LEADING NOTE

9.9a   **9.9b**

If you have followed out the exercise of harmonizing Example 9.7, check
the following points.

1. Are the stems of the notes pointing in the right direction? Soprano and
   tenor should go up; alto and bass should go down.
2. Have you kept the tenor part near the top of the bass stave?
3. Do any of the parts overlap (as in Example 9.10)?

PARTS OVERLAPPING

                                                      9.10

4. Are there any consecutive 5ths or octaves? Look particularly at the first two notes of the second phrase; the harmony is V–VI. You may have to leave out the 5th of one of the chords as in Example 9.9 above.

Exercise

2. Example 9.11 is a similar melody to that of Example 9.7. It can be harmonized using exactly the same chords as Example 9.7 but it is in a different key and the alto and tenor parts will probably have different notes of the triad from those of Example 9.7. Harmonize this melody.

9.11

The Name Bach in Music

The German names for notes differ slightly from ours; our B♭ in German is B; our B is 'H'. The name BACH therefore appears on the stave as shown in Example 9.12. Bach himself was the first of many composers to write music based on his own name.

9.12

Phrygian Cadence

Bach's Brandenburg Concerto No. 3, as we now have it, consists of two movements only. These movements are joined by the two chords shown in Example 9.13. This is a *Phrygian Cadence*. It is frequently heard in Baroque music and, for a piece in a major key, consists of an Imperfect Cadence in the relative minor using the formula IVb V of that key. If the piece of music is already in a minor key, a Phrygian Cadence consists of IVb V in its own key. The 3rd Brandenburg Concerto is in G major; its relative minor is E minor; IVb in E minor = ACE with C at the bass. V = BD♯F♯.

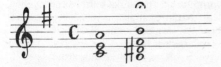

9.13

Suggested Further Reading

David, H. T. and Mendel, A. (eds.) *The Bach Reader* (London: Dent, 1966).
Schweitzer, Albert. *J. S. Bach* 2 volumes, (Dover, 1978).
Steinitz, Paul. *Bach's Passions* (Paul Elek, 1979).
Terry, C. S. *The Music of Bach* (Dover, 1963).
Westrup, J. A. *Bach Cantatas* (London: BBC Music Guides, 1966).
Williams, Peter. *Bach Organ Music* (London: BBC Music Guides, 1972).

10

PART ONE: MUSIC FROM 1740 TO 1780. THE PRE-CLASSICAL STYLE

Transition from the Baroque to the Classical Period

When Bach died in 1750 the Baroque style had already gone out of fashion. From about 1740, secular considerations had led to the feeling that music should be easy to listen to. This resulted in a concentration upon melody in the top line supported by an accompaniment based on chords. The effect of this was to cause composers to rethink the way in which a complete piece of music should be constructed, particularly on a large scale. Baroque music is based on compositional devices which automatically cause it to move forward. It is largely contrapuntal by nature, depending upon the use of sequence and on repeated patterns of notes. The bass part moves equally with the top part, instead of seeking to anchor it. Moreover the Baroque *doctrine of the affections* ensured that a piece, once started, pursued its course at the same speed and in the same mood and with no startling changes of sound level until it came to an end. Thirdly, Baroque music, even when moving quite quickly, gives the impression of dignity and even of seriousness.

With the advent of the new style all this changed. The melodic line, instead of being continuously spun out, was broken up into short, fairly regular phrases. Instead of the doctrine of the affections, deliberate contrast was aimed at; bustling scale passages alternate with chords either repeated or broken up; soft and loud passages jostle one with another; the texture constantly varies. Instead of dignity and seriousness the composers aimed at elegance and grace.

All these ideas formed the starting point for the music of the *Classical* period. At its fullest extent the Classical style may be said to last from 1740 to perhaps as late as 1820. The period is often divided into two: a pre-classical period up to 1780; and the classical style itself, lasting from 1780 to 1810 and beyond. These dates coincide with the mature works of Haydn and Mozart and with some of the works of Beethoven.

The pre-Classical period did not produce composers of such eminence; and although there are important and influential composers in all branches of music during the period, none of them was strong enough to establish a unified pre-Classical style. The result of this was that in the pre-Classical period there are several variations of the newly emerged style which are important enough to be given a classification of their own. They largely reflect national taste.

Rococo, Galant, and Empfindsamer Styles

Rococo is a French cultural term of the early eighteenth century. It is used in connection with architecture, painting, sculpture, and furniture-making, and is also applied to music; it reflects emotions which are neither too lighthearted nor too deep, and is concerned with wit, grace, and charm. The precise musical name for rococo is the *Galant* style, which was used by composers generally throughout Europe and lasted until quite late in the eighteenth century. In Germany a style parallel to the rococo arose, which paid great attention to expressive phrases which give an effect of sentimentality. It is known as the *Empfindsamer* style, and cultivated a singing quality in the melody delighting in the sighing effect of a lingering imperfect cadence. Its phrase lengths varied constantly. The music written in this style begins to be of some importance, for it was during the pre-Classical period that the German domination of music begins and the supremacy of Italian music declines. The German expressive style reached a peak round about 1770 during a period of romantic extravagance in the arts. German literature of the time went through a phase known as Storm and Stress (*Sturm und Drang*); this term is applied also to music.

The Sonata Principle

A style of music based on melody with supporting harmonies poses a problem for its composers, particularly when the melody is broken up into short sections. For when the melody stops the music tends to come to an end. The problem is how to form an extended piece of music from a series of short sections in such a way that it has a sense of balance and an overall coherence – a problem of form. Baroque music tends to generate its own formal structure; Classical music has to have the structure imposed upon it. The solution to the problem lay in exploiting the classical musician's concern with *contrast*. This may be produced by any of the elements of music: melody, harmony, rhythm, speed, dynamics, and so on. But two elements in particular became fused into a single principle of composition, the *sonata principle* which relied on the contrast of thematic material and on the use of keys in such a way as to produce a dramatic conflict of their own.

The application of this principle to the composition of music resulted in a structure which is generally known as *sonata form*, a conventional name which does not necessarily refer to a sonata. Single movements are written in this form; i.e., it is not the form of a symphony or a concerto, but of one of the movements which might make up a symphony or a concerto. It may constitute the form of an entire *Overture*, which is usually a single piece of music. Movements in this form may be analysed by using the *sonata principle* of thematic contrast and tonal drama; but there is a great deal to be gained in the understanding of music from knowing the textbook definition of *sonata form*.

Sonata Form

A movement in sonata form is made up of three distinct sections: *exposition*, *development*, and *recapitulation*. The sonata form structure may be preceded by an introductory piece of music, usually slow-moving; a slow introduction is not part of sonata form but as it is a part of the complete movement it may be made use of during the movement.

The Exposition

A composer who decides to write a movement in sonata form must first invent a musical idea. This is called the *first subject* and usually forms the basis of the movement, in the key of the movement. A really good composer needs no more than the material in Example 10.1 on which to base a movement.

10.1

As a contrast to this, the composer then invents a second theme, the *second subject*, which is in the dominant or relative major key of the movement. It is now necessary to compose a piece of music which will lead the hearer away from the first subject and into the second subject. This is called a *transition* or a *bridge passage*. So far the exposition looks like this:

1st subject–Transition–2nd subject

After the second subject the music proceeds towards another theme, perhaps rather slight and not entirely new, called the *closing theme*. At this point some compositions repeat the first subject in order to tie these various elements together. This section of the movement is then brought to a close with a *codetta* which is Italian for 'little tail'. The exposition now looks like this:

1st subject–Transition–2nd subject–Closing theme–(1st subject)–Codetta

In eighteenth-century movements the whole of the Exposition is repeated; this practice becomes less and less frequent during the nineteenth century.

The Development

The composer now takes some of the material of the exposition and develops from it an argument or a discussion in purely musical terms. A favourite device is to take the music of the first subject and to present it in various guises while at the same time using music from the transition to bind the whole section together. The development section is a test of a composer's creativity and of his skill; it is one of the chief criteria in assessing the value of a symphonic composer.

The Recapitulation

This section presents again the material of the exposition, but it is now heard in the light of the development. The music is not exactly the same as that of the exposition for two reasons, one aesthetic, one practical. Firstly, as the movement proceeds to a close it is necessary to heighten the effect of what the listener has already heard; secondly, the second subject is now presented in the tonic key which means that the composer has to rework at least some of the transition since in the exposition it modulated to the dominant. At the end of the recapitulation the codetta of the exposition turns into a real tail (coda).

The emergence of sonata form triumphantly solved the problem of how to create music on a large scale from small melodic fragments. The form's numerous sections; the opportunity it provides for the contrast of key, texture, dynamics, and mood; its balance of parts and the aesthetic pleasure to be derived from it have all provided scope for the imagination of composers from the mid-eighteenth century up to our own times. Its importance in music has been likened to that of the Parthenon in architecture. In lyrical slow movements sonata form may be used without its development section. The movement then consists of an unrepeated exposition followed by a recapitulation. This is known as *modified sonata form*.

Sonata Rondo

A development of sonata form in another direction was a combination of sonata and rondo forms, known as *sonata rondo* form. A simple rondo consists of five sections ABACA. In a sonata rondo section A becomes the first subject, section B the second subject and section C the Development. This results in the following:

Section	A	B	A	C	A	B	Coda
Content	1st subject	2nd subject	1st subject	Development	1st subject	2nd subject	Coda
Key	Tonic	Dominant	Tonic	Various keys	Tonic	Tonic	Tonic

The Symphony Orchestra

Simultaneously with the emergence of sonata form during the pre-Classical period came the introduction of the *symphony orchestra*. Thus composers were not only equipped with forms to which the new style of music could be adapted, but they also had a flexible and expressive medium of performance for their works. The symphony orchestra sprang directly from the emergence of the string family as the chief instrumental body at the beginning of the eighteenth century; it is fundamentally the same orchestra which we encounter in the concert hall today. The standardization of the instruments which make up an orchestra resulted in the disappearance of a large number of Renaissance and Baroque instruments which have now again become a part of our own musical life.

The *strings* of an orchestra are divided into 1st violins, 2nd violins, violas, and cellos-and-basses, which in the eighteenth century shared the same part. To these the pre-Classical composers added a pair of oboes and a pair of horns. The sharp quality of the oboe sound gave definition to the violin tone; the smoothness of the horn sound bound the whole texture together. In music of a ceremonial nature a pair of *trumpets* and a pair of *drums* were also added. In the Baroque era trumpet music (clarino parts) had been written high in the treble clef and took its full share in the general forward movement of the music, resulting in music of great technical difficulty.

From about 1750 this style of playing went out of fashion; the trumpets descended lower into the treble clef and their parts became fanfare-like. The *bassoon*, which in the Baroque era had been part of the general bass line, now became the bass of the woodwind section in its own right. Soon after 1750 the *clarinet* entered the orchestra and by the end of the century formed a regular part of it. With the standardization of the composition of the orchestra went a standard arrangement of showing the instruments on the printed page: the orchestral score became fixed and arranged instruments in families and in pitch order within each family, as is done today. Only the horn is out of place, being scored above, instead of below, the trumpets; composers tended to think of it as binding together the texture of the woodwind instruments.

The instruments in a score of the Classical period are therefore laid out as shown in the diagram on p. 106. At the beginning of the piece the composer uses a stave for each different instrument whether it is playing or not; but on subsequent pages staves are used only for those instruments playing at that time.

Because of the fixed appearance of an orchestral score it is possible to refer to the instrumentation of any particular piece of music as a series of numbers. For instance 2201 4231 88641 means: two flutes, two oboes, no clarinets, one bassoon; four horns, two trumpets, three trombones, one tuba; eight 1st violins, eight 2nd violins, six violas, four cellos and one double bass.

The most famous orchestra in Europe during the mid-eighteenth century was that at Mannheim. The Elector Karl Theodor had recently built himself one of the palaces which sprang up in Europe at this time in an effort to rival Versailles, the Mannheim castle at Schwetzingen. It employed 1,500 people, many of whom were musicians. Every member of the orchestra was a first class player and many of them were well-known composers of the day. Its leader was **Johann Stamitz** (1717–1757), who was influential as a composer of early symphonies but who also gave to the Mannheim orchestra the qualities for which it became famous. It presented a disciplined and unified sound which resulted from a precision of attack. The bows of all the string players moved together in the same direction. The sound became louder (crescendo) or softer (decrescendo) with a control which caused people to react physically. Its effects were famous enough to be given nicknames such as 'skyrocket' or the term which is today translated as 'steamroller'. By 1780 the court of Mannheim had moved to Munich and although the orchestra's great days were over its effect upon orchestral writing and playing remained.

The Symphony

During the pre-Classical era the *symphony* emerged as the most important form of writing for full orchestra. Towards the end of the eighteenth century and throughout the nineteenth and twentieth centuries, composers have tended to use this form for their most weighty musical thoughts. The standard definition of a symphony is of an orchestral work in four movements; their order is fairly fixed and they are usually referred to as *first movement, slow movement, minuet and trio*, and *finale*. Sonata form plays an important part in symphonic writing; and it is not unusual to find three of the four movements in this form. The first movement, usually a fast one, is commonly in sonata form; modified sonata form fits a slow movement well and many second movements use it. Sonata form is also often used for the finale. The origins of the symphony are somewhat complex but may be summarized as follows:

1. The *Neapolitan overture* (called *sinfonia*) favoured by Alessandro Scarlatti is in three sections, fast, slow, fast. The 1st, 2nd, and 4th movements of a symphony are related to these sections. Several symphonies up to about 1790 consist of only three movements.
2. The movements in a sonata da chiesa and in a concerto grosso are usually marked with directions of mood or of speed, e.g., grave, allegro. Three of the four movements of a symphony follow this practice.
3. The third symphonic movement, minuet and trio, is taken from the *suite*.
4. The early style of symphonic writing, witty, bustling, short-phrased, and tuneful is derived from comic opera (*opera buffa*) of the time.

What is considered to be the first symphony is dated 1740 and is by the Austrian composer **Georg Monn** (1717–1750). Other early symphonists include **François Gossec** (1734–1829) from Paris and **Johann Christian Bach** (1735–1782), the 'London' Bach, who influenced Mozart.

The pre-Classical style came to maturity in the work of two composers in particular. Their lives were almost exactly contemporary. They wrote music which was both important and influential. Between them they covered the entire range of musical forms available to them. They are **Carl Philipp Emanuel Bach** (1714–1788) and **Christof Willibald Gluck** (1714–1787).

C. P. E. Bach

C. P. E. Bach was a keyboard player of some distinction. His style of playing attracted attention, for he seems to have thrown himself about when performing. What is more important is that he reflects the rapid change in the fashion for keyboard instruments during the middle of the eighteenth century; he first devoted himself to the harpsichord and then to the clavichord and finally to the piano which superseded them both. His various sets of keyboard compositions represent the German expressive (empfindsamer) style at its most intense and had a great influence on later composers. Equally important was his book on how to play keyboard instruments which was used as a piano textbook for three-quarters of a century and provides us with a great deal of information about the performance of music at the time.

Bach worked from 1740 to 1747 at the court of Friedrich II (Frederick the Great) of Prussia. Frederick was conservative, military, and musical in equal degrees. Any modern embellishment to the scores of his old-fashioned music was greeted with the threat of flogging. From 1767 until his death Bach directed the music of the churches at Hamburg, a position similar to that of his father at Leipzig. Like his father he wrote no opera.

Eighteenth-century Opera

Operatic activity during the pre-Classical period falls into well-defined divisions. Italian opera appeared in two forms, serious (*opera seria*) and comic (*opera buffa*), although comic (buffo) elements are found also in the very early Italian operas. During the late Baroque period the course of opera seria was largely dictated by the ideas of **Pietro Metastasio** (1698–1782). Metastasio was a fine poet and also a musician. The opera libretti which he supplied were extremely popular with composers almost until the end of the eighteenth century. A Metastasian opera is largely aria-based; the action is often based upon a conflict of human interests and moves slowly towards the point at which someone has to perform an unselfish deed of heroism. Violent contrast in the music is avoided. The orchestral music is subordinate to that of the singers.

Comic opera (opera buffa) arose in Naples, originally as a reaction against the state of opera seria. Its characters were based on those of pantomime figures used in the Italian Commedia dell'arte and on caricatures of real people such as the miserly old bachelor, the fake lawyer or the pert maid. As opera buffa developed it created a style of its own. It gave important parts to the bass voice which had dropped out of currency. It allowed its characters to take part together (ensemble) in swift-moving discussions or arguments. A particular form of this is the 'ensemble of perplexity' where everybody asks everybody else what can possibly be done in such a complicated situation. This type of ensemble is particularly effective at the end of an act.

An early and delightful example of opera buffa which still holds the stage is *La Serva Padrona* (The mistress who is really a maid) by **Giovanni Battista Pergolesi** (1710–1736), who in his short life wrote a wealth of music for church, stage, and drawing room. The French version of opera buffa was the *opéra comique*, which appeared soon after 1700. Opéra comique set out to provide a popular form of entertainment with its characters drawn from the humbler classes of society. Its songs were similar to those of the later *music hall* and were interspersed with spoken dialogue. The form flourished and, in the hands of later eighteenth-century composers, yielded works of some significance.

The German version of opéra comique is the *Singspiel* which is also closely related to the English ballad opera as seen in *The Beggar's Opera*. Both are forms of popular entertainment in which well-known songs are interspersed with spoken dialogue but Singspiel is more sentimental and less satirical than the English form of ballad opera.

Gluck and the Reform of Opera

Although Gluck was born in 1714 he was not brought up in the Baroque tradition, being trained musically in rural Bohemia. His subsequent career was cosmopolitan; he studied in Italy, made a musical tour of Germany, visited England, became a court composer in Vienna, and reaped an operatic triumph in Paris. He wrote numerous operas in various styles but his fame depends upon six of them. In spite of the success of the Metastasian libretto, by the mid-eighteenth century the methods of opera seria had become out of step with the principles of the Classical style. In 1762 Gluck's *Orpheus and Euridice* was performed. This opera contains music of great beauty and well illustrates Gluck's own style of dignified simplicity. It contains the well-known aria 'What shall I do without Euridice?' (*Che farò senza Euridice*) and a very fine flute solo representing the bliss of the after-world. In this opera Gluck put his reforms into action, but it was not until 1767 that he formulated them in the preface to *Alcestis*. They may be summarized as follows:

1. The function of the music should be to support the drama.
2. Music should not interrupt the dramatic action nor weaken it with too much ornament.
3. The da capo aria with its undramatic repeated first section should be banished.
4. Vowel sounds should not be needlessly prolonged.
5. The overture should become an integral part of the opera and should prepare the audience for the action.
6. The orchestral accompaniment to the voice should itself reflect the drama.
7. The transition between recitative and aria should not be abrupt.
8. The whole opera should proceed with a noble simplicity.

In the operas of Gluck these principles are faithfully reflected, for his musical thought was naturally in sympathy with his aesthetic ideals. But his reforms were not finally completely successful. By 1767 Mozart's first opera had already been written; in the best operas of Mozart the musical and dramatic action coincide. But in any case it is arguable that when poetry and music are performed in harness music by its very nature is the more powerful and compelling partner.

Following a Score

Score Reading is a highly specialized musical skill. It requires an acutely trained and sensitive aural imagination together with a ready facility for hearing the sounds of different transposing instruments at their actual pitch at the same time as reading the pitch notated. However, there is a great deal of pleasure and profit to be gained from following the music as it moves along through the score, and this ability can be acquired with practice. Following a score constantly reveals different facets of the music which the ear may pick up or overlook during a performance. It is best done at home with recorded music and the results can then be carried in one's memory into the concert hall. To follow a score at all requires some score-reading skills.

It is perhaps best to start with a Haydn or Mozart string quartet; say the slow movement. If you then move on to the Minuet and Trio remember to account for all the repeats. From a string quartet a good move would be to a Mozart piano concerto where the piano part is prominent on the page. This could be followed by a Mozart or Haydn symphony. (See pp. 106–7 for the view of a score and an orchestra as seen by the conductor.)

There is a great deal of correspondence between the order of the instruments in the score and the seating arrangements by the orchestra. The string players sit in pairs and are referred to as 'desks'; 1st desk, 2nd desk, etc. All other players sit at desks by themselves and have their own part, as can be seen from the score. The standard layout of a symphony orchestra is as shown p. 107. An older arrangement, still used occasionally, was to have the second violins to the conductor's right, balancing the first violins.

FIDELIO
Overture

L. van Beethoven, Op. 72b
(1770-1827)

An orchestral score for a full classical orchestra.

THE STANDARD ARRANGEMENT OF A SYMPHONY ORCHESTRA

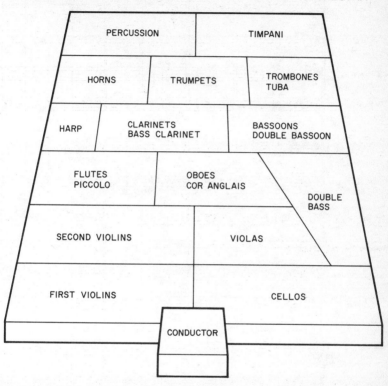

INSTRUMENTAL RANGES

Actual Pitch

o = Exact limit of range

$\bullet$ = Approximate limit of range

$*$ = Transposing instrument (see Chapter 15)

PART TWO: HARMONY

The Interrupted Cadence

An *imperfect cadence* is used at the end of a phrase but not at the end of a piece of music. It avoids sounding complete by merely leaving out the last chord of a perfect cadence. Another way of preventing the music from coming to a full stop is to embark upon a perfect cadence but at the last moment to put another chord in place of the final tonic one. II V I then becomes II V ?. In theory the ?-chord can be anything; in practice it is often chord VI. The progression is then V–VI and is known as an *interrupted cadence*, which the Americans call a 'deceptive cadence' (see Example 10.2). In this example the

V   VI   **10.2**

four parts move quite smoothly, but the progression is very prone to producing consecutive 5ths and octaves (see Example 10.3).

V   VI   **10.3**

Exercise

1. Fill in the alto and tenor parts in the interrupted cadences in Example 10.4.
   i. Make sure that you know the keys which the cadences are in.

10.4

ii. Write out the triads for chords V and VI.
iii. Cross off the notes given and cross off the other notes as you write them
    on the stave.
iv. Check for consecutive 5ths and octaves. If you find any try rearranging
    the alto and tenor parts or double one of the notes given.

We now have three types of cadence: *perfect cadence* (Chapter 7); *imperfect
cadence* (Chapter 9) and *interrupted cadence*.

The Passing Six-Four Chord

So far we have only one way of using the six-four chord (2nd inversion). This
is the use of the six-four chord at a cadence – Ic–V–I (see chapter 8).

Six-four chords may also be used in the middle of a phrase, but their use
remains limited. They may be used in the harmonization of the bottom three
notes of the scale either going down (see Example 10.5, which is the opening

10.5

of 'Three Blind Mice') or going up (see Example 10.6). The standard harmonization of this phrase is shown beneath the notes. Using triads of C major

10.6

(I = CEG : V = GBD) you will see that these chords make the bass move in
the opposite direction from the soprano (see Example 10.7).

10.7

The outer notes thus form a fixed pattern. This is true of the two inner parts also. You will see that the 5th note of the scale G is common to the three chords of the progression. It is therefore best kept in the same part. The remaining notes of the chords are C B C. We have to decide which of these groups of three notes to put in the alto and which into the tenor. If the tenor takes the three repeated Gs and the alto the CBC the result is as shown in Example 10.8(a). The spacing here is not very happy. The alternative in 10.8(b) shows the standard way of dealing with this progression. This use of the 2nd inversion is known as the *passing six-four*. The soprano and bass notes of the $^6_4$ do in fact pass between those of the two outer chords.

10.8

Exercise

2. Fill in the missing parts of Example 10.9. Do not forget to identify the key and write out the notes of the triads as you use them. If you get the pattern of notes right you will not have to worry about consecutive 5ths and octaves.

10.9

Passing Notes

The soprano and bass notes of the passing six-four chord above filled in the space between two notes a 3rd apart – see Example 10.10. These two notes form part of a chord. If they fill in a similar space without being part of a

10.10

chord they are known as *unaccented passing notes*. In the following V–I progression the alto chord notes are G and E. They are joined up by the F
between them, as demonstrated in Example 10.11. The same progression

10.11

without the unaccented passing note F is shown in Example 10.12. The alto G
is now a minim as are all the other notes of the chord. Therefore when you
add a passing note you must alter the value of the note from which it passes.

10.12

I   Ib   10.13

That is, the passing note must be joined to the *first* note and not to the one
after it. Make sure also that the passing note does pass. In the Example 10.13
the B does not belong to anything: it is not part of the harmony and it is not
a passing note.

10.14

10.15

It may seem a good idea to insert a passing note in order to get rid of unwanted consecutives, as shown in Example 10.14, but unfortunately a passing note does not cancel out consecutives if they are already there. It merely covers them up. On the other hand a passing note may create them if they are not there (see Example 10.15)!

Exercise

3. Add passing notes to the melodies shown in Example 10.16.

10.16

Suggested Further Reading

Pauly, Reinhard G. *Music in the Classical Period* (New Jersey: Prentice-Hall, 1973).
Rosen, Charles. *The Classical Style* (London: Faber, 1971).
Open University Course Units A204. *The Rise of the Symphony* and *The Rise of the String Quartet* (Milton Keynes: Open University Press, 1977).

11

PART ONE: HAYDN AND MOZART

A Comparison

By 1780 the Classical style was fully developed. Dozens of centres of music throughout Europe employed musicians who were turning out countless compositions to order. Two men dominated this scene to such an extent that their names have become synonymous with the Classical style itself, **Joseph Haydn** (1732–1809) and **Wolfgang Amadeus Mozart** (1756–1791). Both men are regarded as Viennese composers although neither was born there and the greater part of both of their lives was spent elsewhere.

The lives of Haydn and Mozart are strikingly dissimilar. Haydn had a musical upbringing but as a composer was largely self-trained. He passed a busy and successful professional life followed by a period of travel and a highly respected retirement. Mozart had a celebrated childhood which matured into an erratic search for recognition and even for survival. The continuous succession of his compositions was stopped only by an early death. Mozart and Haydn knew one another well and recognized each other's stature.

The music of Haydn and Mozart also shows marked differences, not only in the types of composition at which they each excelled but also in their individual styles of writing. This becomes apparent only with experience of the music, for it is the Classical sound which overrides their individual voices, if the music is listened to casually.

Haydn's Career

Haydn was born at a little town, Rohrau, in the easternmost part of Austria, almost in Hungary. The local folk-music remained with him all his life. At the age of eight he became a choirboy at the cathedral in Vienna where he stayed for about ten years. He had a lively sense of practical humour; one anecdote relates that he climbed up the cathedral spire and would not come down; eventually the Empress Maria Theresa herself came out and issued a royal command for his descent.

Haydn taught himself theory and composition. The two books which were of most use to him were C. P. E. Bach's handbook on keyboard playing and a famous one on counterpoint called *Gradus ad Parnassum*, by **Johann Fux** (1660–1741) who had only recently retired as director of music at the cathedral. After leaving the cathedral Haydn kicked his heels for a time in some poverty but from 1755 he started getting court appointments. These culminated in his appointment, in 1761, to the musical establishment of one of the wealthiest and most powerful Hungarian noblemen, Prince Paul Esterhazy.

The Esterhazy family were just building at Eisenstadt a palace to rival the one at Versailles. It is estimated to have cost the then enormous sum of £6 million. Here Haydn worked for nearly thirty years in ideal surroundings. He had at his disposal every available kind of musical group; his employer was an amateur musician of no mean accomplishment and for an audience he had a constant succession of visiting European dignitaries. Every winter the whole establishment moved to Vienna, the seat of the Habsburg empire and the centre of European musical life. Haydn became very famous. In 1790 Haydn's patron died; his successor was not musical and Haydn was given his freedom, a pension, and a house in Vienna. Haydn immediately accepted a long-standing invitation to visit London where he arrived on 1 January 1791. He stayed eighteen months and reaped rich rewards, both financial and artistic. In 1794 he returned for a further eighteen months. These visits engendered the music which forms the climax of his career. By 1803 he had ceased to compose. His last work, a string quartet, he left unfinished; and his remaining years were spent in celebrated retirement.

Haydn's Music
Haydn wrote whatever music he was asked to compose; this included some types which have now gone out of fashion. Prince Esterhazy played the *baryton*, an instrument played with a bow and held like a cello. It has six gut strings and some sixteen sympathetic ones. Haydn has left about 200 trios for baryton, violin, and cello. His output also included marionette operas, but he was above all an instrumental composer.

Symphonies
Central to Haydn's œuvre is the *symphony*, whose form he finally established. We now number 104 of these of which 92 were written between 1760 and 1788. The remaining 12, known as the 'London' symphonies, were written in two sets of six for his visits to England.

Several of Haydn's symphonies have distinguishing titles, but these are not Haydn's own. The shape of the symphony did not become fixed immediately with Haydn; for some of the early ones have three movements, or even five, but he increasingly used what has become the standard four-movement form. Some of the early symphonies also seem experimental; Nos. 6, 7, and 8 have programmatic titles, Le Matin, Le Midi, Le Soir (Morning, Noon, Evening) which are accordingly reflected in the music. Other early symphonies give important parts to soloists, No. 31 in D for instance (Hornsignal) has prominent parts for four horns. One of the finest of the early symphonies is No. 44 in E minor, the Trauersinfonie (Mourning Symphony). Its successor, No. 45, is in the unusual key of F sharp minor and is known as the 'Farewell' symphony; for in the last movement the players are instructed to put down their instruments two at a time, take their candles and creep out, as a hint to their employer, at the end of the summer of 1772, that it was time to move to Vienna. Symphonies 82–87 were written for performance in Paris. They include slow introductions which are often thematically related to the following movements.

The two sets of 'London' symphonies represent the culmination of Haydn's symphonic output. They are conceived on a grander scale than any of the previous ones and are scored for large forces. The first set has two each of flutes, oboes, bassoons, trumpets, and drums as well as strings. To these are added two clarinets in the second set. No. 103 in E♭ also has bass drum,

triangle, and cymbals, representing something Turkish. These works also ex-
hibit to a high degree the distinguishing mark of an accomplished symphonist:
the ability to manipulate musical motives into an engaging and coherent
whole. In achieving this Haydn can be deeply serious but his sense of fun is
never far distant. Many of his sonata form movements have no separate
second subject. Instead, at the point where this should occur, the first subject
reappears. The first movement of the 'London' symphony itself, No. 104 in D
is a fine example. The main theme starts as shown in Example 11.1. Of this

11.1

tune Haydn is particularly interested in the part marked with a bracket, a
rhythm defined by two separate notes. This snippet is foreshadowed in the
introduction, as shown in Example 11.2. This phrase forms the basis of the

11.2

development section where Haydn thoroughly explores its implications. The
third movement of this same symphony contains a remarkable joke. Just
before the end of the second section of the minuet there are a trill, a low note,
a high note, an unexplained silence, a longer trill and a noisy cadence.

String Quartets

Haydn's other outstanding contribution to musical literature is the *string
quartet*, a term which has almost become synonymous with chamber music
itself. A string quartet is written for two violins, viola, and cello. The group is
important historically in that it came into being unsupported by keyboard
continuo. The attraction of the medium for the composer is that he has four
agile and expressive instruments of great range, all of the same family. The
lack of tonal contrast enables him to concentrate his musical thinking upon
the music itself. Since the mid-eighteenth century composers have used the
medium for some of their most inward thoughts.

The standard number of Haydn's quartets is eighty-three. Their composition
proceeded equally with that of the symphonies, although it overlaps them at
both ends. Haydn grouped them in sets, mostly of six. They are identified by
opus numbers. Haydn's quartet writing may be divided into three periods, the
first period up to 1772 containing thirty-six quartets ending at op. 20. During
this period Haydn was developing the form and exploring its possibilities.
Prominence is given to the first violin, although the other parts gradually
attain more equal importance. Nearly ten years separates this group from the
next, beginning with op. 33. This set is important historically; Haydn himself
announced, with good commercial sense, that they were written in a new and
special way. He introduced the word *scherzo* (joke) as a title for the third
movement, an idea taken up by Beethoven. These quarters were much admired
by Mozart.

The final group of quartets contains some of Haydn's most remarkable and profound music. They date from 1790. The six quartets of op. 76 are all outstanding works. No. 2 in D minor is known as the 'Fifths' for its first movement is based almost entirely on the interval of a descending fifth. Its minuet is a stark, uncompromising canon. Contrasted to this movement is the warmth of the Largo of op. 76, no. 5, in the remote key of F sharp major. This key allows none of the players to use an open string and causes them to concentrate on the exact tuning of each note they play. The most famous of the op. 76 set is No. 3, known as the 'Emperor' quartet. The tune of the slow movement was written for the birthday of the emperor in 1797; and it remained the Austrian national anthem until well into this century. As an English hymn it is sung to the words 'Glorious things of thee are spoken'. In the quartet the tune forms the basis of a set of variations whose harmony becomes more and more ethereal.

Choral Works

Throughout his life Haydn wrote choral music for the church at which he had received much of his musical training. The style of this music does not differ from that of his secular works. He himself pointed out that he could compose in no other way. His most important choral works were written after 1790. They have two main influences, the first of which is the Handelian oratorio; Haydn's first encounter with the Hallelujah chorus at a massive performance at Westminister Abbey overwhelmed him. The second influence was Haydn's own vast experience of writing symphonic music. Many of the orchestral parts of his late choral works are fully scored symphonic movements, while his choral writing is comparatively simple. After returning from his second visit to London Haydn was required to write six Masses for his new patron, Prince Nicholas II; these works include the 'Mass in Time of War', (1796), the 'Nelson' Mass (1798) and the 'Windband Mass' (1802).

But it is *The Creation* and to a lesser extent *The Seasons* which represent the peak of Haydn's choral writing. *The Creation* is an oratorio in the English tradition and was written as a spontaneous contribution to that tradition and as a work by which Haydn wished to be remembered by posterity. It contains some of the finest orchestral programme music of the eighteenth century. The 'Representation of Chaos' is a remarkable piece of writing which stretches the Classical idiom to its limits. But equally attractive are Haydn's thumbnail sketches of such things as storms, fire, snow, lions, tigers, sheep, and worms. His method is to interpret these in music *before* they are identified in words. The work also contains some very fine arias of which 'With Verdure Clad' is perhaps the most familiar. The choruses of *The Creation* have a Handelian breadth. The C major chord at 'and there was light' has been famous ever since its first performance, while the gigantic simplicity of 'The Heavens are Telling' and 'Achieved is the Glorious Work' derives directly from Handel. In popular esteem *The Creation* outdoes the *The Seasons*, although the latter work also contains some fine choruses and attractive arias. The chorus 'Hark the Deep Tremendous Voice' contains a passage which might well be attributed to Delius, while it is a pleasant surprise to find Haydn's ploughboy going off to work whistling the tune of the slow movement of the 'Surprise Symphony'.

Haydn's influence was immediate and direct. The young Beethoven, coming to Vienna in 1792, took lessons from Haydn. They were not a success, but Haydn's outlook and his musical methods were absorbed into Beethoven's own thinking.

Mozart's Life and Career

When Haydn was twenty-four, in 1756, Mozart was born. While Haydn was in London in 1791 entering upon the outstanding period of his career, Mozart died, leaving behind a body of music, its compositions numbered up to 626, which represents the highest achievement of the Classical style. Mozart is generally regarded as the outstanding example of a musical child prodigy. He played the keyboard at the age of four and was composing by the age of six.

He was born into the musical establishment of the Archbishop of Salzburg where his father, **Leopold Mozart** (1719–1787), was deputy director of music, a violinist and composer of some repute; his work on violin playing, published in the year his son was born, was for a long time the standard text-book on the subject. Leopold Mozart's other child, Marie Anne – four years older than her brother – was also an outstanding young pianist. The father's interest in his children resulted in a series of exhibition tours throughout Europe which lasted for ten years. In consequence Mozart's formative years were spent in almost constant travel and in receiving the attention of the most important people in Europe.

The first of the family's journeys, in 1762, was to Munich and this was quickly followed by a visit to Vienna to play for the Empress, Maria Theresa. The next trip lasted three years over a year of which was spent in London. Mozart's stay is commemorated by a blue plaque at No. 180, Ebury Street. Here, at the age of eight, he composed his first symphony under the influence of J. C. Bach. The final period of Mozart's youthful journeying consisted of three visits to Italy. During the first of these he wrote down from memory, after a single hearing, the nine-part *Miserere* of Allegri, since the music was forbidden to be taken out of the Vatican. The family was back in Salzburg in 1772. Mozart was sixteen and for the first time in his life spent more than a year in his native city.

By this time he had written an astonishing number of compositions – about 200 are catalogued – including concertos, operas, and symphonies. He now had a different Archbishop as an employer, who naturally objected to one of his court musicians spending most of his time away from his work. But Mozart's upbringing and temperament made it difficult for him now to accept the humble status of an ordinary musician. In August 1777 he cut himself free and went off with his mother to try his luck in Paris.

On the way they stayed for a time at Mannheim. The orchestra attracted Mozart, as did the fifteen-year-old daughter of one of its players, Aloysia Weber. The eventual stay at Paris was a disaster. His mother died and Mozart returned home without the commissions he hoped for. Salzburg irked him. Late in 1780 he was invited to Munich to write the opera, *Idomeneo*. During the day he rehearsed and attended upon the court officials. At night, in an unheated room and far from well, he composed. The finished opera is the first of his six masterworks in this form. After its production he spent the spring in Munich relaxing and joined his Archbishop in Vienna later in 1781. Mozart's reappearance resulted in his dismissal; he was actually kicked out of the building.

By now the Weber family had also moved to Vienna. Aloysia had married the actor Joseph Lange, whose unfinished portrait of Mozart is the finest one we have. Mozart moved in with the rest of the family and in 1782 married Aloysia's sister, Constanze. He entered a happy period of composing, teaching, and playing, becoming one of the first free lance musicians. But he was usually short of money and his domestic affairs were not completely satisfactory. The copyright laws were nonexistent and he was constantly disappointed at being unable to find a regular appointment; and neither Mozart nor his wife had a head for business.

During the 1780s his position and his health deteriorated. During the summer and autumn of the year of his death, 1791, Mozart composed an astonishing amount of music. In the middle of this activity, he was commissioned anonymously to write a Mass for the Dead (Requiem). Its composition was wearisome to him, for he felt that he was writing it for himself; and he died writing it. Mozart's years in Vienna, from 1781 to 1791, resulted in some of the world's finest music.

Style

Mozart's style derives initially from the use of his acute musical memory. At the age of six in Vienna he is reported to have identified a concerto whose authorship was a matter of discussion. At the other end of his life he apparently wrote out the individual orchestral parts of the *Don Giovanni* Overture straight from his head without having composed a full score. During his early travels he stored up the essence of every musical style then current in Europe; and he had already formed the habit of composing entire works in his head and writing them down when he had time. But this does not automatically mean that composition was an easy process. His own style, then, became an amalgam of all his influences transmuted through his personal musical vision. Mozart's music evokes a response in its hearers which is difficult to define, for the meaning of the music itself is frequently ambivalent. There is an underlying poignancy to much of it even when it appears to be completely relaxed. On the other hand he is capable of writing full-blooded music of sustained and powerful emotion.

Mozart's character also remains enigmatic and generally eludes those who try to portray it. It is best understood from reading his own letters which give a vivid and detailed account of himself and his daily life. His language is by turns humorous, profound, sad, obscene, childlike, and humanitarian. The begging letters which he wrote to his fellow Freemasons even now make embarrassing reading.

Mozart regarded himself as an opera composer. He earned his living largely by teaching the piano and by playing the keyboard part of his own concerti. He also played the viola. The peak of his achievement is therefore represented by his operas and his piano concerti, although his output contains major works in all the forms in which he wrote. Since 1862 Mozart's works have been identified with the letter K. before a number, according to the catalogue of Ludwig Köchel. This catalogue was revised in 1937 by Alfred Einstein but the original numbering is still in general use.

Piano Concerti

Mozart's piano concerti form a unique body of work. There are twenty-seven of them although the first four are adaptations, by the ten-year-old composer, of sonatas by other composers. Their special importance is as follows:

1. They were written specifically for the piano.
2. The soloist appears as an equal partner with the orchestra with the music of both partners being integrated into a unified whole.
3. The sonata principle is used to provide the structure of the first movement in a way which had no successors.

The first movements of Mozart's piano concerti form a study in themselves. All the concerti have three movements in the order fast–slow–fast. The plan of the first movement, from which Mozart only occasionally departs, is as follows:

1. orchestral exposition;
2. a second exposition with orchestra and piano in which the piano often has a theme of its own;
3. orchestra alone bringing the music of 2. to a close;
4. development using piano and orchestra;
5. recapitulation, piano and orchestra, with a renewed presentation of the material;
6. orchestra alone, leading to a pause on a tonic six-four chord;
7. *cadenza* for piano, ending with trill over the dominant chord (a cadenza is an improvised display piece by the soloist using the movement's thematic material);
8. orchestra alone: coda.

The music moves through this scheme in a sparkling display of controlled inventiveness.

The slow movements are often in the key of the subdominant and are frequently in modified sonata form. The most frequently used forms for the finale are rondo and sonata rondo. All the Viennese concerti, from K.413 onwards, repay whatever attention is given to them. K.453 in G and K.488 in A are among the most delightful, both with slow movements of great intensity. K.466 in D minor is a strong one; its slow movement is the familiar Romanza. K.491 and K.503, in C minor and C major, are both conceived on a grand scale.

Other Concerti

Mozart wrote concerti for instruments other than the piano, including the violin and flute. Of these the Clarinet Concerto K.622 is generally regarded as the finest work in its class, for Mozart was the first composer to write seriously for the clarinet as a solo instrument.

Symphonies

There are forty-one numbered symphonies by Mozart. Of these the last six are works of great importance, but the earlier ones contain some fine compositions. No. 25 in G minor K.183 is a good example of Mozart's tragic use of that key. The scoring includes four horns. No. 29 in A major K.201 is a happy work with a felicitous use of counterpoint. The slow movement of No. 34 in C major K.388, a three-movement work, is an ideal example of Mozart's ability to suggest conflicting emotions at the same time. The later symphonies include the 'Haffner', in D, K.385, the 'Linz' in C K.425 and the 'Prague' in D K.504, another three-movement work. Mozart's last three symphonies were written in the summer of 1788 in the space of six weeks. They are works of the highest order and each represents a different facet of Mozart's art. They are No. 39 in Eb K.543; No. 40 in G minor K.550; and No. 41, the 'Jupiter' in C K.551. The last movement of the 'Jupiter' is an outstanding feat of virtuoso composition being both fugal and in sonata form at the same time. It has five themes which at one point all appear together. The great popularity of the Symphony No. 40 underlines the flawlessness of its composition and the universal nature of its expression.

Chamber Music

Mozart's chamber music takes many forms and includes an impressive number of works of the first order. Among these are: the two piano quartets, K.478 in G minor and K493 in Eb major, both of which reflect Mozart's attitude towards a particular key; the string trio in Eb major, K.563, a difficult medium for composer and performers alike; the piano trio in E K.542 and the clarinet quintet K.581. The most outstanding of the three dozen or so violin sonatas is K.526 in A major; this is a form devised by Mozart himself.

Of Mozart's *string quartets* ten are outstanding and are among the most frequently played works of all chamber music. Six of these are dedicated to Haydn and pay tribute to the importance of Haydn's op. 33 set. In the dedication Mozart says that they cost him much time and effort, which is a healthy corrective to the facile idea that Mozart's compositions appeared to him in a flash, ready made. Each of these quartets, K.387, K.421, K.428, K.458, K.464, and K.465 (the 'Dissonance') will bear being played throughout the whole of a string player's working life. To these must be added K.499 in D ('Hofmeister'). The introduction to K.465 in C major produces some rare melodic clashes; hence its nickname.

Towards the end of his life Mozart hoped that he might be given an appointment by the King of Prussia who played the cello; he therefore projected a set of six quartets with a prominent and difficult cello part. The complete set evaporated with the hope of an appointment and only three were written, K.575, K.589, K.590. For the amateur cellist they still present a challenge. A form of chamber music particularly associated with Mozart is the *string quintet* for two violins, two violas, and cello. (In his orchestral writing Mozart often divides the violas, giving the texture a dark, rich sound.) The string quintets in C major K.515 and G minor K.516 contain the essence of Mozart's thought.

Many people first make the acquaintance of Mozart through the medium of his piano sonatas. These range from the slight but charming, written for his pupils, for example the familiar K.330 in C major, to the fully developed and meaningful works written for himself to play, for example K.310 in A minor, K.332 in F, and K.333 in Bb.

Mozart excelled in the composition of light music. This appears under a variety of titles such as Serenade, Divertimento, Cassation, Notturno. Such works frequently have five movements in the order: Allegro, Minuet, Andante, Minuet, Finale; and the most famous is *Eine Kleine Nachtmusik* K.525. It has only four movements, having perhaps lost its first minuet.

Vocal Music

Mozart's unerring melodic instinct and his deep sympathy with humanity called forth from him music for solo voice of the highest importance. Throughout his life he wrote a series of extended solos to mark particular occasions. The fine movement 'Ch' io mi scordi di te' (how can I forget you) scored for soprano, piano solo and orchestra and addressed to the English singer, Nancy Storace, is of particular significance.

This sympathy with the human voice forms the basis of his operatic writing and resulted in six operatic masterpieces: *Idomeneo* (1781), *Die Entführung aus dem Serail* (1782), *The Marriage of Figaro* (1786), *Don Giovanni* (1787), *Cosi fan Tutte* (1790) and *The Magic Flute* (1791). But what raises Mozart's operas to the outstanding position they hold in the repertoire is his uncanny dramatic instinct. This is immediately apparent in his delineation of character even when the singers are engaged in an ensemble of some complexity. The pace at which the music moves in accordance with the drama is also precisely controlled. The first scene of *Don Giovanni* proceeds from a buffo grumble through a seduction and finally to a duel to the death. All this is presented in music which both guides us and compels our attention with perfect timing until it comes to rest with the victim's last breath.

Mozart's dramatic instinct is also seen in his portrayal of psychological and dramatic truth. The plot of *Cosi fan Tutte* is absurd and yet within the confines of the drama the characters are borne along with passions which soothe them, tear them apart, or overflow with tenderness. Finally, in the major operas Mozart's orchestral writing demands from the opera-goer a pair of ears to itself. The orchestral score of *The Marriage of Figaro*, for example, is in itself a major masterpiece.

Mozart's influence is seen in the work of countless subsequent composers but it also exists largely in the constant devotion of those who come to love his music.

PART TWO: HARMONY

In the last chapter we saw how to avoid making a piece of music come to a final stop at the end of a phrase by interrupting a perfect cadence using the sequence V-VI. We also saw one way of harmonizing a particular fragment of a melody in the middle of a phrase by using a passing six-four chord. Example 11.3 shows both these progressions, and also starts with an anacrusis leading into the first bar.

V   I   I Vc Ib   IIb V   VI

11.3

Chords whose Roots Move by a 4th or a 5th

If we consider yet again the sequence II V I we find that it provides a clue to one of the most useful ways of choosing chords for the middle of a piece of music. In C major the bass notes of II V I are shown in Example 11.4. Here

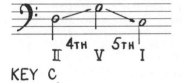

11.4

KEY C

the bass note of II, D, moves up a 4th to G which then moves down a 5th to C. If the D and C were an octave higher the moves would be down a 5th and up a 4th. Whichever way the bass moves the chords are strong and agreeable. This is true of all successive chords whose roots move by a 4th or a 5th, up or down. Both the 4th and 5th are fairly large intervals and this type of sequence causes the bass to jump about. But consider what happens if we put II into its first inversion (see Example 11.5). The bass now becomes smoother.

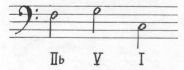

IIb   V   I

11.5

Remember that the *bass note* of IIb is F but the *root* is still D (triad = DFA). Example 11.6 is a piece using chords whose roots move up or down a 4th or a 5th.

124   *Music*

11.6

Chords whose Roots Fall by a 3rd

Another useful general rule is that successive chords whose roots fall by a 3rd sound well, as illustrated in Example 11.7.

11.7

Example 11.8 includes examples of roots moving up or down a 4th or a 5th and roots falling by a 3rd. All the chords, except IIb which is shown, are in root position.

11.8

Exercises

1. Fill in the alto part.
2. Identify the chords with Roman numerals.
3. Add passing notes where possible.
4. In Example 11.9 the alto and tenor parts are missing. Fill in the alto and tenor parts, label the chords with Roman numerals and add passing notes.

11.9

Suggested Further Reading

Einstein, A. *Mozart* (London: Cassell, 1946)

Hughes, R. *Haydn String Quartets* (BBC Music Guides, 1966)

Hutchings, A. *A Companion to Mozart's Piano Concertos* (Oxford University Press, 1950)

Landon, H. C. Robbins. *Haydn Symphonies* (BBC Music Guides, 1966)

Landon, H. C. Robbins and Mitchell, D. *The Mozart Companion* (London: Faber, 1965)

de Saint-Foix, G. *The Symphonies of Mozart* (London: Dobson, 1947)

12

PART ONE: BEETHOVEN

It is not difficult to become familiar with a large proportion of the major works of **Ludwig van Beethoven** (1770–1827). They are frequently played, have been recorded many times, and in most cases their impression is immediate and renews itself with each hearing. Beethoven himself directed the publication of his works throughout his career and assigned to each one an *opus number*; he was the first composer to exert this type of control. In the earlier part of his working life he sometimes grouped works of a similar nature under the same number to form a single opus, in the eighteenth century manner. A list of Beethoven's major works together with their dates of composition and opus numbers is given in Appendix III on p. 260 as an example of the means by which a composer's works are identified by the musical public.

Beethoven was born at Bonn, the provincial capital of the Elector of Cologne. His grandfather was court director of music and his father a singer in the choir. As a boy Beethoven became involved in the flourishing musical life of the court, as organist, viola player, teacher, and composer. Throughout his life he associated himself with the aristocracy whom he came to regard on equal terms. At Bonn these included Count Ferdinand von Waldstein to whom Beethoven later dedicated his op. 53, and the family von Breuning who had a love of literature and music. These people decided to send him to Vienna when he was sixteen to have lessons, they hoped, from Mozart.

His visit was short-lived for he returned home almost immediately on the death of his mother. But in 1792, at the age of 22, he set out for Vienna and remained there for the rest of his life. He was now an experienced composer but his immediate impact on Viennese society was as a pianist. He was much in demand at social gatherings particularly for his extraordinary ability to improvise at the piano. He was equipped with an impressive personality but did not cultivate social graces. Nevertheless he asserted himself over his distinguished audiences by his presence and his playing. Success of this kind did not deflect him from the seriousness with which he regarded his position as a composer. He put himself under the guidance of no fewer than three teachers, one of whom was Haydn. At the same time his compositions began to appear. Traditionally Beethoven's output has been divided into three stylistic periods which also roughly correspond to the changing fortunes of his life.

First Period

The first period coincides with his early years in Vienna, from 1792 until about 1802, and includes the works from op. 1 to about op. 31. The music of this period can be called 'early' only in a comparative sense, for the works are those of a mature, individual, and important composer. In its directness of expression and in its rough good humour the music is related to that of Haydn; in its expressiveness it derives from C. P. E. Bach. But such influences are quite absorbed in Beethoven's individual style. It is not surprising that a large number of Beethoven's first period works are for piano solo or for piano with other instruments; into these years fall twenty of the thirty-two piano sonatas.

From the very first these sonatas are all individual works, each with a strong character of its own. The piano itself was becoming a more expressive and powerful instrument during the 1790s; at this time, for instance, metal braces were first applied to its frame. Beethoven's sonatas exploit both the percussive and the expressive qualities of the instrument. He also rethinks and reorders the form of the sonata itself. For example all the op. 2 set have four movements instead of the traditional three; and in two of them the Minuet is replaced by the more powerful Scherzo. In the familiar 'Pathétique' sonata in C minor, the music of the introduction twice interrupts the course of the first movement. The key of this sonata is a favourite one with Beethoven and often produces from him music of a stormy character. The 'Moonlight' sonata, starting as it does with a slow movement, is an example of Beethoven's unconventional attitude towards tradition. The marking of this sonata *'quasi una fantasia'* may give the impression that this particular movement meanders in a wayward fashion. But Beethoven's instruction translates *'as though it were* freely composed': the movement is a textbook example of sonata form. The last movement of the 'Moonlight' sonata exhibits one of the main characteristics of Beethoven's style, that is the rhythmic drive which compels the listener's attention.

One of Beethoven's most popular works in his lifetime was the Septet in E♭, op. 20. This is a tuneful and uncomplicated work. Later, when Beethoven was writing music which was only partially understood, people asked why he did not write more works like the Septet. Of Beethoven's seven concerti two belong to the first period, both of them for piano and orchestra. The first movement of the First Piano Concerto, which was in fact written second, is based upon a favourite device of Beethoven's, the use of tonic and dominant harmony. In his later works he is able to raise this simple progression to heights of great expressiveness.

The first two of the nine symphonies also belong to the first period, although the spirit of the second symphony really belongs to the later Beethoven. This work is conceived on a large scale; the outer movements are both propelled along by energetic rhythmic devices while the slow movement luxuriates in an abundance of melody. The first six of Beethoven's seventeen works for string quartet also belong to his early years in Vienna. They were published as a set as op. 18 and were carefully arranged in two groups of three, each group starting with a quartet of some substance. The finest of the set is therefore perhaps op. 18, no.1. Its first movement is built on a thematic fragment from which the composer constructs a movement of great originality (see Example 12.1). In contrast the slow movement, in D minor, is dominated by a long theme

12.1

of great intensity. The quartet op. 18, no. 4, standing at the head of the second group of three, is in Beethoven's C minor manner.

When Beethoven was about twenty-eight he began to notice that he was becoming hard of hearing. By the time he was thirty he realized that he was going deaf. At first he tried to hide this affliction from the world, while society attributed its effects to his absent-mindedness or to the erratic nature of his character. But when the fact of his deafness could no longer be hidden Beethoven began to carry with him a notebook for people to write down what they wanted to say. Many of these conversation books have been preserved. They are both fascinating and frustrating documents, for they contain only what people said to Beethoven and not what he said to them. Beethoven's deafness resulted in a personal crisis; he retreated to the village of Heiligenstadt and on 6 October 1802 wrote a personal document which reads as if his life were at an end. But he came back from Heiligenstadt and faced the world afresh. From this time there is in his music a new spirit, of defiance and of heroism. He immersed himself in composition and during the decade 1802–1812 produced an unparalleled series of masterpieces, which form his second period. They were consciously addressed to all mankind and are a remarkable document of the composer's power of concentration and of the exploration of the human psyche.

Second Period

The first result of Beethoven's new approach to composition was the *Eroica Symphony*, with which he broke into a new stylistic world. The symphony is of great length – using the composer's own metronome speeds it lasts about an hour. Such a time scale is necessary for Beethoven to work out the implications of his musical material.

In the first movement the sonata principle of conflict and tonal drama is subjected to vast processes of thought as the music moves into areas from which it can retreat only gradually and over a period of time. The slow movement is a funeral march in C minor; for the whole work was originally dedicated to Napoleon who embodied Beethoven's ideals of freedom and of the brotherhood of all mankind. When in 1803 Napoleon declared himself Emperor Beethoven saw this as a betrayal of his principles and scored his name from the title page. The Eroica's third movement has removed itself entirely from the eighteenth-century minuet. Its three horns proclaim a spirit of hopefulness and of heroism. In this movement Beethoven's use of syncopation, even when familiar, still has a startling effect. The last movement provides wit, humour, and intellectual delight, all of which are gathered up and borne along by the powerful stride of the music. With this work Beethoven's attitude towards the symphony became fully apparent. His influence upon the form may be summarized as follows:

Beethoven and the Symphony

1. Beethoven's attitude towards the *structure* of the symphony is based upon his treatment of *sonata form*; he tended to give greater importance to the second subject group and extended the development section. Balance was therefore achieved by extending the coda so that it takes on the nature of a second development.

2. Each symphony presents a *unity of mood*. This is reinforced by the joining together of the last three movements of No. 6 and of the last two movements of No. 5. Furthermore the main idea of the first movement of No. 5 is used also in the third movement, while the fourth movement of No. 9 quotes each of the other movements in turn.
3. Greater importance is attached to the traditional third movement; it is given greater rhythmic vitality and increased musical weight.
4. The finale of a Beethoven symphony crowns the whole work.

Beethoven's technical innovations are:

1. an increase in the size of the orchestra; after the No. 1 his standard orchestra contains double woodwind, two horns, two trumpets, and timpani. To these are added an extra horn in No. 3; three trombones in No. 5; piccolo and double bassoon in No. 6; and double bassoon, two extra horns, three trombones, percussion, four soloists and chorus to No. 9.
2. there is greater freedom in writing for the instruments and increased technical demands upon the players, for example the cello and double bass solos in the third movement of No. 5 and the virtuoso horn writing in the trio of No. 3.

Increased size does not not necessarily result in greater quality of music; but Beethoven as a symphonist is a vast musical thinker and an emotional volcano.

Method of Composition

The composition of music for Beethoven was a protracted and difficult business, and was accompanied by a great deal of systematic hard work. He always carried with him a *notebook* into which he jotted musical ideas as they occurred to him. These ideas were then transferred to a *sketchbook* and subjected to a series of amendments until he found the shape he wanted for them. The work of composition was then begun. Beethoven was an untidy worker and not governed by any routine. Moreover, the agitation arising from his attempts to play and sing what he was hearing in his imagination produced disorder and confusion in his surroundings; he had to change lodgings frequently and is reported sometimes not to have remembered where he was living. In addition he was in the habit of working at more than one composition at the same time; the list of works from op. 53 to op. 61 gives some impression of the overlapping of this gigantic feat of concentration.

As a professional composer Beethoven remained financially independent. He professed to have little idea of money and yet his dealings with his publishers, playing them off one against the other, display a shrewdness which sometimes transcends the bounds of honesty. Moreover, in 1809 he was granted a pension by three of his patrons and in spite of the subsequent devaluation of the currency this remained a comfortable source of income to him. His patrons were handsomely repaid. One of them, the Archduke Rudolf, has for instance the following opus numbers dedicated to him: 58, 72, 73, 81, 96, 97, 111, 123, and 133.

Beethoven's most important concerti belong to the second period. They comprise the Third, Fourth, Fifth Piano Concerti, the Triple Concerto, op. 56, and the Violin Concerto op. 61. The Third Piano Concerto with its clear outlines became a model for the nineteenth-century concerto. The Fourth Piano Concerto starts with the soloist, an idea which Mozart had already used in the concerto in E♭, K.271. In both these concerti the piano, after its initial solo, remains silent during the rest of the orchestral exposition. However, in the 'Emperor' concerto (Piano Concerto No. 5) the piano makes its appearance together with the orchestra at the beginning of the first movement and remains in partnership with it throughout the work.

Beethoven's Violin Concerto is perhaps the most outstanding and most successful example of the form. The technical difficulties of writing a concerto for violin and orchestra are considerable. Unlike the piano, a violin is basically a single-line instrument and its tone forms the background of the orchestral sound against which it is competing. There are, moreover, several instruments in the orchestra which are powerful enough by themselves to swamp the sound of the violin. In the Beethoven concerto these problems do not seem to exist. It is a spacious and relaxed work which in performance provides no problems of balance.

Beethoven's attitude towards the string quartet was just as original as his attitude towards the symphony; and the second period quartets are all outstanding works. The three Rasumovsky quartets (op. 59 nos. 1–3) are all on a large scale and of such striking originality that it was at first thought that they had been written as a joke. The quartet, op. 95 is, on the other hand, a model of terse expression. Its first movement lasts about three and a half minutes and manages to range over large areas of emotional experience.

The second period piano sonatas follow those of the first period in unbroken sequence. They continue to explore the medium in a great range of structures, styles, moods, and piano sonorities. The best known are the 'Waldstein' and the 'Appassionata' each of which sums up Beethoven's methods and intentions at this time.

Beethoven's only opera, 'Fidelio', gave him more trouble than any other of his compositions. He worked at it, on and off, from 1803 to 1814. Its first version was performed in 1805. The plot is concerned with unjust political imprisonment, heroism, and freedom, all ideas which appealed to Beethoven. It is a type of work known as a *rescue opera*, which was a popular form at the beginning of the nineteenth century. For the opera's various revisions Beethoven wrote no fewer than four overtures. Of these 'Leonore No. 3' is now the most familiar. In common with all Beethoven's overtures it is often performed as a separate concert item.

Third Period

From 1812 Beethoven's music moves into its third period. His hearing was by now for practical purposes nonexistent; his general health was poor; and he was for a number of years beset by domestic troubles; he had also given up the hope of finding security in marriage. For a few years his compositions dwindled to practically nothing. But from 1816 until his death he produced a series of works dominated by a style which had become far removed from the standard ideas of Classicism. Some of these works are public ones and of gigantic stature; others reflect the inward thoughts of a man who has ceased to be influenced by external events. Into the former category fall the Ninth Symphony, the *Missa Solemnis*, the 'Hammerklavier' sonata and the 'Diabelli

Variations'. The C minor piano sonata, op. 111, partakes of both worlds. Into the second category come the last string quartets.

Late Style

The characteristics of Beethoven's final style are:

1. The working out of themes to the limit of their capabilities;
2. a concern with the technique of variation;
3. the merging of the structural elements of a composition into one another;
4. the introduction of improvisatory passages into an otherwise formal movement;
5. an interest in contrapuntal textures;
6. an interest in new sonorities, for example, all the late piano sonatas include passages using the extreme ends of the keyboard with the middle of the texture completely absent;
7. the evolution of formal Classical structures into new patterns, for example, the string quartet op. 131 contains seven movements of which only the last is in sonata form.

Beethoven's achievement may be summed up as follows: his *attitude* was that of a professional composer addressing himself to the whole of mankind. His music therefore has a direct seriousness of purpose. These aims are achieved by a boldness of formal treatment, powerful rhythms, and unexpected modulations. This results in music of startling originality and urgent inevitability which demands the listener's attention. For much of his working life Beethoven dominated musical Europe. He stood at the junction of the Classical and Romantic periods but belonged to neither. His influence both upon music and the world in general is incalculable.

The Italian terms given in Appendix II are found at the head of a piece of music as an indication of the pace and mood which the composer wishes the performer to adopt. Starting with Beethoven expression marks and indications of the manner of performance became increasingly common during the course of a piece of music.

PART TWO: HARMONY

The Alto and Tenor Clefs

As we have seen one of the most important forms of music to arise from the Classical era was the string quartet, for two violins, viola, and cello. The compass of the viola is given in Examples 12.2 and 12.3. However, most viola

12.2   **12.3**

music uses the lower two octaves only. It therefore fits comfortably neither into the treble clef nor into the bass clef. The use of either clef by itself would produce constant ledger lines; the use of both clefs would result in frequent changes from one to the other. What is wanted is a clef which puts Middle C (the centre of the instrument's working range) into the middle of the stave. This is achieved by the use of the *alto clef* (see Example 12.4.) The alto clef is

12.4

a *C clef*, and its centre indicates the position of Middle C. It is one of the two C clefs in general use. The other one is the *tenor clef* (see Example 12.5). As

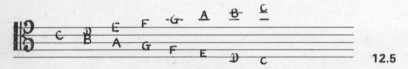

12.5

with the alto clef, the centre of the tenor clef indicates Middle C. The passage in Example 12.6 is the first three bars of the viola part of Mozart's String Quartet in G, K.387. It is written using the treble and bass clefs.

12.6

Example 12.7 shows how it appears to a viola player. The music lies comfortably on the stave. Notice the key signature of one sharp (F♯) indicating G major.

12.7

Practically all viola music is written in the alto clef. The *tenor clef* is used for the same reason as the alto clef, i.e., to avoid an excessive use of ledger lines or a frequent change of treble and bass clefs. The tenor clef is used mainly by three instruments: the cello, bassoon, and tenor trombone. All three employ the bass and tenor clefs, while cello and bassoon music may also be written in the treble clef. Example 12.8 is taken from the cello part of the

12.8

Minuet of Mozart's String Quartet in G K.387. It is written in the bass clef and then in the tenor clef. The passages in Example 12.9 are taken from Haydn's 'Emperor' Quartet, op. 76 No. 3 in C major.

VIOLA

12.9a

CELLO

12.9b

Exercises

1. Using the above two passages put the viola music into the alto clef and the cello music into the tenor clef.

2. Example 12.10 is taken from the last movement of Beethoven's last string quartet, op. 135 in F major. Put the viola part into the treble clef and the cello part into the bass clef. There is often a tendency, particularly when

KEY F MAJOR

12.10

changing viola music from the alto the treble clef to write the whole of it an octave too low. Remember that the alto and tenor clefs both indicate *Middle* C.

Chord III – The Mediant Chord

From the last chapter we saw that when harmonizing in four parts a smooth progression is obtained by choosing chords whose roots move by a 4th or a 5th, e.g., I–V–II–VI; or whose roots fall by a 3rd. Chord III results from the use of both these progressions (see Example 12.11). Another very pleasing use

KEY C MAJOR

of the mediant chord is as part of the harmony of a scale descending from the tonic. The harmony here is I–III–IV–V. This is particularly effective because of the movement of the outer parts (see Example 12.12).

Exercises

3. Fill in the alto and tenor parts of the above example. Check for consecutive 5ths and octaves.

The harmonization of the complete descending scale seen in Example 12.13 sounds well. You should be able to account for all the chord progressions.

KEY C MAJOR

I   III   IV   V   II   Ic   V   I

12.13

Suggested Further Reading

Arnold, D., and Fortune, N. (ed.) *The Beethoven Companion* (London: Faber, 1973).
Fiske, R. *Beethoven Concertos and Overtures* (London: BBC Music Guides, 1970).
Kerman, J. *The Beethoven Quartets*, (Oxford: OUP, 1967).
Lam, B. *Beethoven String Quartets* (London: BBC Music Guides, 1979).
Matthews, D. *Beethoven Piano Sonatas* (London: BBC Music Guides, 1968).
Simpson, R. *Beethoven Symphonies* (London: BBC Music Guides, 1970).
Sonneck, O. G. (ed.) *Beethoven, Impressions by His Contemporaries* (Dover, 1967).
Sullivan, J. W. N. *Beethoven* (London: Unwin, 1927).

13

PART ONE: ROMANTICISM IN MUSIC

The nineteenth century is the era of Romanticism in music. During the first quarter of the century the Classical period merged into the Romantic one, although several of the characteristics of Romanticism are already apparent in the Classical style itself.

The main features of Romantic music are:

1. Its lyricism, particularly as expressed in emotive melody.
2. This is closely allied to *chromatic harmony* used for expressive rather than for decorative purposes.
3. Priority is given to the *emotional aspect* of a work over its formal structure.
4. Formal cohesion is therefore sought in such devices as cyclic structure and the use of recurring ideas such as the idée fixe, leitmotiv and motto theme.
5. An interest in *literature*. This occurs in two ways:
   (a) composers *used* literature as a basis for their compositions;
   (b) they themselves wrote works of an aesthetic or critical nature.
6. *Programme music.*
7. The composition of small, independent pieces illustrating a title, sometimes called character pieces.
8. An idealized view of *nature*; Beethoven's Pastoral Symphony was a main influence.
9. The rise of *nationalism* in music.
10. The enhanced *status of the composer* and the view of the artist as a genius set apart from the rest of society.
11. This is seen in the adulation given to the *virtuoso performer*.
12. A love of the distant past, often romanticized, expressed, for instance, in an interest in Bach and Palestrina.
13. During this period the scientific study of music known as *musicology* was first developed.

Some of these characteristics are found as early as 1770 in the period of Sturm und Drang. They occur in much of the music of Beethoven and **Franz Schubert** (1797–1828). They gather momentum with **Carl Maria von Weber** (1786–1826). Finally Romanticism dominated music from the 1820s throughout the nineteenth century and it continues as one of the many strands which make up the music of our own century.

The First Viennese School

Franz Peter Schubert was the last of the four composers who form what is sometimes called the First Viennese School, the others being Haydn, Mozart, and Beethoven. Schubert was the only one of the four born in Vienna. The name *First Viennese School* is implicit in the use of the term *Second Viennese School* given to Schoenberg and his followers in the twentieth century. The grouping together of Haydn, Mozart, Beethoven, and Schubert is perhaps useful in the way in which it relates four major composers to the European musical capital of the time. It also serves to unite their output of *chamber music* which in practice forms the point of departure for subsequent music of this kind. However, the fact remains that Beethoven was the only one of the four who knew the other three, and while it is true that Haydn influenced Beethoven and Beethoven influenced Schubert, Schubert himself has more in common with Mozart than with Haydn.

Schubert

At the beginning of the nineteenth century Vienna was a city of about a quarter of a million people. It housed both Beethoven and Schubert, who met for the first time a week before Beethoven's death. Schubert, a fanatical admirer of Beethoven, was one of the thirty-six torchbearers at his funeral. He himself died the next year at the age of thirty-one. Schubert was trained as a singer in the same choir-school as Haydn. He left at the age of sixteen and did a year's teacher training at the end of which he joined the staff of his father's school. But his gift for composition was spontaneous and it was this which directed the course of his life. Before he was twenty he gave up teaching and spent his time in composition. Sociable by nature and much liked, he was surrounded by a circle of friends, literary and artistic, who did not let him starve. Their evening gatherings for music and poetry came to be known as Schubertiads.

Schubert's first compositions date from 1810; by 1812 his music was impressive, and by 1815 he was composing the first masterpieces of the Romantic era. Schubert composed rapidly and sometimes uncritically, rarely revising what he had written, but the spontaneous flow of his ideas gives coherence to his music. His works are now identified by the letter D. followed by a number, according to their appearance in the catalogue of Otto Deutsch. But the opus numbers which were used in Schubert's lifetime are by no means obsolete. Among his compositions are 9 symphonies, 22 piano sonatas, 35 chamber works, 6 Masses, 17 stage works, over 300 short piano pieces, and 603 songs.

Songs

All Schubert's music springs from his gift for melody and it is this which forms the basis of his pre-eminence as a writer of songs. The German art-song (the *Lied*, prounced 'leed', plural *Lieder*) existed long before Schubert, but because of his achievement the history of nineteenth century German Lieder starts with him. Schubert's songs were composed for informal, domestic performance. Today, a Lieder recital is a formal public occasion, which illustrates the degree of importance which has been subsequently attached to his songs.

Basically, a song may be either *strophic*, that is having all its verses set to the same tune, or *through-composed*, that is with the music continuously moving forward as it follows the course of the words. Schubert uses both these methods. In his mature work, that is from the age of eighteen, he adapts the strophic form so that the music of the verses varies to catch the meaning of the words. Some of his early through-composed songs are in the form of an operatic scene, that is a structure made up of several sections. Schubert's songs are distinguished by being a perfect union between the poem, the voice, and the piano. His first masterpieces appeared in 1815, a year in which he wrote over 140 songs. *Gretchen am Spinnrade* (Gretchen at the Spinning-wheel) is in modified strophic form and is the first of the many Schubert songs set to poems by **Johann Wolfgang von Goethe** (1749–1832). The girl's heart is like lead as she sits and spins and recalls her lover, his laugh, way of speaking, the touch of his hand, and of his lips. The music is simple and direct and unerringly catches the erratic movement of the treadle, the succession of the girl's thoughts, and the weight of her emotions. In the *Erlkönig* (Elf king), also of 1815, there are four characters, a galloping horse carrying a sick boy who clings to the back of his father, and Death in the form of the Erlkönig. Throughout the song the horse gallops swiftly and constantly through the night; the Erlkönig tries to entice away the frightened child while the father seeks to calm him as he tries to get to the shelter of an inn on time. The suspense which Schubert creates is released only in the final bars' recitative relating the Erlkönig's victory. Schubert wrote two *song cycles*, *Die Schöne Müllerin* (The Maid of the Mill) (1823), and *Winterreise* (Winter Journey) (1828); a third cycle *Schwanengesang* (Swan Song) was compiled after his death.

These are not the earliest examples of a collection of songs presented as a unity, for Beethoven's *An die ferne Geliebte* (To the Far-off Lover) is dated 1816. Both of Schubert's major song cycles are concerned with love. The miller in The Maid of the Mill is sad because his girl has gone off with a huntsman who is much more lively than he is. But there are consolations in the world of nature about him. *The Winter Journey*, on the other hand, is a remarkable document of the feeling of bleak desolation. A man comes into a town in spring and falls in love. The seasons symbolize his joy and fulfilment. It is now winter; he is walking away from the town alone and it is the end of a cold day. As he walks on the only other human figure to be seen is the begging hurdy-gurdy man who grinds out a tune to which no one listens.

The Symphonies

Of Schubert's nine symphonies two rightly belong to the standard repertoire: No. 8 in B minor, the 'Unfinished'; and No. 9 the 'Great C Major'. A third symphony, No. 5 in B♭, has the power of raising the spirits whenever it is heard. Why the Eighth Symphony remains unfinished is a matter for speculation. Its two movements seem complete in themselves, although this is probably because we have got used to it in that form. It is a Romantic symphony in its lyricism, its orchestral colour, and its shifts of key. It also contains sudden outbursts of gruffness, which are characteristic of Schubert's music but not apparently of his personality.

The word 'Great' given to No. 9 does double duty, distinguishing the symphony from No. 6, also in C major, and at the same time expressing the judgement of posterity regarding No. 9. The work is very long and much more highly organized than is usual with Schubert. It is thought to have been composed in March 1828, Schubert's final year. The amount of music he composed in that year, much of it of the highest order, is remarkable, and it may be that the Ninth Symphony was composed three years earlier. The length of the 1st, 3rd, and 4th movements is sustained by an insistent rhythmic drive in the manner of Beethoven. But the effect is completely different from Beethoven because of the exuberance of Schubert's melodic invention. It is this gift of melody which guides the slow movement along in music which is both carefree and nostalgic. The symphony was not performed in Schubert's lifetime; and its manuscript was discovered by Schumann in 1839. It was first performed, under Mendelssohn's direction, that year. In 1844 Mendelssohn was unable to perform the work in London since the orchestra found the music grotesque and broke down at rehearsal in helpless merriment.

Chamber Music

The chamber music of Schubert forms an enduring part of the basic repertoire. The most important works are two piano trios, four works for string quartet, two quintets, and an octet. The piano trios, in B♭ and E♭, were written in 1827, and are examples of domestic music-making at its happiest.

Of the works for string quartet one consists of a single movement, (*Quartettsatz*) in C minor; the remainder of the quartet was not completed. The existing movement is a personal outpouring by the composer, music of nervous energy relieved by the sweetly contrasting second subject. It was not performed until 1867. Of Schubert's outstanding complete quartets those in A minor and D minor are contrasting works, both written in 1824. The A minor quartet is pleasant, accessible music, tinged with melancholy. Its slow movement is based on a tune familiar from its appearance in the *Rosamunde* stage music. The quartet in D minor is a grim, persistent work. It is sub-titled 'Death and the Maiden' since all of its movements are related to Schubert's song of that name. The slow movement is a set of variations on the song itself. The quartet in G, of 1826, is Schubert's most ambitious work in the medium. It is written on a large scale and is technically difficult. The first movement is perhaps the most outstanding example of one of Schubert's most characteristic idioms for the movement hovers between the major and minor forms of the same triad. Music of a happy, domestic nature pervades the 'Trout' quintet of 1819, scored for the unusual combination of violin, viola, cello, double bass, and piano. It has five movements, the extra one being a set of variations on Schubert's song *Die Forelle* (The Trout) which is placed between the scherzo and the finale. The Octet in F of 1824 is clearly modelled on Beethoven's Septet in E♭, op. 20, and is scored for string quartet and double bass, clarinet, horn, and bassoon. The work was commissioned by a clarinettist, Count Ferdinand Troyer and in consequence the clarinet part is both prominent and delightful.

Undoubtedly Schubert's masterpiece in the field of chamber music is the String Quintet in C major, another work from the year 1828, scored for two violins, viola, and two cellos. In this respect it differs from Mozart's string quintets which include two violas and one cello, and is more akin to the quintets of Boccherini. But the music is pure Schubert, and he extracts an extraordinary range of sonorities from the combination. The music itself is of the utmost lyricism, the moods ranging from nostalgic serenity to something like despair in the Trio. On the surface the last movement sounds like café music, but there are disturbing undercurrents.

Piano music

Schubert's piano music is of three different kinds. Firstly, there are over 300 marches, waltzes, and national dances, either for piano solo or for piano duet. The most familiar of these is the *Marche Militaire*, which is one of a set of three. Next come fourteen short pieces, six with the title of *Moment Musical* and eight named *Impromptu*. These are all perfect little works which became the model for subsequent small, unpretentious piano pieces during the century. Lastly there are several extended duets, eleven sonatas, and the technically demanding work in C major known as the *Wanderer Fantasia*. Schubert's piano sonatas are quite distinct from Beethoven's. They regularly have four movements in the traditional order; they are lyrical and expansive rather than dramatic. They culminate in the three sonatas of 1828, in C minor, A major, and B♭ major. This last sonata is Schubert's most important work in this medium, much of it inhabiting the same world as the *Winterreise* song cycle.

Music for Church and Stage

Schubert wrote a great deal of music for the stage: operas, operettas, and incidental music. Much of it was not performed in his lifetime, and his operas suffer from the undramatic nature of the texts; but the incidental music to *Rosamunde* has been popular since it was composed, in 1823. Another delightful and familiar work is *Der Hirt auf dem Felsen* ('The Shepherd on the Rock'), composed on the model of a Rossini aria, and scored for soprano, clarinet, and piano. Schubert's church music, composed throughout his life, suffers from a lack of motivation on the composer's part, although certain of the Masses receive regular performances.

Style

Schubert's music has many influences including Mozart, Beethoven, and the operas of Rossini which swept Vienna in 1817; but these are all absorbed into his own musical thinking. Technically, he often hovers between the minor and the major modes; he is fond of unexpected moves to the mediant or to the flattened submediant; he likes Neapolitan harmony, i.e., that based on the key of the flattened supertonic, and chords of the augmented 6th (see Chapter 21). Above all his music constantly sings. Given the characteristics of Romanticism at the start of this chapter, we can see that Schubert is a firmly Romantic composer.

Early Romantic Opera

Nowhere is the onset of Romanticism in music seen more clearly than in the development of opera. During the first half of the century opera was centred in Paris which played host to three distinct national traditions: Italian, French, and German.

The tradition least affected by Romantic ideals was Italian. In the works of **Gaetano Donizetti** (1797–1848) and **Vincenzo Bellini** (1801–1835), the long-established Italian operatic tradition continued to pursue an orderly development. Donizetti was a prolific composer who wrote for immediate effect. His operas are compounded of catchy tunes, stock harmonies, and blood-and-thunder situations. Between 1818 and 1844 he wrote about seventy operas, perhaps the most familiar of which is *Don Pasquale* (1843). But several others still hold the stage, including *L'Elisir d'amore* (1832) and *Lucia di Lammermoor* (1835).

Bellini's work is in direct contrast to that of Donizetti. His music has a delicate strength; and his melodies are carefully constructed and are supported by a sensitive harmonic palette. He treats chorus and orchestra with equal care. His writing for his principal characters, particularly for his heroines, is technically demanding. It is possible that he both influenced and was influenced by the music of Chopin; certainly their distinctive idioms have much in common. Of Bellini's ten operas the chief are *la Sonnambula* (The Sleepwalker) (1831), *Norma* (1831) and *I Puritani* (1835).

Rossini

The most successful Italian composer of the period was **Gioacchino Rossini** (1792–1868), who had both a head for business and a flair for bringing the house down. He entered into a business partnership with Domenico Barbaia (1778–1841) who had been a waiter but eventually controlled in turn the opera houses at Naples, Vienna, and Milan. Perhaps Rossini's association with Barbaia had some effect upon the later success of his dinner parties for which he cooked some of the food himself. The first Rossini opera appeared in 1810. *The Barber of Seville*, one of the most popular of all operas, appeared in 1816. His others include *La Cenerentola* (Cinderella) (1817) and *L'Italiana in Algeri* (1813). A Rossini opera includes astute characterization, the exact placing of arias and ensembles to gain maximum effect, and the famous Rossini *crescendo*. This usually consists of a slow build-up of a repeated melody with a catchy rhythm by the means of constantly adding voices and instruments until everybody is involved. The effect is often hypnotic. During the crescendo the dramatic action is completely suspended and the audience's attention is fixed only on the slowly expanding music.

In 1825 Rossini was engaged to write operas for Paris at an enormous annual salary. He wrote two such works before retiring: *Le Comte Ory* (1828), which includes a reference to the second movement of Beethoven's Eighth Symphony, and which marked the beginning of French light opera; and *William Tell* (1829) a five-act grand opera in the French tradition. This was Rossini's last opera. For the next forty years he lived a comfortable and active life of pleasure, occasionally writing little pieces to amuse his friends, 'the sins of my old age'. Amongst these is the full-scale *Petite Messe Solennelle* (Small Solemn Mass) of 1863.

At about the same time as Rossini came to Paris there arrived also the German-born **Giacomo Meyerbeer** (1791–1864). He was born Jakob Beer and was both wealthy and cultured. After the retirement of Rossini he increased both his fame and his fortune with a series of spectacular and enormously successful operas. It is from him that the term 'grand opera' came into the European languages. It is a phrase little used nowadays but was intended to distinguish French serious opera with its five acts, its important parts for ballet and chorus from the lighter type of entertainment represented by opéra comique with its three acts and spoken dialogue.

It was not however, from the grand French opera that the main line of nineteenth-century Romantic opera developed but from the much humbler German Singspiel (see Chapter 10). By the beginning of the century this type of entertainment had developed many aspects of Romanticism, and it was in the hands of Carl Maria von Weber that these were moulded into the definitive form of German Romantic opera. Weber is a composer of great originality. Of his instrumental works the two clarinet concerti are perhaps now the most familiar. The turning point of Romantic opera arrived with his *Der Freischütz* (The Marksman) of 1821. This work inhabits a completely different world from that of French and Italian opera. It is concerned with the supernatural, the wild and mysterious, and the distant past as portrayed in the Gothic novels of the time. Its characters can be seen as symbols of supernatural forces; and all of these elements are presented with such force in *Der Freischütz* that the work became the main influence in the development of nineteenth-century opera. Weber's other important operas are *Euryanthe* (1823) and *Oberon* (1826). He died in London preparing for a performance of the latter work.

The Guitar

The start of the nineteenth century saw the beginning of that interest in the guitar which has lasted until our own day. A number of virtuoso players arose at the main centres who were also teachers and composers. In Paris were Matteo Carcassi whose Guitar Method was much in demand, and Napoléon Coste who was a composer of some talent. In Vienna was Mauro Giuliani whose guitar concertos were much played for many years. Perhaps the most important guitarists were **Fernando Sor** (1778–1839) and **Dionisio Aguado** (1784–1849). Sor worked in London from 1809 where he became a famous figure in English musical life as a guitar teacher and performer and as a composer of operas. Aguado worked in Paris; his collection of studies for the guitar is of great value and both his and Sor's Methods are still in use.

PART TWO: HARMONY

The Plagal Cadence

The rise of Romanticism saw the reintroduction of a final cadence which had largely been in abeyance during the Classical period. This is the *Plagal Cadence*. It consists of the chord progression IV I: subdominant – tonic, and has a rather more spacious effect than that of a perfect cadence. It can sound somewhat grandiose and archaic. It often forms the final cadence of a Handelian chorus. A fine example occurs at the end of the The Beatles' 'Yesterday'. It is more weighty and generally moves slower than a perfect cadence (see Example 13.1).

13.1

Exercise

1. Fill in the alto and tenor parts of the Plagal Cadences in Example 13.2.

13.2

It was a plagal cadence which was used for the singing of 'Amen' at the end of a nineteenth-century hymn. This gives a clue as to one of the main ways of using it. A piece of music can end with a perfect cadence which then merges into a plagal cadence, or with an interrupted cadence merging into a plagal cadence giving the sequences V–I–IV–I and V–VI–IV–I (see Example 13.3).

Subdominant Chord

Another way of using the *subdominant chord* is in place of the supertonic in the cadential sequence II–V–I making instead IV–V–I, as in Example 13.4.

In this progression IV–V–(I) the root moves up from one note of the scale to the next, by step. We have already met this type of movement in the

13.3

13.4

sequence I–III–IV (see Chapter 12) and in the Interrupted Cadence (V–VI). All these progressions sound well. We may add to these the progression I–II which also sounds agreeable.

In general, then, if the roots move up a step the progression is acceptable, and in particular the following may be used, in the key of C: C to D; E to F, F to G; G to A. There is, however, a built-in danger when chords move in this way, since all the notes of the chord move together consecutively (see Example 13.5.) causing a great possibility of consecutive 5ths and octaves.

13.5

Added to this there is a special difficulty which applies only to the progression IV–V, concerned with the interval of the augmented 4th, the tritone, which was known in the Middle Ages as *diabolus in musica*.

The two major 3rds in the progression IV–V form between them a tritone, as shown in Example 13.6. It is advisable to avoid making these two parts

TRITONE

13.6

move in this way if possible. A way of minimizing these difficulties and dangers is to make the soprano and bass parts move in different directions, preferably towards one another. This causes the other parts to move smoothly. (See the harmonization of the descending scale at the end of Chapter 12).

Suggested Further Reading

Einstein, A. *Music in the Romantic Era* (London: Dent, 1947).

Einstein, A. *Schubert* (London: Panther, 1971).

Capell, R. *Schubert's Songs* (London: Pan, 1957).

Longyear, Rey M. *Nineteenth-Century Romanticism in Music* (New Jersey: Prentice-Hall, 1973).

Orrey, Leslie. *Bellini* (London: Dent, Master Musicians Series, 1969).

Robertson, A. and Stevens, D. (eds.) *The Pelican History of Music, Vol. 3* (London: Penguin, 1969).

Stevens, D. *Musicology* (London: MacDonald, 1980).

14

PART ONE: MENDELSSOHN AND SCHUMANN

Throughout the nineteenth century, Paris continued to be the centre of a vigorous musical and artistic life. However, from the beginning of the Romantic era German composers became increasingly aware of the importance of their own music. Among early Romantic composers this trend is clearly represented by Mendelssohn and Schumann.

Mendelssohn: Life and Works

Mendelssohn, or **Felix Mendelssohn-Bartholdy** (1809–1847), was a remarkable man. He would have been important in music even if he had not written a note of it and would probably have been successful in whatever career he chose to follow. He was wealthy, intelligent, well-connected, with an agreeable personality and attractive good looks. He was a good classical scholar and linguist, a water colourist of more than average ability, an excellent chess player, an athlete, swimmer and horseman; he had a head for business and for organization and was devoted to his family; musically he was a child prodigy, composing fluently as a boy and developing into one of the outstanding organists of the day. His music is much loved and has accompanied countless brides on their journey into married life.

From the age of ten Mendelssohn received lessons from **Carl Zelter** (1758–1832) who was director of the Berlin Choral School (Singakademie) and an ardent admirer of the music of Bach. Mendelssohn wrote about a dozen symphonies for strings while studying with Zelter; in them the influence of Bach is clearly heard. Zelter had a manuscript score of Bach's St Matthew Passion which he was unwilling to be made public for fear that the work would not be appreciated. Mendelssohn came to know this score and at the age of fourteen was given a copy of it as a Christmas present by his grandmother. During his teens a wish to perform the work gradually possessed him. Meanwhile at the age of sixteen he composed his first work of outstanding merit, the *Octet* for strings (four violins, two violas, two cellos), in E♭, op.20. This is a remarkably mature work. In it many of Mendelssohn's stylistic characteristics may be seen: although it is a Romantic work it looks back to the Classical period, for all its four movements are in sonata form. The main theme of the first movement is wide-ranging, extending over three octaves; the slow movement has the loose lyricism of the Songs without Words; the mood of the Scherzo is fleeting; the instrumental writing is fluent and the textures transparent; the whole work has a tautness of structure and an immediacy of effect common to much of Mendelssohn's music.

In August of the next year, 1826, Mendelssohn completed the *Midsummer Night's Dream Overture*, also an outstanding work, and one of great fascination. It is, firstly, an excellent example of sonata form, for instance in the way that Mendelssohn shortens the recapitulation without sacrificing any of his musical material; secondly, it is a model of instrumental clarity; it is scored for double woodwind, two each of horns, trumpets and timpani and strings. The instrumentation also includes an *ophicleide* which was a large keyed bugle, and is now obsolete, the part usually being played by the tuba; thirdly, and quite apart from its formal structure, it is an exploration of what can be done with four descending notes; most of the main themes are based on them as well as many of the accompanying and cadential figures. Finally, the overture is a superb translation into musical terms of the ideas, mood and characters of Shakespeare's play. The development section is particularly notable, for in it Mendelssohn presents the wood in which the central portion of the play takes place; the music teems with tiny creatures, some playing miniature instruments; the atmosphere is at first mysterious and eerie, but gradually becomes real and of human dimensions, until Hermia enters and sinks down wearily to four descending notes.

The Concert Overture

Mendelssohn completed the remaining incidental music, including the Wedding March, much later, in 1842, for an actual performance of the play. But the Midsummer Night's Dream Overture is one of the first examples of a *concert overture*; that is, an independent orchestral piece, complete in one movement, with a title which the music illustrates, and often in sonata form. With the completion of the Octet and the Midsummer Night's Dream Overture Mendelssohn had reached musical maturity. After this his style did not develop but he nevertheless continued to compose a series of important works throughout his life,

At about the time of the Midsummer Night's Dream Overture Mendelssohn started rehearsing the St Matthew Passion. Fortunately the family garden ran to several acres in which was a pavilion large enough to accommodate all the performers. With a fine sense of occasion the work was presented on Good Friday – March 11 – 1829, the first performance having been given by Bach at Leipzig on Good Friday 1729. Mendelssohn's performance was a Romantic one rather than a Baroque one, in the instruments he used, the size of orchestra and choir, and the interpretation of the score, but it is one of the cornerstones of the nineteenth-century Bach revival.

After this performance Mendelssohn went on a grand tour which included Scotland and Italy. This resulted in the *Hebrides Overture* (1830), the *Italian Symphony* (1833), and the *Scottish Symphony* (1842) which was dedicated to Queen Victoria. The *Hebrides Overture* is a superbly evocative piece of music, recalling as it does the spaciousness and clarity of a seascape on a fine day and, given its title, it is everybody's impression of certain parts of Scotland. In this way it is more successful than the Scottish Symphony which openly tried to imitate Scottish music. In the overture the great wave with its spindrift which ushers in the recapitulation is a fine musical stroke. The Hebrides's opening theme, which suggests the swell of the sea, is also the basis of all the other musical material in the work. Its relationship to the second subject is apparent in the last bar but one, when both themes take leave of the work together.

The *Italian Symphony*, No. 4 in A major, is probably Mendelssohn's most successful large-scale orchestral work; it combines all the virtues of scoring and form which have been noted above. The interest starts even before the wide-ranging first subject of the 1st movement; the very first chord is a model of scoring.

Piano Works and Concerti

Between 1829 and 1845 Mendelssohn composed and gathered into seven volumes the *Songs without Words*. They were intended as affectionate contributions to autograph albums and many of them are sentimental; some of them are familiar, such as No. 29 in A, the Venetian Gondola song; No. 30, also in A major, the Spring Song; and No. 34 in C major, The Bee's Wedding; some of them suggest that the recipients were quite accomplished players. Mendelssohn's sets of variations for piano contain much stronger music; this is particularly the case with the *Variations Sérieuses* of 1841.

The brilliance of Mendelssohn's piano writing is seen in the two piano concerti; the first in G minor (1831), op. 25 is more familiar than the second in D minor (1837), op. 40. But more important and more well known than either of these is the *Violin Concerto*, in E minor (1844), op. 64. This is an extremely successful work, for the capabilities of the solo instrument are fully exploited but always within the bounds of musicality. These concerti show some modifications to the traditional form in that the opening orchestral exposition is abolished; the movements are also interlinked while the cadenzas have a functional rather than a decorative purpose; that of the first movement of the Violin Concerto serves to introduce the recapitulation.

The literature of the organ in the nineteenth century is quite limited. Mendelssohn's contributions to it are important and show his devotion to the music of Bach, particularly in the three Preludes and Fugues (1837), op. 37 and six sonatas (1844–1845) op. 65.

Elijah

Mendelssohn visited England seventeen times, the last two of these, in 1846 and 1847, were mainly concerned with the oratorio '*Elijah*', which was written for the Birmingham Festival of 1846. This work has maintained its popularity with choral societies and is successful because it meets Handel on his own ground. It is a dramatic work and it contains a series of fine choruses which are interspersed with memorable solos. Perhaps the finest chorus of all is No. 29 'He, watching over Israel'. During Mendelssohn's last visit to England the ceaseless activity over the years had begun to take its toll, and the death of his sister was the final blow. In September 1847 the finest of his six string quartets, op. 80 in F minor, was composed in her memory. When Mendelssohn died in November, the effect upon Europe was as if a great statesman had died. Such had already become the status of a musician in the Romantic era.

Of Mendelssohn's many public appointments two in particular deserve notice, both of them connected with Leipzig. In 1843 the Leipzig Conservatory was founded by Mendelssohn with him as its first director. The musical academy represented part of the general spread of musical education throughout Europe in the nineteenth century, starting with the Paris Conservatoire in 1793. The Royal Academy of Music was the first of the London schools in 1822. The Leipzig Conservatory was important from its foundation, including among its staff and students a brilliant series of musicians, many of them

English. Unfortunately it was the weaker side of Mendelssohn's music which they emulated.

Mendelssohn's other important appointment in Leipzig was as director of the *Gewandhaus Concerts*. These were started when Bach was at Leipzig and carried enormous prestige. Mendelssohn's standards as a conductor were exacting; he helped to raise the standard both of public concertgiving and of orchestral playing.

Schumann: Character and Early Life

The music of **Robert Schumann** (1810–1856) is largely autobiographical. It is not merely bound up with the external events of his life but also constantly reflects a fantasy world of his own creation. The music is full of allusions and private messages; many of these no doubt still lie undetected and the significance of others is lost upon us. But fortunately the music itself is of sufficient calibre for this not to matter. Schumann is an excellent example of the literary Romantic musician. His father was a dealer in books at Zwickau, about fifty miles south of Leipzig, where Schumann was born; and in his early years Schumann devoted as much time to literature as he did to music. When writing or composing he imagined himself as various pantomime characters, especially Florestan if feeling fierce, or Eusebius if feeling dreamy. He also identified himself with the biblical David who killed Goliath and he invented a band of Davidites to fight against the Philistines.

The year 1828 was an important one for Schumann. During this year he first met the poet **Heinrich Heine** (1797–1856) whose lyrics appealed to him throughout his life. He also started to take piano lessons at Leipzig from Friedrich Wieck (1785–1873) whose daughter, Clara, then aged nine was already an accomplished pianist. At this time he was also a student at Leipzig University, supposedly reading law although he did not do any work. He transferred to Heidelberg University but spent much of his time there practising the piano and toying with several compositions. At Heidelberg he heard and was impressed by the virtuoso violinist **Niccolò Paganini** (1782–1840). He returned to Leipzig in 1830 and continued studying with Friedrich Wieck. But by 1832 he had given up any thought of being a concert pianist, for his right hand was not strong, either through some hereditary weakness or as a result of damage inflicted by himself while trying to strengthen it.

In 1834 Schumann started a successful newspaper devoted to musical criticism which he edited for the next ten years. Its first mention of Chopin started with the words 'Hats off, gentlemen, a genius'. Also in this year there came to board at the house of the Wiecks a girl of seventeen called Ernestine von Fricken. Within ten weeks Schumann was engaged to her; Clara Wieck was then fifteen.

The Music

Schumann's compositions during the 1830s are mostly for solo piano. The works are made up of short allusive pieces bound together by an overall title. Schumann's op. 1, for instance, is a set of variations on the notes A B E G G this being the surname of a girl he met at a dance. Op. 6, of 1837, is a set of eighteen pieces making up the 'Dances of the Society of David' (*Davidsbündlertänze*). These are dedicated to the poet Goethe 'by Florestan and Eusebius'. But the work which most revealingly sums up Schumann's life to this point is *Carnaval* op. 9, of 1834. It consists of twenty pieces, most of them based on the letters A–S (E♭ in German) C–H (B in German). Asch is the village where Ernestine von Fricken came from but these letters are also the musical ones in the name *SCHUMANN*. As the carnival passes we see both Eusebius and Florestan among other pantomime figures, Clara (Chiarina), Ernestine (Estrella), Chopin, Paganini, and the Davidites marching against the Philistines. Schumann's most successful extended piano composition of this period is the *Fantasy in C major*, op. 17 of 1836.

On New Year's Day 1836 Ernestine was jilted and in 1837 Schumann proposed to Clara Wieck. Her father was not amused; but Schumann was persistent and a quarrel between the two men dragged on for nearly two years. In the end Schumann went to law to get permission for the marriage; while the case was proceeding he went to Vienna with the idea of setting up home there. In Vienna he met Schubert's brother who allowed him to go through Schubert's unpublished manuscripts among which Schumann came across the Great C Major Symphony. In 1840 the marriage between Schumann and Clara Wieck took place. Its effect on Schumann was to release in him a flood of lyric song writing. During the year he wrote about 140 songs which immediately place him, with Schubert, among the outstanding Lieder writers of the nineteenth century. The four song cycles of 1840 include the *Frauenliebe und -Leben* (A Woman's Life and Loves) and the *Dichterliebe* (The Poet's Loves). Schumann's songs differ from those of Schubert in that their mood is generally more introspective and the parts of the piano and voice become much more interdependent with the piano frequently having the last word in a postlude which sums up the whole feeling of the song.

The Schumanns' marriage was a happy one but the partners were not equally matched. Clara Schumann was a much more forceful and stable character than her husband. She was becoming internationally famous as a concert pianist while he was still a comparatively unknown composer of piano pieces. Schumann therefore turned to the composition of large-scale orchestral works and in 1841 wrote the first two of his four symphonies and a Fantasy in A minor for piano and orchestra which we now know as the first movement of the Piano Concerto. Schumann's First Symphony in B♭ major, the 'Spring' Symphony, op. 38, is a joyous work, overflowing with songlike Romantic themes and moving forward with boundless energy. The second symphony in D minor was extensively revised in 1851 and published as No. 4. It is a much more introspective work and shows Schumann developing the cyclic method of symphonic writing. All the four movements flow into one another and the thematic material is largely derived from the first movement's introduction.

In 1842 Schumann's principal chamber works were composed. These consist of three string quartets, a piano quartet and a piano quintet. The string quartets, op. 41 are influenced by Beethoven although they are all Romantic in feeling, particularly op. 41, No. 3 in A major. Both the *Piano Quartet*, op. 47 and the *Piano Quintet*, op. 44 are fine examples of Schumann's mature, Romantic style; the slow movement of the Quartet is particularly beautiful.

The years 1843 and 1844 both provide examples of the difficulties which beset Schumann. Mendelssohn had been at Leipzig since 1835 and had been a source of constant support to Schumann, making his works known and giving him advice both musical and personal. When the Leipzig Conservatory opened Schumann was appointed as a piano teacher and conductor, but the appointment was not a success and before the end of the year Schumann had resigned. In the next year Clara Schumann made a highly successful concert tour in Russia which brought her international acclaim. Her husband spent a lot of time in dressing rooms during the concerts waiting for her to return after she had received all the applause. On their return they moved to Dresden and it was here in 1845 that the remaining two movements of the Piano Concerto were written.

Schumann's *Piano Concerto* in A minor, op. 54 is justly one of the most popular in the repertoire. Although its composition extends over five years it is a remarkably integrated work, with both a rhythmic and a thematic unity; the most outstanding feature of the main themes of all of the movements is the rising octave leap but this itself is part of a phrase common to all the themes. The concerto's orchestration is most effective and the integration of piano and orchestra is effortless. The rhythmic complexity of the third movement is probably the most successful of Schumann's many experiments in this direction, and the sustained invention of the work's final pages is a matter of wonder at each performance.

Schumann's Second Symphony in C Major, op. 61 was written in 1846. It is the least memorable of the four, although its slow movement has the haunting quality of Schumann's best music. The Third Symphony in E♭ (the 'Rhenish') of 1850 is a fine work. It has five movements the first of which is vigorous and compelling. The solemn fourth movement which evokes the Rhine and Cologne cathedral is an expression of the growing feeling of German unity.

Between 1847 and 1850 Schumann wrestled with his only opera, *Genoveva*. In spite of the quality of some of the music it is not a successful stage work. In 1848 he gathered together, for his daughter's birthday, the pieces known as 'Album for the Young' (*Jugendalbum*), op. 68.

In 1850 Schumann was persuaded to accept the post of director and conductor of the concert society at Düsseldorf. At this time the position of orchestral conductor had begun to assume something of the importance which we now attach to it, through the example of musical directors such as Weber, Mendelssohn, and Berlioz. Schumann's appointment was disastrous. Within six months the morale of the orchestra had disappeared and Schumann's direction had become ineffectual although he did not officially resign until 1853. It is sometimes held that the thickness of Schumann's own orchestral scoring resulted from his fear of having to direct performances of his works on the assumption that even if some of the players stopped the music would still go on. However, subsequent attempts to rescore Schumann's symphonies are not a success and they are now usually played as he wrote them, on the grounds that the scoring is just what he intended.

In 1853 the Schumanns befriended the twenty-year-old Brahms and welcomed him into their home; Schumann's musical influence is seen directly in the music of Brahms. In 1854 Schumann became insane and threw himself into the Rhine, but was rescued. He spent the next two years in an asylum where he died in 1856. Clara Schumann lived until 1896 pursuing a distinguished career as a pianist, composer and teacher. She and Brahms remained devoted to one another throughout this period and her death fore-shadowed that of Brahms a year later.

Schumann's style is seen most clearly in his piano writing, with its richness of part-writing and his precise use of the pedal. Both melody and harmony contribute to the sense of nostalgia and of introspection. Paradoxically Schumann's music creates a feeling of warmth and security. The short piano pieces form the basis of all his other writing; the songs are another aspect of it; in the larger works the music does not develop but teems mosaic-like with ideas.

PART TWO: HARMONY

The Dominant Seventh

A chord of the seventh may be formed on any degree of the scale by adding to the triad a 7th above its root (see Example 14.1). Of these chords the *dominant seventh*, V_7, is the most frequently used. In C major the dominant 7th (V_7) consists of GBDF. This would be referred to in popular music as G_7: G_7 and the dominant 7th of C major are the same thing.

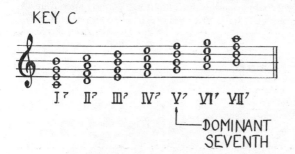

14.1

The dominant seventh is a rich-sounding chord and if used too frequently has a cloying effect. One of the charges against Mendelssohn is that he was overfond of it but his music also contains some very effective uses of it (see Example 14.2). Since chords of the 7th consist of four notes they have *3*

14.2

inversions in addition to the root position (see Example 14.3; the figuring of these chords is also shown. Since V_7 is an enrichment of V the progression

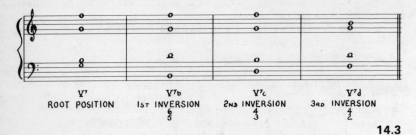

14.3

V–V_7 increases the interest while V_7–V is disappointing. V–V_7 is often found at cadences with the 7th being used as a passing note, as in Example 14.4. There

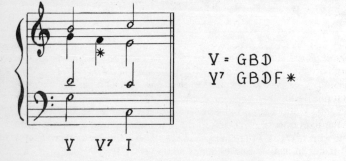

$V = GBD$
$V^7 \ GBDF*$

14.4

is a standard way of resolving V_7 in whatever position it is used: the 3rd should rise and the 7th should fall (see Example 14.5).

KEY C

$V^7 \ GBDF$
3RD 7TH

14.5

Use of the Dominant Seventh

1. *Root position*, V₇I as above or V₇VI as in a Perfect and an Interrupted
   Cadence (see Example 14.6).

   *In the progression V_7I one of the chords has to have its 5th left out in order
   to avoid consecutive 5ths.* In Examples 14.4 and 14.5 the second chord – I –
   consists of CCCE.

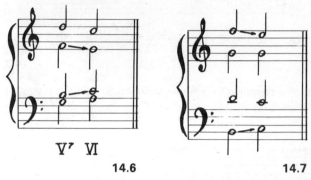

14.6   **14.7**

2. *1st Inversion*, V₇bI. This is the easiest form to use: the four notes of V₇b
   go naturally to the four-part chord of I (see Example 14.7).
3. *2nd Inversion*, V₇cI. V₇c is best used in the same way as a passing ⁶₄ chord,
   as in Example 14.8.
4. *3rd Inversion*. V₇dI. This progression cannot be used as a final cadence
   because the bass note of V₇d falls to the 3rd of I, making a 1st inversion
   chord. A very effective progression is V–V₇d with the bass leaping up a
   minor 7th, shown in Example 14.9.

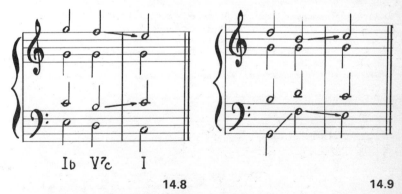

14.8   **14.9**

In order to form the dominant 7th in any key,

1. Write down the notes of the dominant triad (refer to the table of triads on
   p. 74); e.g., in D major the dominant is AC♯E.
2. Add the note in the scale of D which is a 7th above A (the root of the
   dominant), in this case = G. The dominant 7th of D therefore = AC♯EG.

Exercises

1. Write down the names of the notes of the dominant 7th in the keys of (a) C (b) D (c) A (d) B♭ (e) E♮ (f) A♮

2. Example 14.10 shows dominant 7ths in their root position. Resolve them

14.10

on to the following tonic chord (V₇–I). Remember that the 3rd of V_7 must rise and the 7th must fall.

3. Supply the missing notes in the progressions of Example 14.11.

14.11

Suggested Further Reading

Chissell, J. *Schumann*. (London: Dent, Master Musicians, 1979).

Gal, Hans. *Schumann Orchestral Music* (London: BBC Music Guides, 1979).

Horton, J. *Mendelssohn Chamber Music* (London: BBC Music Guides, 1972).

Radcliffe, P. *Mendelssohn* (London: Dent, Master Musicians, 1967).

Radcliffe, P. *Mendelssohn Orchestral Music* (London: BBC Music Guides, 1972).

Walker, A. (ed.) *Robert Schumann, The Man and His Music.* (London: Barrie & Jenkins, 1976).

15

PART ONE: THE FLOWERING OF ROMANTICISM

During the 1830s the spirit of Romanticism found full expression in the work of the many writers, painters, and musicians congregated in Paris. Among the writers were Victor Hugo and Alexandre Dumas the elder, and the two women novelists: Aurore Dudevant, better known as George Sand, and the Comtesse d'Agoult who wrote under the name of Daniel Stern. The musicians included Rossini, Meyerbeer, the virtuoso violinist Niccolò Paganini (1782–1840), the equally brilliant pianist Charles Morhange (1813–88) known as Alkan, and the commanding figures of Chopin, Berlioz, and Liszt.

Chopin

Frédéric Chopin (1810–49) arrived in Paris in 1830. He was already famous both as a pianist and as a composer, having made a successful tour in Berlin and in Vienna the previous year. He was born near Warsaw and brought up in the prevailing French culture. From 1830 Paris remained his home for the rest of his life. He gave a few public concerts but was much happier as a teacher than as a concert pianist. His pupils were for the most part aristocrats from whom he commanded high fees. He visited Germany in 1834 and in 1835 and met Mendelssohn and Clara and Robert Schumann.

In 1836 he first met George Sand. The relationship between them, which lasted until 1847, was complicated by the presence of George Sand's two children and by the tuberculosis of the throat which was beginning to affect Chopin. These four spent the winter of 1838–39 near Palma, in Majorca. The stay was disastrous, for the local populace was suspicious of Chopin's illness and the party had to move away to a deserted monastery. Moreover, it rained constantly; but Chopin's piano had been sent over from the mainland and he continued composing. By 1847 George Sand's children were grown up and the domestic situation became even more complex. Chopin broke with the family that year. He made a final visit to England before he died. Chopin is one of the few nineteenth-century composers to have escaped the influence of Beethoven. His style is highly individual but may be traced from Mozart through three pianist-composers in particular. These are **Muzio Clementi** (1752–1832), **Johann Nepomuk Hummel** (1778–1837), and **John Field** (1782–1837). Clementi is remembered for his keyboard works, which exploit the fullness of tone and the dynamic range of the newly-developed piano. Hummel cultivated a lighter and less dramatic style of writing. Field's influence on Chopin is direct. He came from Dublin to London where he took lessons from Clementi who had set up in the capital a firm of piano manufacturers and distributors. Field became the demonstrator of Clementi's pianos in London and later in St Petersburg where he died as a result of a life of dissipation. Field wrote seven piano concerti and eighteen *Nocturnes*, a title which he is believed to have invented. Chopin's Nocturnes derive directly from Field's.

Chopin's Works

When Chopin came to Paris he brought with him two Piano Concerti: No. 1 in E minor, op. 11 and No. 2 in F minor, op. 21. His style of writing for the piano was already fully developed but he was not happy writing for orchestra and the main bulk of his total output is for piano solo. A large proportion of his piano works are small, typically Romantic pieces, with a title indicating their scope, but he is by no means a miniaturist. He was much influenced by traditional Polish music, although his view of it was perhaps somewhat idealized. Throughout his career he wrote Polish dances such as the Mazurka, in $\frac{3}{4}$ rhythm with an accent on the second beat; and the Polonaise, also in $\frac{3}{4}$ time with dotted rhythms and softened cadences.

But Chopin's cosmopolitan outlook is also represented by collections of waltzes, impromptus, preludes, nocturnes and studies. The twenty-four Preludes, op. 28 were completed in Majorca. There is one Prelude in each major key followed by another in its relative minor. They start in C/A minor and then move up by 5ths to G/E minor, D/B minor, and so on. The two sets of Études (studies) opp. 10 and 25 each contain twelve pieces and each separate study deals with some technical aspect of keyboard playing; this fact is overshadowed by the musical quality of the pieces themselves. Op. 10, no. 12 is the familiar 'Revolutionary' Study, in C minor. The Études tend to be brilliant by nature; the Nocturnes, on the contrary, are generally reflective and contemplative. They are not grouped in sets but were composed throughout Chopin's career. Most of them are based on striking musical ideas which are perfectly worked into a simple overall structure.

Chopin's large-scale works include four Ballades, four Scherzos and three sonatas. Chopin was apparently the first composer to use the term 'Ballade' and his works in this form, especially op. 23 in G minor and op. 52 in F minor, give the impression of a continuous narrative springing from the initial material. The Scherzos bear little relation to earlier uses of the term and are strong, passionate works in tautly organized forms. Of the sonatas the second in B minor, op. 35 (the Funeral March sonata) and the third in B minor, op. 58 are both fully Romantic works, unconventional in their form, but dramatic and intensely lyrical.

Chopin's Style

Much of Chopin's music is introspective, but without the slightest trace of sentimentality, although it contains some of the nostalgic quality found also in Schumann. On the other hand the music can be dramatic without being theatrical. Chopin's melody is sharp and clearly defined, as are his formal structures. In performance his music lends itself to *tempo rubato* (literally 'robbed time'), that is, a discreet holding back of the phrases of the right hand while the left hand continues in strict time. Chopin's lyricism has much in common with that of Bellini although the extent to which one composer influenced the other is difficult to determine. Chopin's harmony is generally chromatic and often modulates unexpectedly. His piano music is inseparable from the instrument itself; in his spacing of chords, his sonorities and in his creation of pianistic figuration and ornamentation his influence was considerable; but his personal style is inimitable.

The Piano

The piano did not completely displace the harpsichord until the end of the eighteenth century, but its eventual triumph was considerable for it is perhaps the outstanding instrument of the nineteenth century.

As a keyboard instrument the piano combines the mechanism of the clavichord – whereby a string is struck by a hammer – with that of a harpsichord, whereby the resultant tone can be dampened. In order to achieve this three problems had to be overcome:

1. how to propel the hammer freely towards the string;
2. how to allow the hammer to fall back freely once it has struck the string;
3. how to dampen the sound as soon as the player releases the key.

The construction of an instrument which successfully overcame these difficulties is first attributed to **Bartolomeo Cristofori** (1665–1731) at Florence in 1709. The main lines of development which followed this invention were as follows:

In Germany, Gottfried Silbermann (1683–1753) about 1740, solved the problem of allowing a note to be rapidly repeated. His brother, Andreas Silbermann (1678–1734), about 1770, improved the escapement mechanism of the hammer.

In England, Silbermann and Johannes Zumpe, in 1775, improved the tone and gave the instrument greater sonority. They produced the English square piano. John Broadwood applied scientific principles to the mechanism of the instrument and in 1783 decided the exact point at which the string should be struck for maximum effect.

In France, Sébastien Erard produced his first piano in 1777. Erard pianos eventually combined the rapid action of German instruments with the sonority of the English ones.

The iron frame was introduced and improved by the firms of Broadwood, Erard and the American Chickering and Sons during the early years of the nineteenth century. The system of overstringing by which the longer bass strings are crossed over the shorter higher ones was introduced in 1827 by the Parisian firm of Blanchet and Rollet. By the 1840s the concert grand for which Chopin wrote was recognizably the same instrument as we have today, although during the remainder of the nineteenth century the piano was further strengthened and subject to various refinements by individual firms.

Hector Berlioz

The nineteenth-century development of the piano was accompanied by the evolution and enlargement of the orchestra. **Hector Berlioz** (1803–1869) stands in much the same position towards the orchestra as does Chopin towards the piano. It is true that some of Berlioz's most important works include voices but it is the expertise of his instrumental scoring which gives his music its special character. His handling of the orchestra is marked by a mixture of sensitivity and flamboyance. His own personality was extrovert and forceful; sometimes his excesses led him into embarrassing situations, financial, domestic, and artistic. He has left us an excellent account of himself in his *Memoirs* and letters. He came to Paris from Grenoble in 1821 to study medicine, but turned instead to music. In 1826 he entered the Paris Conservatory and eventually won the scholarship known as the *Prix de Rome*. This has been offered annually by the French Ministry of Culture (Académie des Beaux-Arts) since 1803 and allows the holder to study in Italy for four years. Berlioz won it in 1830 but by 1832 had returned to Paris. His return was not unconnected with the Irish actress Harriet Smithson, whom he eventually married but towards whom his dealings up to then had been a trifle bizarre. It was because of her, however, that he wrote his first major work, the *Fantastic Symphony* (*Symphonie fantastique*), subtitled 'An Episode in the Life of an Artist'. This work is autobiographical and is derived from de Quincey's 'Confessions of an English Opium-Eater'. It is a *programme symphony* and Berlioz intended that the audience should listen to it following a detailed description of the course of events. It is in five movements, each of which conveys a different aspect of the hallucinatory effects of taking opium. The artist's amorous obsession, which eventually leads him to suicide, is represented by an *idée fixe*, a constantly recurring theme which binds the whole symphony together (see Example 15.1). The work is of considerable historical importance.

15.1

Among Berlioz' other symphonies is one entitled *Harold in Italy*, a four-movement work which again makes use of a motto theme, or idée fixe, and which has an important part for solo viola which was written for Paganini. The *Romeo and Juliet Symphony* has seven movements, four of which use soloists and chorus. This work is operatic in character but is still recognizable as concert hall music. The *Funeral and Triumphal Symphony* was written for a national event and is chiefly notable for the exuberance of its scoring which includes 110 violins, hundreds of voices, and four brass bands. A similarly large-scale work is the *Te Deum* for three choirs, orchestra, and organ.

Berlioz' symphonies lead in two directions: as purely orchestral works they point towards the symphonic poems of Liszt; but because of their increasing use of voices and looseness of structure they tend to become indistinguishable from Berlioz's own dramatic works for the stage and his religious works of the oratorio type.

Stage Works

Berlioz is very important in the history of nineteenth-century French opera. His works include *The Damnation of Faust*, which he called a dramatic legend; *The Childhood of Christ* from which the 'Shepherds' Farewell' is justly celebrated; and *Benvenuto Cellini*, a grand opera – in the French sense – based upon the life of a character with whom Berlioz had much in common. But Berlioz's main operatic achievement is the five-act *The Trojans* (*Les Troyens*) (1856–1858). This was composed as a single work lasting five hours but was later divided by Berlioz into 'The Capture of Troy' and 'The Trojans at Carthage'. Berlioz devised the text himself from the Latin epic poem (the Aeneid) by Virgil. The opera – like his *Romeo and Juliet* – does not present a continuous narrative but deals with a succession of events conveyed in a series of dramatic scenes interspersed with all the paraphernalia of a French grand opera – ballets, choruses, and processions. But the exuberance of Berlioz's treatment of the epic does not make for looseness of structure. On the contrary, every part of the music is made relevant to the text by the acuteness of Berlioz's psychological perception.

Berlioz's Position in Musical History

Until well into the twentieth century, Berlioz's standing as a composer was a matter of considerable disagreement. His detractors maintained that his melodies sounded contrived, that his harmonic progressions were unmusical, and that his counterpoint was nonexistent. These sins, combined with his bombastic ideas, caused him to be damned. But today his works are more readily available and he is recognized as a composer of considerable ability and influence; his fine rhythmic sense and his superb feeling for orchestral texture have never been doubted. His Treatise on Instrumentation of 1844 is still a valuable guide to the way in which instruments may be used in combination. He typifies perfectly the romantic artist; and in his precise translation into music of psychological drama he is a composer of a very high order.

Berlioz's Orchestra: The Development of Orchestral Instruments

As a young man Berlioz devised his ideal orchestra. It consisted of 417 players as follows: 120 violins, 40 violas, 45 cellos, 37 double basses, 14 flutes, 12 oboes, 5 saxophones, 15 clarinets, 16 bassoons, 16 horns, 18 trumpets, 12 trombones, 3 ophicleides, 2 tubas, 30 harps, 30 pianos, organ, and percussion.

The first chapter of his Treatise on Instrumentation lists 44 different sorts of instrument. During his lifetime improvements were made to all sections of the orchestra: woodwind, brass, percussion, and strings.

To the *woodwind section* were added new instruments such as the saxophone; the old instruments were improved by the addition of keys and by new methods of fingering. Mainly responsible for these improvements were **Theobald Boehm** (1794–1881) and **Adolph Sax** (1814–94).

The *brass section*: all the brass instruments with the exception of the trombone were improved by the addition of valves. In the orchestra this section was enlarged to include four horns, tenor and bass trombone and sometimes four trumpets, in place of which or in addition to which French composers often preferred cornets.

Percussion: From the mid-nineteenth century dates the introduction of the great variety of pitched and non-pitched percussion instruments with which we are familiar today. In this section also must be included the harp.

Strings: Paganini had greatly extended violin technique. Great improvements were also made to the violin bow by **François Tourte** (1747–1835) who made a delicate and finely balanced bow with the stick curving towards, instead of away from, the hair. His bows are today still used and greatly sought after by violinists.

Transposing Instruments

There are several orchestral instruments whose music does not sound at the pitch at which it is written. This may seem odd but it generally makes for convenience of performance. Such instruments are known as *transposing instruments*. They may be divided into three groups:

1. Instruments whose sound is so high or so low that their part would appear almost entirely on ledger lines if written at its proper pitch. Amongst these are the piccolo, glockenspiel, and celesta whose music is written an octave lower than it sounds; and the double bass, whose music is written an octave higher than it sounds.

2. Instruments which are made in different sizes and whose basic scales therefore differ in pitch. The player learns a single fingering for all sizes of the same instrument. The written music is then transposed in such a way that the player always applies the same fingering to the same written notes; the actual sound then varies according to the size of the instrument. For instance, a player of a B♭ clarinet sees a written C and fingers accordingly; the actual sound is B♭. He then picks up an A clarinet and again plays a written C using the same fingering; the sound this time is A. This means that the music of a clarinet in B♭ is always written up a tone, e.g., a piece of music in G major would be written in A major, and the music for a clarinet in A is written up a minor 3rd, e.g., a piece of music in G major is written in B♭ major.

    Music for a quartet of saxophones is written in the treble clef for all the instruments. The music sounds lower than it is written, as follows: the Soprano sax in B♭ sounds a tone lower than written (as for clarinet in B♭); the Alto sax in E♭ sounds down a major 6th; the Tenor sax in B♭ sounds down a 9th (octave and a tone); and the Baritone sax in E♭ sounds down an octave plus a 6th.

3. The horn, whose basic scale (of the natural horn) is F major. Before the introduction of valves the notes available to a natural horn were limited; and so in order to allow the instrument to be played easily in various keys the player kept by him a number of 'crooks', each crook corresponding to a different key. The composer indicated the crook to be used, writing the music always in C major. The player played in C major but the crook which he inserted ensured that the music sounded in the key the composer wanted. With the introduction of valves the horn in F remained the standard instrument but the use of crooks was discontinued. This meant that every horn note sounded a 5th lower than it was written. However, all horn music continued to be written with the key signature for C major, i.e., no sharps or flats, the composer adding the appropriate accidentals as he went along for whatever key he was writing in.

    But a difficulty now arises whenever a horn player (with a horn in F) meets a pre-valve part written for a crook, say, in E♭. In this case the player has to make his own transposition in addition to that assumed by the composer. All horn parts in the treble clef transpose *downwards*. But up till about 1900 horn parts in the bass clef sound upwards. In the twentieth century composers have tended to use key signatures for horn parts.

Liszt

Franz Liszt (1811–1886) was born in Hungary on the Esterhazy estate, and although 154 years separate the birth of Haydn from the death of Liszt there were no doubt many people connected with the Esterhazy family who knew them both. But whereas Haydn had been a model eighteenth-century musical servant Liszt was the complete nineteenth-century Romantic artist.

There were three main influences upon Liszt. In the first place, the great technical virtuosity of Paganini appealed to his love of display and presented a challenge for his own formidable piano technique. There were also Chopin and Berlioz, the one writing a new sort of piano music and the other producing novel orchestral sounds. To these influences must be added the Romantic concern with the works of Bach and Palestrina. Liszt himself became as famous for his virtuosity as was Paganini. The list of his compositions is quite remarkable; and in considering Liszt's public image, it is easy to overlook the enormous amount of time which he must have devoted to composition.

His career falls into three periods. During the first from about 1830 to 1848, he appeared as the star performer in a period of outstanding composer/pianists. In the 1820s he acquired and perfected a formidable technique and in the 1830s dominated Paris with his playing. His Bohemian outlook and aristocratic way of life attracted attention. During this period he formed a liaison with the Comtesse d'Agoult. They had three children, one of whom, Cosima – named after Lake Como – became the wife of Wagner.

From 1839 Liszt made a series of immensely successful concert tours of Europe. They were conducted in grand style; his personal carriage contained a small piano for practice and his extensive wardrobe included 365 cravats. He was mobbed by the populace and showered with honours by royalty. The music of this period contains many showpieces for piano. Many of them are transcriptions of works such as the Beethoven symphonies or versions of well-known operatic arias the themes of which stand out amid a display of pianistic fireworks. But Liszt did also start work on several original compositions. Amongst these are the *Transcendental Studies* which derive from Paganini's *Caprices*; a volume of evocative mood pieces entitled The Years of Travel (*Années de Pélerinage*) and a number of Hungarian Rhapsodies, which are based on gypsy music rather than on folk music.

In 1842 Liszt was appointed musical director at the court of Weimar but he did not go there to live until 1848. By this time the Comtesse d'Agoult had been succeeded in his affections by the Russian Princess Carolyn Sayn-Wittgenstein. During this second period of his career Liszt devoted himself to conducting, teaching, and composing; in each of these areas his work was of importance. As a conductor he championed the works of avant-garde composers such as Berlioz and Wagner. As a teacher his pupils came to him from all over Europe. As a composer he not only completed the bulk of his piano works but turned also to orchestral composition. His most important contribution in this field is the *symphonic poem*.

The third period of Liszt's career, from 1861, is dominated by the spiritual side of his nature. This had always sat somewhat uncomfortably beside his love of flamboyance; but now late in life he took minor orders in the Roman Catholic church and divided his time between Weimar and Rome. To this period belongs a series of religious choral works, but during the last five years of his life he turned again to the piano and produced several pieces whose harmonic idiom looks well into the twentieth century.

Liszt's works include two piano concerti, a Sonata in B minor, a 'Dante' and a 'Faust' symphony, twenty Hungarian Rhapsodies and an organ fantasia and fugue on BACH. He preferred to couch his largescale works in a single movement which nevertheless contrived to contain the forms and overall structure of a classical work with separate movements. An important compositional device associated with Liszt is the transformation, or metamorphosis, of themes.

The Symphonic Poem

The term *symphonic poem* was coined by Liszt. It represents a work for orchestra in a single movement. The movement consists of separate sections which are bound together by a common musical idea. The work is programmatic and each section represents a part of the unfolding programme. As the work progresses the music springs continuously from the various transformations of the theme. At Weimar Liszt wrote twelve symphonic poems the most famous of which is 'Les Préludes'. To this set he added a thirteenth in 1882. The idea of the symphonic poem was immediately successful and was adopted particularly by nationalist composers who wished to express aspects of their native country, and resulted in such works as Smetana's 'Má Vlast', Borodin's 'In the Steppes of Central Asia' and Sibelius's 'Finlandia'. Richard Strauss is often regarded as the successor of Liszt in this type of composition for which he preferred the name 'Tone Poem'.

PART TWO

Writing a Melody (1)

A simple and effective way of inventing a melody is to base it on a common chord. For example the tonic chord of C major can produce the melody in Example 15.2. Each of these chords is formed into a melodic phrase indicated

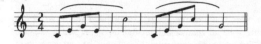

15.2

by a phrase mark. These phrases have a clear melodic outline which gives shape to this miniature composition. Properly phrased, practically any arrangements of the notes of this chord can yield an effective melody.

If we now take a simple chord progression such as I–V–II–V–I a melody such as Example 15.3 can be produced. This melody has been made to start

15.3

and end on the keynote rather than on the 3rd or 5th. This is probably the safest thing to do although it is not necessary. A tune which starts with an anacrusis will probably begin on the dominant note.

The above examples are in $\frac{2}{4}$ time but the idea may be adapted to any time signature. Example 15.4 shows the start of the melody in $\frac{3}{4}$ and in $\frac{6}{8}$.

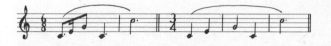

15.4

There are only three ways in which the notes of a melody may follow one another; they may leap, as in the above examples; or they may repeat the previous note; or they may move by step, i.e., to the next note of the scale up or down. *Repeated notes* are very effective provided that they are rhythmical; otherwise they produce an anticlimax (see Example 15.5). To make the melody *move by step* add passing notes to the basic chord notes as shown in Example 15.6. The phrases of a melody can be given rhythmic shape by using dotted

15.5

15.6

15.7

notes (see Example 15.7). Example 15.8 shows the basic chord sequence
I–V–II–V–I, with dotted notes and passing notes.

15.8

Exercise:

1. Experiment with the tune shown in Example 15.9 by adapting it in the
various ways suggested above.

15.9

Modulation (1)

When music passes from one key to another it is said to *modulate*. An extended
piece of music often nods in the direction of various keys as it moves along.
However, modulation does not take place unless the new key is firmly established, usually by means of a perfect cadence (V I) in that key. It is quite
possible to modulate from any key to any other key.

The most usual modulations are to the keys of II, III, IV, V, and VI.
These keys from the key of C major would be D minor, E minor, F major, G
major, and A minor. These are the five *nearly related keys*.

The standard way of modulating is to make use of a chord (or chords)
common to both the old key and the new key. Such a chord is called a *pivot*

chord. The music enters the pivot chord in the old key and leaves it heading for a perfect cadence in the new key.

OLD KEY————→PIVOT——→V I of NEW KEY.

A modulation always involves the use of accidentals *after* the pivot chord.

Modulation to the Dominant.
The most common of all modulations is to the *dominant*, e.g., from C major to G major.

KEY C————→PIVOT——→DF♯ A GBD = KEY G
                                          V   I

If you look at the list of triads of C and G on page 74 you will see that four chords are common to both keys:

	CEG	EGB	GBD	ACE
KEY C	I	III	V	VI
KEY G	IV	VI	I	II

Of these chords the last is the most useful because it leads neatly into a II–V–I cadence in G major. A modulation to the dominant appears in all sorts of guises. In Example 15.10 it is in a very direct form:

15.10

Modulation to the Subdominant

This is a modulation e.g. from C major to F major. The possible pivot chords are: CEG, DFA, FAC, ACE.

In this case the dominant of F major (the new key) is the chord of C (tonic of the old key). But neither of these chords contains an accidental and so merely to make the music end with these two chords (F followed by C) does not produce a modulation (see Example 15.11). A very common way of intro-

15.11

ducing an accidental here is to turn V–I in F major (CEG–FAC) into V_7–I (CEGB♭–FAC) as shown in Example 15.12.

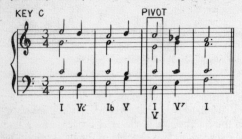

15.12

Exercises

2. Name the five nearly-related keys to (a) G, (b) F, (c) D, and (d) B♭ major.
3. Fill in the missing notes in the modulation to the dominant shown in Example 15.13.

15.13

4. Fill in the missing notes in the modulation to the subdominant shown in Example 15.14.

15.14

Suggested Further Reading

Baines, Anthony. *Musical Instruments Through the Ages* (Penguin: 1971).

Berlioz, Hector. *Memoirs* (trans. David Cairns. London: Gollancz, 1969; Panther, 1970).

Ehrlich, C. *The Piano: A History* (London: Dent, 1979).

Einstein, A. *Music in The Romantic Era* (London: Dent, 1947).

McDonald, Hugh. *Berlioz Orchestral Music* (London: BBC Music Guides).

Searle, Humphrey. *The Music of Liszt* (Dover, 1966).

Sitwell, Sacheverell. *Liszt* (Dover, 1967).

Summer, W. L. *The Pianoforte* (London: MacDonald, 1971).

16

PART ONE: WAGNER, BRAHMS, VERDI.

Richard Wagner

The music of **Richard Wagner** (1813–1883) represents the most complete expression of nineteenth-century Romanticism, and was one of the most important steps leading towards the breakdown of classical tonality. As a man Wagner was both revered and detested; he was capable of the most admirable and the most despicable of actions. As a musician he is unimpeachable and his influence upon subsequent composers was very great and lasted well into the twentieth century. Moreover, his prose writings, which occupy ten volumes and are on a variety of subjects, had considerable influence upon nineteenth-century aesthetic and political thought.

All of Wagner's important works are for the stage. There are eleven of them, four of which were written before 1850 and seven after 1850. The pre-1850 group are examples of *opera*: two of these, *Rienzi* (1842) and *Tannhäuser* (1844) are grand operas in the French manner; the other two, *The Flying Dutchman* (1843) and *Lohengrin* (1848) are German Romantic operas. The stage works which Wagner wrote after 1850 are cast in a new form which Wagner invented and are known as *music-dramas*, a type of work towards which the pre-1850 group had been steadily progressing. The music-dramas consist of: *Tristan und Isolde* (1857–59), *The Mastersingers* (*Die Meistersinger von Nürnberg*) (1862–67), *Parsifal* (1877–82) and the four works which together make up the cycle known as the *Ring of the Nibelung*; *The Rhinegold* (*Das Rheingold*) (1853–54), *The Valkyrie* (*Die Walküre*) (1854–56), *Siegfried* (1856–69) and *The Dusk of the Gods* (*Götterdämmerung*) (1869–74). All Wagner's stage works are generally referred to as operas.

Music-drama

A music-drama for Wagner is a work which embraces all the arts; it is called into being and controlled by one person, the Artist, a class of person of which Wagner recognized himself as the perfect example. Fortunately Wagner was primarily a musician, since music is the main constituent of music-drama; but he did write the words himself and control every aspect of the production of his works.

Wagner's Life

Wagner was born in Leipzig and came into contact with the theatre as a boy, both through his own family and through the work of Weber at Dresden. Between the ages of twenty and twenty-six he held a series of local operatic conducting posts, and during this time he married the actress Minna Planer. Throughout his life the love of a woman was vital to Wagner's musical creativity and many of his works deal with the idea of redemption through love. However, by 1839 he was overwhelmed with debts which he could not pay. One night he managed to escape his creditors, having first piled everything he could into a carriage, and set out for Paris via London. This was the Paris of

Rossini, Meyerbeer, and Liszt and his circle. Wager maintained an existence through the generosity of his friends, but even so was forced to do the hackwork of copying and arranging music in order to earn money. Both *Rienzi* and *The Flying Dutchman* were written in Paris.

From 1843 to 1849 Wagner worked as musical director at the court of Dresden. This was a settled and productive period of his life. In it he wrote *Tannhäuser*, produced at Dresden in 1845, and *Lohengrin* which received its first performance under Liszt at Weimar in 1850. He also, in 1846, produced a memorable performance of Beethoven's Ninth Symphony. This work was for Wagner a point of departure for his own later musical thinking.

Wagner became implicated in the revolutions of 1848 and was forced to flee a second time. Owing to the good offices of Liszt, he was able to settle in Zürich. He lived in Switzerland for ten years and during this period began the germination of the whole of his subsequent musical output. During the rest of his life, with dogged persistence, with an enormous effort of will, and with a sublime belief in his own destiny, he brought his music-dramas to fruition one by one, even though at the time there was no opera house thought capable of staging them. During this period, too, many of Wagner's prose works were written. The most important of these are *The Art Work of the Future* (1850) and *Opera and Drama* (1851).

By 1857 Wagner had completed the first two parts of the 'Ring' cycle and was halfway through *Siegfried*. At this point he fell in love with Mathilde Wesendonck, the wife of one of his wealthy patrons. His passion for her was intense and inspired the music of *Tristan and Isolde*, a work which may fairly be said to contain some of the most passionate and erotic music in existence. It is the music of *Tristan and Isolde*, also, which did more than anything to blur the outlines of classical harmony. In 1860 Wagner left Switzerland and for some years wandered through Europe looking for a direction in which his life was to move.

In 1864 the throne of Bavaria fell to the eighteen-year-old Ludwig II. This eccentric and passionate young monarch had since the age of fifteen fallen under the spell of Wagner, both the man and the musician; he was also addicted to the building of particularly dramatic and grandiose castles, and had a preoccupation with swans. Ludwig sent for Wagner, installed him in Munich and provided him with a sizeable pension. He also summoned the young conductor **Hans von Bülow** (1830–1894) who had in 1857 married Liszt's daughter Cosima, and who was a champion of Wagner's music. In 1865 von Bülow conducted the first performance of *Tristan and Isolde*. But the people of Munich were suspicious of Wagner's designs upon their country's finances and an intimacy had sprung up between Wagner and Cosima von Bülow. Wagner was forced to retire from Munich. Meanwhile plans were going ahead for the building of an opera house at Bayreuth capable of staging Wagner's music-dramas. The theatre was opened in 1876 with the first complete performance of the 'Ring' cycle. The occasion was attended by the elite of Europe. In 1870 Wagner married Cosima von Bülow. She outlived him by nearly fifty years, dying in 1930 at Bayreuth, where she had ensured that every detail in the performance of Wagner's operas was meticulously attended to. Wagner's final opera *Parsifal* was performed at Bayreuth in 1882. This is a mystical and religious work in which the idea of redemption is still a dominant feature.

Wagner's Method.

Each act of a Wagner music-drama consists of a continous piece of music, which is woven out of what Wagner himself called 'endless melody'. This musical texture is constructed out of a number of separate musical ideas. Each idea is known as a *Leitmotiv* and represents an object, a person or an emotion. Wagner's mastery is shown in his handling of the leitmotivs, for by their use he can show what his characters are thinking even when they remain still and silent on the stage; he can immediately evoke any component part or aspect of the drama with which he is dealing; he can manipulate the audience's thinking and reactions. And all the time the music is superbly constructed and controlled.

Wagner regards the voices and the orchestra as a single musical entity. For this reason the vocal parts often become embedded in the orchestral texture but he can at will make them soar above the orchestra in long lines of pure melody. The voices and the orchestra have separate functions, however. The voice parts, as they declaim the text, give us the narrative of the drama; the orchestra is used to keep up a continuous commentary and reflection upon what the characters are saying and doing. The sound of Wagner's music is persuasive and all-embracing. It was written with the intention of intoxicating and overwhelming the listener. It is very easy to fall under its spell. But to become a perfect Wagnerite, to follow the spacious and complex workings of Wagner's dramatic and musical thoughts requires patience, persistence and a great deal of application. Once the spell is woven it is there for life.

Johannes Brahms

The music of **Johannes Brahms** (1833–1897) combines strength with tenderness. It is essentially lyrical and Romantic in feeling. However, both by training and by aptitude Brahms delighted in orderliness and in the discipline of writing in strict forms. Consequently he has the ability to create towering musical edifices within well-defined limits. He did not compose as a result of artistic theorizing, nor was his music prompted by the events of his private life. Instead he regarded himself as an entirely professional composer. He studied the works of the Netherlands school of the fifteenth and sixteenth centuries and of Bach and Beethoven, and saw himself as the inheritor of an unbroken tradition. His importance as a composer was recognized as early as 1853 when he was acclaimed by Schumann in a lengthy article. As a result of Brahms's conservatism he was used as a rallying point by those who found the avant-garde thoughts of Liszt and Wagner difficult to follow.

Life

Brahms was born in Hamburg of working-class parents. His father, who played the double bass, saw to it that he had the best teaching available in the city. By the time Brahms was fourteen he was a powerful pianist and earned money by playing in cafés and in dockside inns. His meeting with the Schumann family in 1853 affected the rest of his life and was crucial to his development as a composer; after Robert Schumann's death in 1856 Brahms maintained a warm friendship with Clara which lasted until her death in 1896. Brahms received an appointment at Detmold in 1854 but preferred throughout his life to be free to follow his career. He moved to Vienna in 1862 and settled there in 1869.

Brahms's published works contain 122 opus numbers. These may be divided into: works for orchestra, with or without soloists; chamber music; songs; works for piano solo; and choral works; Brahms wrote no operas.

Orchestral Works

Chief among Brahms's orchestral works are four symphonies: in C minor and major, op. 68; in D major, op. 73; in F major, op. 90; and in E minor, op. 98. They are classical in form, each having four movements, with the main weight of each work in the outer movements. They are romantic in their lyricism; and they each have a motto theme which occurs in all four movements. One motto is shown in Example 16.1: Brahms's symphonic movements in sonata

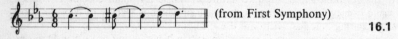 (from First Symphony)

16.1

form have a greater number of themes than is common in Beethoven, but the thematic material is given coherence by the use of the motto: Brahms's development sections have more in common with variation technique than with motivic development. Brahms was traditional enough to indicate a repeat of the exposition in the first movement of each of the first three symphonies; he attached great importance to the writing of symphonies and did not release his First Symphony until he was forty-three. The introduction to the last movement is romantic in its scoring and apparent waywardness. The main theme of the movement has two bars in common with the main theme of the last movement of Beethoven's Ninth Symphony; in 1876, this caused the supporters of Wagner to become indignant.

Brahms's Second Symphony is pastoral in character. The apparently insignificant motto theme forms the basis of a remarkably complex structure. The Third Symphony is an extrovert work, and has much the same feeling as the E♭ Symphony of Schumann. The notes of its motto FAF represent Brahms's personal motto *frei aber froh* (free but happy). Brahms's Fourth Symphony is notable for its last movement which is in the form of a passacaglia. This consists of thirty-two variations woven around a constantly recurring theme and is a fine example of Brahms's ability to create a splendid movement within the strictest of limitations.

Two of Brahms's four concerti are for piano and orchestra. No. 1 in D minor, op. 15, is a forceful and somewhat sprawling work which gave the composer considerable trouble in its composition. The Second Piano Concerto, in B♭, op. 83, is a large-scale work of great power. It has four movements, and is uncompromising in its demands upon the performer's technique and stamina. Brahms's Violin Concerto in D major, op. 77 was written for the renowned violinist **Joseph Joachim** (1831–1907). It is a fine work and a successful essay in solving the problems of writing a romantic concerto for the violin.

Brahms's last concerto is for the unusual combination of violin, cello and orchestra, op. 102 in A minor. The division of labour between the two soloists is admirably handled, and the concerto has a certain mellowness about it although the last movement is in Brahms's Hungarian gypsy style. The *Variations on a theme of Haydn*, op. 56a (op. 56b is a version for two pianos) is a work in which Brahms's great technical competence is used for purely musical ends. It is finely scored and full of delightful invention. The familiar theme is characteristic of both Haydn and Brahms in that it consists of five-bar phrases. Brahms's two overtures, the *Academic Festival Overture* and the *Tragic Overture*, have consecutive opus numbers, 80 and 81. They form a completely contrasting pair with the title of each one accurately reflecting the mood of the music.

Chamber Music

Brahms is the most considerable writer of nineteenth-century romantic chamber music, for the ideals of Romanticism do not readily lend themselves to the restrained and intimate nature of music for small ensemble. Brahms wrote twenty-four chamber works, each of which is worthy of consideration. Outstanding amongst them are the F minor Piano Quintet, op. 34; the three Violin Sonatas, op. 78 in G major, op. 100 in A major and op. 108 in D minor; the two String Sextets, op.18 in B♭, and op. 36 in G major; and the Clarinet Quintet in B minor, op. 115. This last work is one of the very few for this combination of instruments and makes a worthy companion to Mozart's Quintet in A major K.581.

Songs

As a songwriter, Brahms maintains the tradition established by Schubert and Schumann and is one of the outstanding writers of German Lieder. He wrote about 240 songs and his treatment of them tends to follow Schubert rather than Schumann, for although the piano part has a life of its own it forms an accompaniment to the voice rather than sharing the thematic interest with it. Many of his songs reflect the serious side of his nature; this flowers into rich Romanticism in the 'Magelone' song cycle, op. 33, and finds a mood of restrained intensity in the 'Four Serious Songs' (*Vier ernste Gesänge*), op. 121. But Brahms also wrote some fine spirited songs, for example, 'von ewiger Liebe', op. 43, No. 1 or the well-known 'Der Schmied', op. 19, No. 4. Op. 49, No. 4 is known as 'Brahms's Lullaby'.

Piano Music

Brahms wrote piano music throughout his whole career. His output starts by being classical, at least in outline, with three sonatas, op. 1 in C major, op. 2 in F♯ minor, and op. 5 in F minor. After this Brahms turned to smaller forms and to sets of variations, the most outstanding of which are the Handel Variations, op. 24 (1861) and the two sets of Paganini Variations, op. 35 (1863). Both of these sets contain studies of some technical difficulty. Brahms did not then publish any further piano music until 1878. From this date there appear a series of pieces romantic both in mood and in design with titles such as Capriccio, Intermezzo, and Rhapsody. These works explore the sonorities and the textures of the now fully developed grand piano, and include the eight pieces of op. 76 and the two ebullient Rhapsodies of op. 79. Towards the end of his life Brahms wrote a series of introspective and truly romantic pieces from op. 116 to op. 119.

Choral Music

The most outstanding of Brahms's choral works is the Requiem, op. 45. This has the title *A German Requiem* for it bears little relation to the Roman Catholic Mass. It is for soprano and baritone soloists, chorus and orchestra; it presents a rewarding challenge to a competent amateur choral society. The work is based on a motto theme which consists of the first three notes sung by the sopranos. These three notes – dominant, leading note, tonic – form the basis of much of the subsequent thematic material, including that of the familiar 'How lovely are thy Dwellings'. The motto theme finds its fullest expression at the fugue of No. 6 'Worthy art Thou, Lord' where from bar 282 it strides from the lowest to the highest orchestral instruments taking in the chorus parts as it passes.

Brahms wrote neither any opera nor any programme music. He was an extremely self-critical composer and destroyed even completed works if he was displeased with them. His compositions depend heavily on the techniques of variation. In an age when many musicians were concerned with the art of the future he showed that it was possible to carry forward the traditions of the past.

Giuseppe Verdi

As a native Italian opera composer **Giuseppe Verdi** (1813–1901) was heir to a tradition stretching back to the beginning of the seventeenth century. With the work of Rossini, Donizetti, and Bellini opera in the nineteenth century had become an important part of Italian popular culture. Verdi accepted this tradition and brought Italian opera to a point of excellence which has not been surpassed. He wrote twenty-six operas over a period of fifty-four years. During that time his method and style of writing remained constant although his work shows a continuous development in the direction of refinement of both outlook and technique.

Verdi's work is usually divided into three groups, the first of which contains fifteen operas written between 1839 and 1850. His second period starts with three outstanding works: *Rigoletto*, *Il Trovatore*, and *La Traviata*, and finishes with *Aida* in 1871. To the last group belong the two remarkable operas of Verdi's old age, *Otello* and *Falstaff*. Verdi's work also includes a string quartet in E minor and the Requiem (1874) written in memory of the writer Alessandro Manzoni. The Requiem inhabits the same world as the operas in its intensity and directness of expression.

Life

Verdi was born near Parma in northern Italy at a small hamlet called Le Roncole where his parents kept an inn and general stores. He was given music lessons by the local church organist and in 1832 received a grant to study at the Milan Conservatory. However, he was not accepted as a student and studied instead with one of the music staff of La Scala opera house. It was here in 1839 that his first opera, *Oberto*, was performed. He had married in 1836 but his wife and their two children all died before before 1840. He formed a friendship with the opera singer Giuseppina Strepponi, who supported him loyally and actively and eventually became his second wife. His succession of operas made him both wealthy and famous and in 1848 he bought a farming estate near his birthplace which he ran with much success.

During Verdi's early life Italy was under the dominion of Austria; the Italian national spirit, seeking freedom and the unification of Italy, was stifled. In 1842 Verdi's opera *Nabucco* (Nebuchadnezzar) was produced. This deals with the people of Israel in captivity at Babylon and contains the fine chorus 'Fly my thought on wings of gold', in which the Jews long for freedom. This chorus and its composer became a rallying point for the patriotic spirit. Later it was discovered that the letters of the name VERDI form an acrostic of the Italian 'Victor Emmanuel, king of Italy' (Vittorio Emmanuele Re D'Italia) and the cries of 'Viva Verdi' had a patriotic as well as an artistic significance.

Operatic Style

Verdi's operas are quite often based on creaking plots which contain implausible situations and improbable coincidences. The action is swift and develops strong, emotional situations depending upon violent and often brutal contrasts. There are plenty of crowd scenes giving ample opportunity for operatic chorus work. Verdi gives plausibility and dramatic truth to such plots with direct, hard-hitting music of passionate vigour. It is music which is conceived for the human voice and entirely suited to it. The orchestral accompaniment both supports and heightens the effect of the vocal line. His writing for the chorus is direct, often rousing, and always immediately effective.

A typical Verdi opera consists of four main sections which form either four acts or three acts preceded by a prologue. Of these four sections the second usually ends with a rousing finale, the third contains a big duet often for the hero and heroine and ends with a grand ensemble. The fourth section opens in complete contrast with the heroine meditating or in prayer, and the opera usually ends swiftly in tragedy. As a musician Verdi shared the common nineteenth-century admiration of the work of Beethoven; as a dramatist he became throughout his life more and more drawn to the works of Shakespeare.

Career

Verdi's early works are notable for their choruses, but as his career developed interest increasingly focused on the delineation of the individual characters, so that by 1851 with *Rigoletto* Verdi wrote a work in which the melodic line is entirely at the service of the dramatic situations and the presentation of the characters. Verdi's second period includes two five-act grand operas for the Paris stage, *The Sicilian Vespers* (1855) and *Don Carlos* (1867). *Aida* was commissioned for the opening of the Suez canal in 1871, and is a festival opera with spectacular scenes, but is also imbued with a sense of tragedy which is made explicit in the beautiful final scene.

Sixteen years separate Aida from *Otello*, written when Verdi was 74. In this opera his style has not changed but his musical thought has become more subtle and his expression more refined. The music gives the impression of continuous movement within each act, although it is in fact still divided into sections. *Otello* was followed six years later, in 1893, by *Falstaff*, Verdi's last opera. Here the foibles and the frailty of humanity are examined gently and kindly while the comedy is borne along continuously over a kaleidoscope of orchestral sound.

PART TWO

Harmony in Minor Keys

Before studying the following section read again the section on Minor Scales in Chapter 4. Triads in a minor key are formed in exactly the same way as those in a major key. Because there are two forms of the minor scale there are more triads possible in a minor key than there are in a major one. Some of these are not used very often: those minor triads most used are shown in Example 16.2. The minor triads less often used are shown in Example 16.3.

16.2

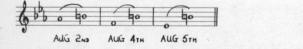

16.3

Chord progressions in minor keys follow the same pattern as they do in major keys. The following points are worth remembering:

1. Chord V is the *dominant* chord. It is formed from a *major* triad; in its alternative form, it is not being used as the Dominant. As a dominant chord in minor, its 3rd *always* has an accidental. It is particularly important to remember this when writing a V I cadence in the minor.
2. The harmonic minor scale produces some augmented intervals. These should be avoided in part writing (see Example 16.4).

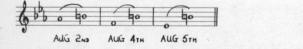

16.4

3. This means that individual parts should move according to the melodic minor scale.
4. A piece of music in a minor key contains frequent accidentals. If the accidentals become fewer until they cease this means that the piece has moved into the relative major, e.g., a piece of music with three flats which contains no accidentals is in Eb major.
5. It is possible to double the root or the 3rd or the 5th of a minor triad.
6. Sometimes the very last chord of a piece of music in a minor key has its 3rd made into a major one giving a sense of completeness. This is known as a *'Tierce de Picardie'* (Picardy Third).
7. In an interrupted cadence in a minor key (V–VI) the major 3rd of VI must be doubled in order to avoid consecutive 5ths or octaves.

Exercise

1. Try filling in the remaining notes of the cadence in Example 16.5.

V VI

16.5

Example 16.6 shows the other cadences in C minor.

PERFECT   IMPERFECT   PLAGAL

V   I   I   V   IV   I

16.6

8. It is useful to remember an acceptable harmonization of the top half of a melodic minor scale, such as Example 16.7. It is given in C minor and in A minor.

KEY A MINOR

I IV V I   I VIIb IV   V

16.7a

KEY C MINOR

I IV V I   I VIIb IV   V

16.7b

A convention is sometimes used whereby major scales are referred to by capital letters and minor scales by small ones, e.g., A major, a minor. You may even find the letters used in this way by themselves, e.g., Brahms's Fourth Symphony in e (= E minor).

Exercises

2. Fill in the alto and tenor parts of the cadences in Example 16.8.

16.8

3. Fill in the alto and tenor parts of the passages in Example 16.9. Make the second passage end with a Tierce de Picardie.

16.9

Writing a Melody (2)

In the last chapter we saw how a melody can be constructed from a chord sequence with interest being given to the shape of the tune by the addition of passing notes. Another very useful way of adding interest to a melody is by the use of *auxiliary notes*. An auxiliary note occurs when a harmony note moves to the note above or below it and back again immediately (see Example 16.10). A very good example of the use of auxiliary notes occurs in the first

16.10

two phrases of 'Silent Night', given in Example 16.11. Auxiliary notes are also

16.11

used in such figures as that in Example 16.12 which is based on the two
harmony notes shown in Example 16.13.

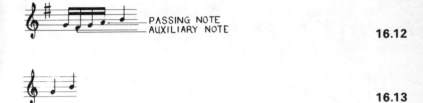

16.12

16.13

Satisfying melodies can be written using every possible arrangement of notes
formed into every imaginable phrase structure. But a tune made up of four
phrases is as good a starting point as any. Perhaps the most frequent version
of the four-line tune is found in the scheme AABA.

In this arrangement the tune frequently modulates to the dominant or to
the relative major or minor during the second or third phrase. It also reaches
a point of climax at about the same time. A climax can be brought about by a
high note, or a low one, or by a pause. The melodies in Example 16.14 are

16.14a

16.14b

both harmonically based and use the scheme AABA. The first one is in C minor and the second in G major. They include passing notes (1), auxiliary notes (2), modulation (3), and points of climax (4).

You can experiment by writing tunes beginning as shown in Example 16.15

16.15

and using various four line schemes such as AABA ABBA ABAB AAAA or even ABCD. Make them modulate and give them a point of climax.

Suggested Further Reading

Blunt, W. *The Dream King* (London: Hamish Hamilton, 1970).
Gutman, R. W. *Richard Wagner* (London: Penguin, 1968).
Horton, J. *Brahms Orchestral Music* (London: BBC Music Guides, 1972).
Hussey, D. *Verdi* (London: Dent, Master Musicians, 1974).
Keys, I. *Brahms Chamber Music* (London: BBC Music Guides, 1973).
Latham, P. *Brahms* (London: Dent, Master Musicians, 1975).
Newman, E. *Wagner Nights* (London: Pan, 1977).
Newman, E. *Wagner as Man and Artist* (London: Gollancz, 1963).
Sams, E. *Brahms Songs* (London: BBC Music Guides, 1972).
Walker, F. *The Man Verdi* (London: Dent, 1962).

17

PART ONE: MUSIC IN RUSSIA
FROM THE MID-EIGHTEENTH CENTURY

Western influences on the music of Russia begin to appear from about the middle of the eighteenth century. Before that time Russian music sprang mainly from two sources: the liturgy of the Greek Orthodox Church, and a strongly established folk culture. In the early part of the century Peter the Great (1672–1725) developed a policy of westernizing Russian culture which was continued by his granddaughter Catherine the Great (1729–96). One result of this policy was the formation of the Russian Imperial Ballet in 1738. The music for the ballet however was imported complete, from Italy, for it was at this time that Italian musicians were also flooding into England, France, and Germany.

But towards the end of the century native-born Russian composers began to appear, and from this time Russian music possesses a continuity of style and aim which has lasted until our own day. The first Russian composer of consequence is **Dmitri Bortniansky** (1752–1825). His operas and keyboard pieces are dominated by the Italian style. But Russian native influences also began to make themselves felt in his work and that of other composers. The first composer to effect a synthesis of the two styles is **Mikhail Ivanovich Glinka** (1804–57). In his music the Russian folk idiom is harnessed to the western tonal system. Glinka's achievement had an immense influence on subsequent Russian composers. In 1830 Glinka embarked upon a long study tour of Europe in which he met Donizetti, Bellini, Berlioz, and Mendelssohn. Glinka is best remembered for his two operas, *A Life for the Tsar* (1836) and *Russlan and Ludmilla* (1842). The first of these has a historical plot and the second is a folk or fairy tale; most subsequent Russian operas fall into one of these two categories.

Glinka was immediately followed in Russian musical history by **Alexander Dargomizhsky** (1813–69). His music contains the type of soaring melody which is later found in Tchaikovsky, but on the other hand his opera *The Stone Guest* (the Don Giovanni story) has the words set one by one in a declamatory style which influenced Mussorgsky.

In the middle of the nineteenth century Russian music began to develop in two quite separate directions. On the one hand the ideals of Peter the Great were carried to their logical conclusion with Russian music entering the main stream of European music; on the other hand a group of composers arose whose aim was to assert the purely Russian characteristics of their music. The first group, which was much opposed to the ideals of the second, was led by **Anton Rubinstein** (1829–94). Rubinstein was a pianist of international fame whose ability was said to rival even that of Liszt. In 1862 he set up in the capital St Petersburg a conservatory of music which was very much influenced by the work of Mendelssohn at Leipzig. With his brother **Nicholas Rubinstein**

(1835–81) he also set up the Moscow conservatory in 1864. Neither of the Rubinsteins was influential as a composer and in fact the development of Russian music remained with the nationalist school. This was led also by an outstanding pianist, **Mily Balakirev** (1837–1910).

The Five

Balakirev's musical training was somewhat haphazard but his enthusiasm for national music was intense. In 1861 he began to form a group of nationalist musicians and in 1862 founded, also at St Petersburg, a Free School of Music. The main members of the nationalist group are known as *The Five*; they consist of Balakirev, **César Cui** (1835–1918), **Alexander Borodin** (1833–1887), **Modest Mussorgsky** (1839–1881) and **Nicholas Rimsky-Korsakov** (1844–1908). These men were united in their aim but differed in their backgrounds, talents, outputs and influence.

Balakirev was attracted to folk music and to the oriental aspect of Russian music. He composed slowly, often spending several years on a single composition. His handling of the folk idiom is seen in two overtures, one based on Russian themes (1858) and the other called *Russia – 1,000 Years*. Both of these works provided his fellow composers with musical material. Balakirev's interest in the oriental is seen in the fantasy for piano *Islamey* (1869) and the symphonic poem *Tamara* (1866–82). His two symphonies, in C major (1866–98) and in D minor (1907–8) show the influence of Western composers such as Berlioz, Schumann, and Liszt. Balakirev had a possessive interest in the work of his group, often literally watching over them and trying to direct them as they wrote. His importance lies not so much in his own work as in the use which some of the others made of his particular interests.

The member of The Five whose music has least survived is Cui. He was an officer in the Russian army and a professor of military science at St Petersburg. His musical talent was for small-scale compositions, but he seems to have been unaware of this – he wrote ten operas. He is remembered today as a writer of salon music, but he ably served the cause of The Five with his pen; his writings promoted their interests and made their work known.

Even less of a professional composer was Borodin, but he was gifted with a natural talent for composition and was a competent performer on four instruments. He worked as a professor of chemistry at St Petersburg Military Academy and led an extremely busy professional life, working on the aldehydes. He discovered aldol. His musical works are few but important; he was a spontaneous writer of rich, broad melodies but without the desire, or perhaps the ability, to develop them. He had though the ability to create a sense of oriental splendour. These characteristics are fully displayed in the opera *Prince Igor* with its superabundance of tunes and the splendid, familiar *Polovtsian Dances*. *Prince Igor* was started in 1869 but left unfinished. Also suggestive of the East is the symphonic poem *In the Steppes of Central Asia*. On the other hand the first movement of the second of Borodin's three symphonies, in B minor, is motivated by a single, striking idea. A more directly lyrical work is the Second String Quartet, in D major, whose hauntingly beautiful Nocturne has been separately scored for string orchestra.

The most outstanding member of The Five is Mussorgsky. He was the son of a wealthy landowner, but when in 1861 the system of serfdom was abolished in Russia, the family found itself in financial difficulties and Mussorgsky entered the civil service as a clerk. He was of a nervous disposition and subject to epilepsy. When his compositions met with little success his mode of life deteriorated and he died in poverty.

Mussorgsky's natural mode of musical expression is rough, direct, even brutal. He was a fine pianist but not versed in Western harmony. He therefore worked out his chord sequences painfully at the piano. They frequently result in sustained passages of sonorous splendour. For him music was a means of *communicating* rather than a way of expressing abstract beauty. His most familiar work is *Pictures at an Exhibition* (1874), originally written for solo piano but perhaps best known today in the orchestral version scored by Ravel. Of Mussorgsky's own orchestral works the symphonic poem *A Night on the Bare Mountain* is a splendid evocation of a Witches' Sabbath.

But his masterpiece is the opera *Boris Godunov*. This is divided into four acts and a prologue but is in fact made up of ten separate scenes. The opera concerns the remorse of Boris, a sixteenth-century Tsar who had usurped the throne by the murder of a child. The plot gives ample opportunity for massive crowd scenes, splendid ceremonial and for the portrayal of the innermost thoughts of the main characters. Mussorgsky's declamatory style, derived from that of Dargomizhsky, is an ideal vehicle for his direct and biting realism. *Boris Godunov* was written between 1868 and 1869 and was revised three years later. It was further revised, in 1896, by Rimsky-Korsakov, who rewrote much of it, made some extensive cuts, and added some music of his own. It was this version which held the stage until well into our own century. The opera is now usually given in Mussorgsky's own final version although it is rarely performed in its entirety. Mussorgsky left two operas unfinished, *Khovanshchina* and *Sorochintsy Fair*. The first of these was revised and finished by Rimsky-Korsakov in 1886.

All members of The Five were songwriters but Mussorgsky's songs are outstanding as a result of his ability to evoke an immediate picture when setting a poem. Each of his three song cycles is important musically; *The Nursery* (1868–72), *Without Sun* (1874) and *Songs and Dances of Death* (1875–77).

Mussorgsky's impact on subsequent composers was considerable. His use of apparently unrelated chords and his declamatory style have influenced such composers as Janáček and Bartók while the fluid harmonic style of his songs appears in the work of Debussy.

Rimsky-Korsakov, like many late Romantic composers, was a fine orchestrator. Basing his methods upon Berlioz's Treatise of 1844 he wrote his own *Principles of Orchestration* between 1896 and 1908. Although he was a member of The Five his outlook was cosmopolitan and he united the two opposing traditions of Rubinstein and Balakirev, for in 1871 he was appointed professor of composition at the St Petersburg Conservatory. Before that he had been an officer in the Russian navy. He worked at his Symphony in E♭ op. 1 while his ship was berthed at Greenwich. He was the most prolific of the Russian composers of the late nineteenth century. His works included fifteen operas, four symphonies, three concerti, and five symphonic poems. His best and most popular music is contained in the operas and symphonic poems, particularly when he is dealing with the fantastic, exotic and fairytale world. The sym-

phonic suite *Scheherezade* (1888) is an outstanding example of this style. Of
the operas *The Golden Cockerel* (1907) is most often performed; and *Sadko*
(1894–96), perhaps the best of them, deals with both historical medieval Russia
and the make-believe world of the water-maidens. The opera is set under the
sea. Rimsky-Korsakov's operas are spectacular and include exotic effects and
transformation scenes. Rimsky-Korsakov was an outstanding teacher and
numbered Stravinsky among his pupils.

Nineteenth-Century Russian Opera

The characteristic features of nineteenth-century Russian opera from the time
of Glinka may be summarized as follows:

1. Frequent use of folk melody;
2. the chorus is an important part of the drama;
3. ballet is also used as part of the action;
4. tragedy often mixed with comedy (*Boris Godunov* is an exception);
5. the main characters are individuals, not types;
6. the libretti are works of literature in their own right;
7. the setting of the words echoes the cadences of Russian epic poetry.

Among the pupils of Rimsky-Korsakov are **Anatol Liadov** (1855–1914) and
Alexander Glazunov (1865–1936). Liadov was a miniaturist, whose best work
is for the piano in which his style of writing is indebted to Chopin. His
orchestral scoring was highly regarded by Rimsky-Korsakov. His symphonic
poems include *The Enchanted Lake* and *From the Book of Revelation*, both
works finely composed and beautifully orchestrated.

Glazunov was a somewhat more considerable musical figure. He possessed
a remarkable memory and could recall complete works after a single hearing,
down to the smallest detail. His works tend to follow the classical tradition
rather than the ideals of Russian nationalism, although the ballet score
Raymonda, which is sometimes heard, captures national feeling in highly
coloured and energetic music. His earlier work, also, includes symphonic
poems on national themes. He wrote no opera. His eight completed symphonies reflect serenity and triumph rather than struggle.

Tchaikovsky

Peter Ilyich Tchaikovsky (1840–1893), was for the school of Rubinstein the
sort of champion it had been seeking; as a composer he is thoroughly Russian
but his outlook is cosmopolitan and his mode of expression international.
Tchaikovsky was a graduate of the first intake at Rubinstein's St Petersburg
conservatory. Upon finishing his studies he was immediately appointed to a
teaching post at the Moscow conservatory. He was not a good teacher for as
a person he was extremely sensitive and given to bouts of melancholy and
depression; but he maintained the position for several years.

Tchaikovsky's earlier works were not particularly well received. In 1877 he
contracted a disastrous marriage, a mode of life which was alien to his nature.
After nine weeks of married life he fled; but at about the same time he formed
a curious friendship with a woman ten years older than himself. This was
Nadezhda von Meck, a wealthy widow of strong character with a good head

for business, eleven children and an admiration for Tchaikovsky's music. She provided Tchaikovsky with an annual allowance to enable him to compose at his leisure on condition that the two never met. The friendship was conducted by correspondence and lasted thirteen years. Tchaikovsky's death at the age of fifty-three was from cholera after drinking unboiled water.

By his training and through his musical inheritance Tchaikovsky was influenced by French, German, and Russian composers. He was devoted to the music of Mozart. In his own music he uses Russian rhythms and authentic folk melodies but submits them to a westernized treatment. Unlike Balakirev and Rimsky-Korsakov he owes very little to the East.

Tchaikovsky's themes are usually ample and memorable. His orchestration is rich and effective but not spectacular. He preferred to work in the traditional formal structures of Western music. In extended movements he sometimes exhibits a weakness of structure particularly when passing from one section of a movement to another; for having created great tension he finds it difficult to relax the music and pass naturally into the following section. Two very familiar examples of this occur in the First Piano Concerto, when the grandiose introduction to the first movement passes into the movement's main theme; and in the *Pathétique Symphony* at the transition to the second subject of the first movement. On the other hand the *Romeo and Juliet Overture*, for all its expansiveness, exhibits a remarkable economy of material and a tautness of structure.

In Tchaikovsky's music there is a broad division of style between those works in a major key and those in a minor key. In a major key he can show an almost classical restraint. Among such works are the Serenade for Strings, op. 48, the Third Symphony in D major, op. 29 (the only one of Tchaikovsky's six symphonies in a major key), the Second Piano Concerto in G major, op. 44, and even the Violin Concerto in D, op. 35, while quite a few of the movements from the *Swan Lake*, *The Nutcracker Suite* and *Sleeping Beauty* ballet scores are precisely stated musical gems.

But it is the works in minor keys which perhaps give rise to Tchaikovsky's great popularity. In them the composer abandons himself to soaring lyricism, with rising sequences and with melody which expands until it reaches bursting point. The extreme subjectivity of Tchaikovsky's thought evokes an immediate response in the hearer. Much of this music is undoubtedly sentimental but it also has a toughness and a strength which enable it to withstand repeated performances. Among such works are: the last three symphonies, No. 4 in F minor, op. 36, No. 5 in E minor, op. 64, and No. 6 in B minor, (*Pathétique*), op. 74 and the *Manfred Symphony*, op. 58; and the overtures *Francesca da Rimini*, *Hamlet*, and *Romeo and Juliet*. Tchaikovsky's best work is probably the opera *Eugene Onegin*, op. 24 (1877–78) in which there is a synthesis of both his Classical and his Romantic styles.

The spiritual heir of Tchaikovsky was **Alexander Arensky** (1861–1906). He is now chiefly remembered for his piano trio in D minor, op. 32. Much of his music is in Tchaikovsky's Romantic vein but without Tchaikovsky's immediacy and individuality. Arensky was, however, the teacher of two twentieth-century composers of distinction, one of whom, Rachmaninov, carried on the Romantic tradition while another, Scriabin, pointed the way to some of the developments of twentieth-century music.

Rachmaninov

The music of **Sergey Rachmaninov** (1873–1943) has much in common with that of Tchaikovsky. Rachmaninov has the same vein of lyricism and a competent handling of the larger forms, but he lacks Tchaikovsky's incisiveness. His music too sometimes contains a sense of bitterness which is lacking in Tchaikovsky. It is cosmopolitan in style but is firmly rooted in the traditions of Russia. Rachmaninov's style shows a distinct development; his earlier works partake of a lush Romanticism which gradually became less effusive and more sinewy and his final works are characterized by restraint and understatement.

Rachmaninov was an immensely successful international concert pianist. As a result certain of his piano works achieved great popularity and tended to obscure his overall achievement. Of his four Piano Concerti, No. 2 in C minor, op. 18, and No. 3 in D minor, op. 30 rightly remain popular. No. 4 in G minor, op. 40, is a late work and suffers from the weakness of its slow movement. The Rhapsody on a Theme of Paganini (1934) is mainly in the composer's late style, in spite of the Romanticism, and popularity, of the eighteenth variation.

Rachmaninov's two sets of Preludes for piano solo, op. 23 and op. 32, and two sets of Études-Tableaux, op. 33 and op. 39, are technical studies, many of them of some difficulty, but are satisfying and well-wrought compositions. Of Rachmaninov's three symphonies the finest is No. 2 in E minor, op. 27. Although this work owes much to Tchaikovsky its strong and individual lyricism finds expression in a finely conceived orchestral texture. The tone poem, *The Isle of the Dead*, op. 29, is an intense evocation of the underworld of classical mythology while *The Bells*, op. 35, for soloists, chorus, and orchestra is a rewarding work rarely performed. Rachmaninov is a rounded composer who justly deserves his popularity.

Scriabin

Alexander Scriabin (1872–1915) also followed the career of a concert pianist but his musical career is strikingly different from that of Rachmaninov. Of the seventy-four opus numbers into which Scriabin's work is collected, sixty-eight are for piano solo. The earlier sets of pieces are in the style of Chopin. But Scriabin also came under the influence of the Eastern aspects of Russian music, while he himself was a visionary and a mystic and fascinated by the occult. His theories about music and about the arts developed continously throughout his career and as they became more fascinating so they became less attainable.

Scriabin's final intention was to create a work embracing all the arts, including colour and perfume, which was to induce a state of unutterable mystic rapture and to end in the transformation of the world. The two possible venues he considered for the performance of this work were Tibet and England. Although somewhat idealistic, these theories greatly influenced those of his compositions which remained within the bounds of possibility. In particular Scriabin devised a mystic chord, based upon the interval of a 4th, which provides the starting point for his later works, and which resulted in a harmonic vagueness which amounted to atonality (see Example 17.1).

Scriabin's stylistic development can be followed in his orchestral works, starting with his three symphonies, in E major, C minor and C major, through the
Poem of Ecstasy of 1908 to *Prometheus; the Poem of Fire* of 1910. This last
work the composer intended to be accompanied by shifting coloured lights
rather in the manner of a celestial disco.

17.1

PART TWO

Modulation (2)

Consider the degrees of the scale I II III IV V VI, i.e., leaving out VII. We have seen in Chapter 15 how to modulate from I (tonic) to IV (subdominant) and from I to V (dominant). This leaves three triads from the group, II III and VI. They are all minor triads. They are each the *relative minor* of the triad a minor 3rd above them, that is, II is the relative minor of IV, III is the relative minor of V, and VI is the relative minor of I. Using the triads of C major this means that D minor (d) is the relative minor of F major, E minor (e) is the relative minor of G major, and A minor (a) is the relative minor of C major. For these reasons the keys of II III IV V and VI are known as *nearly related keys* to the tonic I (see p.166). Because they are nearly related they are quite easy to modulate into.

The following examples show the commonest ways of modulating to II, III, and VI.

Modulation to II (supertonic): Use II itself as a pivot chord as in Example 17.2.

17.2

Modulation to III (mediant): Use VI as a pivot chord. The example is shown twice in Examples 17.3 and 17.4; the second time, passing notes have been added.

17.3

*= PASSING NOTES   **17.4**

Another very effective way of moving to the mediant is to arrive at the chord of IIIc (following III in its root position) which then becomes Ic of the new key and introduces the cadential six-four procedure, as shown in Example 17.5.

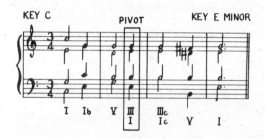

17.5

Modulation to VI (submediant): Many ways are possible: the key is, after all, the relative minor of the tonic. Use II IV VI or VII as pivot chords, as shown in Examples 17.6 and 17.7

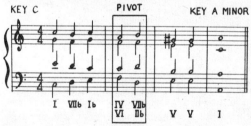

17.6

17.7

Exercise

1. Fill in the alto and tenor part of the passages in Examples 17.8 and 17.9, modulating as indicated. Remember (i) use a pivot chord (=a chord common to both the old and the new keys); (ii) after the pivot chord (but not necessarily *immediately* after it) establish the new key with a V I cadence.

17.8

17.9

Writing a Song

Song-writing is a pleasant pastime in its own right. Many examinations ask for the setting of words to music. Here is the first verse of Thomas Gray's Elegy, a nostalgic and emotive poem.

> The curfew tolls the knell of parting day
> The lowing herd wind slowly o'er the lea,
> The ploughman homeward plods his weary way,
> And leaves the world to darkness and to me.

1. Read the words slowly. Let them suggest their own time signature. Most passages can be set quite satisfactorily to several different time signatures. The above verse might well be in $\frac{2}{4}$.
2. Put the words beneath the stave with the time signature inserted (see Example 17.10).

17.10

3. Draw in the bar lines where the strong stresses fall.
4. Write in the rhythm of the music on one note. There should be at least one note to every syllable. The tails of notes belonging to different syllables are not joined together (see Example 17.10).
5. Let the words suggest a melody, remembering the advice given in Chapters 15 and 16.
6. Be aware of the structure of the song so that the phrases balance one another (see Example 17.11).

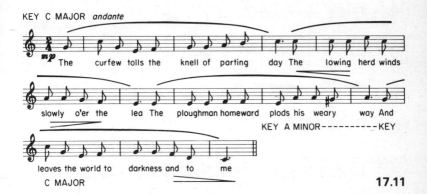

KEY C MAJOR *andante*

np The curfew tolls the knell of parting day The lowing herd winds

slowly o'er the lea The ploughman homeward plods his weary way And

KEY A MINOR --------- KEY

leaves the world to darkness and to me

C MAJOR

17.11

7. Try to *suggest* the meaning of the words in your music but do not *imitate* the words. The sound of bells and of mooing in the above passage would be grotesque.
8. Add performing directions, phrase marks and dynamics.

Below are some words for practice song writing, with suggested time signatures.

    (a) Dear Thomas, didst thou never pop
        Thy head into a tin-man's shop? $\frac{2}{4}$

    (b) Love in her eyes sits playing
        And sheds delicious death
        Love in her lips is straying
        And warbling in her breath $\frac{6}{8}$

    (c) I am: yet what I am none cares or knows,
        My friends forsake me like a memory lost
        I am the self-consumer of my woes,
        They rise and vanish in oblivious host $\frac{4}{4}$

    (d) You went away / Without me /
        I find no joy / Without you $\frac{4}{4}$

Exercise

2. Here is the second verse of Gray's Elegy. Experiment with a melody, starting with Example 17.12.

KEY C MINOR

17.12

Now fades the glimmering landscape on the sight,
And all the air a solemn stillness holds,
Save where the beetle wheels his droning flight,
And drowsy tinklings lull the distant folds;

Suggested Further Reading

Calvocoressi, M. D. *Mussorgsky* (London: Dent, Master Musicians, 1977).
Culshaw, John. *Sergei Rachmaninov* (London: Dennis Dobson, 1949).
Piggott, Patrick. *Rachmaninov Orchestral Music* (London: BBC Music Guides, 1974).
Swan, Alfred J. *Russian Music* (John Baker, 1973).
Warrack, John. *Tschaikovsky* (London: Hamish Hamilton, 1973).
Warrack, John. *Tschaikovsky Symphonies and Concertos* (London: BBC Music Guides, 1974).

18

PART ONE: NATIONALISM IN MUSIC

Bohemia: Smetana and Dvořák

The most prominent of nineteenth-century national schools was that of Russia; but during this period several other countries also produced music based upon national characteristics. The ancient kingdom of *Bohemia* was of particular importance in this respect as a result of the work of Smetana and Dvořák. Bohemia was the westernmost of the three provinces from which modern Czechoslovakia was founded. During the classical period and into the nineteenth century music had played an important part in the country's national life; Johann Stamitz, founder of the Mannheim orchestra, was only one of several eighteenth-century Czech musicians whose work was of international importance. Smetana and Dvořák are in many ways complementary to one another. Smetana was influenced by Liszt and championed the cause of Wagner; Dvořák followed in the steps of Brahms. Smetana is remembered for his symphonic poems and his operas; it was by means of programme music that he celebrated his country's history and its natural beauty. Dvořák, on the other hand, is a symphonist of some importance and an outstanding writer of chamber music and choral works. He is a writer of absolute music. He uses no programme but rather expresses the *spirit* of his native land particularly through the use of dance rhythms.

Bedrich Smetana (1824–84) was engaged from the outset of his career in fostering his country's native music. In 1848, aged twenty-four, he founded the Prague Conservatory. In 1856 political events caused him to move to Göteborg in Sweden. On his way there, he was received and encouraged by Liszt at Weimar. During that decade Liszt was developing his idea of the symphonic poem, a fact which had great influence on Smetana.

Smetana returned to Czechoslovakia in 1861. In the following year an important event took place in the opening of the Czech National Theatre in Prague. It was in this theatre that all Smetana's eight operas, celebrating either his country's history or its national way of life, were first produced. Among the first group are *The Brandenburgers in Bohemia* (1863), *Dalibor* (1867), and *Libussa* (1872). But it was in the second group that Smetana produced an opera which has become part of Czech national culture, *The Bartered Bride* (1866). Folk music as such is not found in this opera, but the work's freshness and spontaneity and its glimpse into the everyday world of the Czechs have carried it around the world.

About 1874 Smetana began to go deaf and suffered from noises in his head. He continued to compose, however, and it was during this time that he wrote six symphonic poems under the title of *Má Vlast* (My Country). These are: *Vyšehrad*, the name of the ancient citadel at Prague; *Vltava*, the epic of the river Moldau; *Šárka*, illustrating a story of love and revenge surrounding a folk-heroine; *From Bohemia's Fields and Forests*; *Tábor*, the city most closely associated with Bohemia's struggles for religious and political freedom; and *Blanik*, the place where the ancient warriors lie buried. Of these the most familiar are numbers 2 and 4. Smetana entitled his First String Quartet, in E minor (1876) *From my Life*. In all these works, and in his piano music, Smetana succeeded in creating a type of national music which places him among the leaders of nineteenth-century nationalism.

Antonin Dvořák (1841–1904) wrote in a wider variety of forms than did Smetana. He expressed himself spontaneously in music that is fresh and original, and which abounds in fascinating melodic, harmonic, and rhythmic ideas. He has a sure handling of the larger forms and is an excellent orchestrator.

Dvořák was of peasant origin; the simplicity of his life and his love of nature remained with him even when he had become world-famous. He profited greatly by the advice of Brahms who also did much to get his work published and known. Dvořák began to travel in 1884. He visited England, where his music was much liked, several times. He was director of the New York Conservatory from 1892–95 but resigned in order to return to his native land. Dvořák wrote nine symphonies of which the 9th in E minor *From the New World* is the most familiar. The folk melodies to be heard in this work have an affinity with both those of the Negroes and of Bohemia. Symphony No. 7 in D minor is rich in thematic material, finely constructed and somewhat tragic in character. By contrast the Eighth Symphony in G major is a sunny and expansive work and also contains splendid themes. Among Dvořák's other fine orchestral works are the *Symphonic Variations* and the cycle of three concert overtures *In Nature*, *Carnival*, and *Othello*.

Dvořák is important as a writer of chamber music. The String Quartet in F major, op. 96 (American) shares with the New World Symphony a feeling of folk music. The Piano Quintet in A major is a notable example of a work for this medium. Outstanding among Dvorak's choral works are the *Stabat Mater*, op. 58, the *Requiem*, op. 89 and the *Te Deum*, op. 103. Each of these depends for its effect on the exact rendering of every performing indication given by the composer. His Cello Concerto in B minor, op. 104 is a striking example of a work in this difficult medium.

Dvořák's desire to honour his country with music is seen in the series of operas which followed the lead of Smetana. However, apart from *Russalka* (1900) they have not kept the stage. Much more immediately and lastingly successful are the two sets of Slavonic Dances for piano duet, op. 46 and op. 72; although these works were entirely created by Dvořák they admirably capture the folk idiom. In his many fine songs and in the series of character pieces for solo piano Dvořák shows himself a true Romantic composer. Even Dvořák's less important music is attractive; as a composer he has had few detractors.

Norway

The best known of all Scandinavian composers and the most distinctly national is **Edvard Grieg** (1843–1907). Through him Norwegian music has become a part of Western culture. He was trained at the Leipzig Conservatory but was not in sympathy with the Mendelssohn tradition which he found there. However, the immediate outcome of this period of training was the composition of a symphony in C minor (1863–64), a work which owes more than its key to the example of Beethoven's Fifth Symphony. In 1867 Grieg banned further performances of the work and it was not until the spring of 1981, when it was recorded, that it was heard again. For instead of the traditional compositional methods Grieg came to prefer Norwegian traditional rhythms, and scales such as that with a sharpened 4th or a flattened 7th, and the drone bass. In traditional harmony he was fond of chords of the 9th and 13th. He was one of the many composers to whom Liszt gave advice and encouragement.

Grieg is not usually regarded as a major composer but a surprising amount of his work remains in the concert repertoire. He is undoubtedly a miniaturist without the ability to handle large forms successfully and yet the Piano Concerto in A minor, op. 16, remains one of the most popular of all such works. It is said that Liszt, upon being presented with the score played it through at sight. Among Grieg's other extended works are the Piano Sonata in E minor, op. 7, and the Sonata for Violin and Piano, op. 36. In these works his traditional training is apparent. But it is in his smaller works that his individual voice is most clearly heard. The ten books of *Lyric Pieces* for piano, his numerous songs, and the two orchestral suites from the incidental music to *Peer Gynt* contain many small-scale works perfect in design and in musical content.

Sweden and Denmark

In **Franz Berwald** (1796–1868) Sweden produced a composer of note whose six symphonies stand comparison with those of Mendelssohn and Schumann. Of Danish composers **Niels Gade** (1817–90) was a teacher of importance and a facile, prolific writer of music in the German tradition. On the other hand the six symphonies of **Carl Nielsen** (1865–1931) play an important part in the history of twentieth century symphonic writing. Nielsen's First Symphony (1894) in G minor is in the Romantic tradition and is indebted to Brahms. But from that time his work shows a continuous development, particularly in his treatment of tonality. In his later work he frequently shifts the tonal centre and often writes in more than one key at the same time (*polytonality*). But in spite of such devices his music remains approachable by the ordinary listener.

Nielsen gave his symphonies titles, signifying the works' general characters but not providing programmes for them in the manner of Berlioz. Nielsen's Fourth Symphony, *The Inextinguishable* (1916) sums up the composer's attitude towards his art 'Music, like life, is inextinguishable'. Perhaps the Fifth Symphony (1922) represents his most important achievement. It is in two extended sections both of which are unconventional in form and original in conception.

Finland

The composer of Finland is Sibelius. Like Nielsen **Jan Sibelius** (1865–1957) is primarily a symphonist and although the music of both composers reflects their country of origin in both cases it transcends the bounds of nationalism. Sibelius was influenced by Borodin, Greig, and Tchaikovsky; but his work also reflects three particular aspects of his native Finland: the sombre vastness of its forests and lakes, its collection of folk tales known as the *Kalevala* and its people's desire for independence from the Russians, which they achieved in 1917. Sibelius's achievement as a national composer was recognised at the age of 32 when he was given a state pension to enable him to devote his time to composition.

He was known first as a writer of salon pieces of which *Valse Triste* is the most familiar example. But early in his career he embarked upon a series of tone poems (symphonic poems) some of which are based on episodes from the *Kalevala*. Among these are *En Saga* (1892) and *The Swan of Tuonela* (1893) with its evocative use of the cor anglais. The Finnish landscape is evoked in the *Karelia Suite* (1893) while *Finlandia* (1899) provided a nationalist call for liberty. Among Sibelius's larger works is the Violin Concerto in D minor of 1905, which is fully in the European Romantic tradition and is splendidly written for the solo instrument.

But it is in his seven symphonies that Sibelius's most individual voice is heard. These were composed between 1899 and 1924. They are works of great originality and show a sure handling of symphonic form. The first two are conventional in the late Romantic tradition but thereafter Sibelius developed a symphonic method which is in some ways the reverse of the traditional procedure. For instead of announcing his material at the outset of a movement and then proceeding to explore its possibilities, he builds up his movements from isolated fragments which gradually turn themselves into themes and are finally woven into a continuous symphonic texture. This method is first apparent in the Third Symphony in C major (1907), a work in three movements.

Sibelius's scoring is clean-sounding and sparse; he tends to write for instruments in their lower ranges and to keep them separate from one another, not mixed together in families. He is fond of building up a climax over a repeated (ostinato) bass, as in the last movement of the Second Symphony, and he has a highly original method of opposing speed and tempo: the notes may follow one another quickly and yet the music may feel as if it is moving slowly; on the other hand the notes may be few but yet generate a feeling of great speed. Both of these methods of writing are found in the Fifth Symphony in E♭ (1915), a popular and triumphant work. This work is in contrast to the Fourth Symphony in A minor (1911), tense, emotional music which explores the interval of an augmented 4th, (C–F♯), heard in the opening phrase. Symphony No. 6 in D minor (1923) is intimate in character, while No. 7 in C (1924) combines in one continuous movement all the aspects of a classical symphony.

Spain

The national music of Spain needs no introduction. Its dance rhythms and the cadences of its melodies have long been international currency. The earlier part of the nineteenth century is important for the resurgence of music for the guitar (see Chapter 13); the most important Spanish figure during the latter part of the century was **Felipe Pedrell** (1841–1922). Pedrell composed, amongst other things, six operas but his importance lies not so much in his music as in the fact that he collected, edited, and published the music of others. He was an outstanding *musicologist*. By his own music he sought to establish a national school, which was brought to fruition by two composers from Catalonia, Albeniz (z = th) and Granados.

Isaac Albeniz (1860–1909) was a child prodigy, giving his first piano recital at the age of four. When he was thirteen he ran away from home and played his way through North and South America, thence to London and Leipzig. In 1878 he took lessons from Liszt and also studied for a time in Paris. In 1891 he settled in London with a handsome commission from the banker, Lord Latymer, who had written six opera librettos and retained Albeniz to set them to music. Albeniz is chiefly remembered for his piano music, in particular for the set of pieces entitled *Iberia* (1906–09) which consists of twelve pieces in four books of three each. The music of *Iberia* is colourful and of virtuoso standard and makes much use of Spanish dance rhythms.

Enrique Granados (1867–1916) was also primarily a pianist, although he took lessons in composition from Pedrell. Like Albeniz, he was able to capture the flavour of music from parts of Spain other than his native Catalonia. His main works for the piano are contained in two collections; of *Danzas españolas*, arranged in four sets of three; and *Goyescas*, a set of pieces inspired by the paintings of Goya (1746–1828). In *Goyescas* Granados succeeds in capturing the stark reality and fervour of the paintings in music which is tinged with melancholy.

The principal Spanish composer of the early twentieth century is **Manuel de Falla** (1876–1946). He was also a pupil of Pedrell and came to prominence in 1905 with his opera *La Vida Breve* (*Life is Short*). Between 1907 and 1914 he lived in Paris from which time his music is subject to French influence. His main works are *Nights in the Gardens of Spain* (1916), consisting of three pieces for piano and orchestra, and two ballet scores, both of 1919, *'El Amor Brujo'* (Love, the Sorcerer) and *'The Three-cornered Hat'* both of which contain elements of popular Spanish music. His mature works are the Concerto for Harpsichord and Five Solo Instruments of 1926 and the puppet opera *Master Peter's Puppet Show*. In both of these scores the fire of the Spanish idiom is transmuted into a style of classic serenity.

Brazil

The Brazilian composer **Heitor Villa-Lobos** (1887–1959) is of some importance. He was immensely active as a teacher, cellist, founder of the Brazilian music academy, collector of folk songs, a musicologist, and the composer of a large body of works many of which are experimental. He arranged the music of Bach for various combinations of instruments under the general title of *Bachianas Brasileiras*. The fifth of these is an evocative piece for eight cellos and soprano voice. Villa-Lobos also invented a new type of composition called a *chôro*. This is a work in a popular idiom consisting of a set of variations for soloist and different combinations of instruments. There are 14 chôros. Villa-Lobos was also given to organizing and conducting events consisting of a great many people. His festival of 1940 included a choir of 40,000.

England

During the nineteenth century England produced no composer of great importance. This is neither odd nor reprehensible. There was, however, a great deal of musical activity throughout the land. Anglican church composers continued to be very active in spite of a certain amount of religious heart-searching in the middle of the century, and in 1861 the first edition of *Hymns*

Ancient and Modern was published. In the secular field the *Brass Band movement* became increasingly important as the century advanced.

The earlier bands, during the first quarter of the century, were made up of both woodwind and brass instruments, formed on the pattern of the military band. A typical early band consisted of the following instruments: a trumpet, a bugle, two french horns, a serpent, two bassoons, a bass horn, four flutes, four clarinets, cymbal, drum and triangle. With the introduction of valves for brass instruments from the 1840s it became possible for a band to consist entirely of brass and percussion. At the same time the expansion of the railways provided cheap and easy travel, with the result that *contesting* became an important part of the brass band movement. The first big contest was held at Belle Vue in Manchester in 1853 with eight bands taking part. In 1860 the first London contest took place at the Crystal Palace attended by 170 bands. By the end of the century it is estimated that there were over 20,000 bands in existence. British brass bands have always been amateur organizations and have traditionally raised their own funds for the purchase of instruments. They have always been supported by business interests and by interested amateurs. Today many bands are trained by a professional conductor. A Bandsmen's College of Music exists and it is now possible to get a Diploma in Brass Bandmastership.

The Music Hall

The music hall emerged about the 1840s. It was originally centred around the working-class public houses which provided music as well as food and drink. But from 1850 custom-built halls began to appear and by 1860 there were about 260 such halls in London with perhaps 300 in the rest of the country. By the 1890s businessmen developed chains of halls which attracted people from all classes of society. This was the golden age of the music hall. A star system of performers developed, the most famous name perhaps being that of Marie Lloyd. The entertainment catered for a mostly urban audience with songs relating either to city life or to the towndweller's idealized view of the country. Apart from such ballads the music included glees, catches and operatic excerpts.

Gilbert and Sullivan

An important part of London's musical life during the 1870s and 1880s were the operettas of Gilbert and Sullivan at the Savoy theatre. These works have always had an immense audience appeal. They have wit; their plots are deftly handled; they move from sentimentality to disarming moments of merriment; and they are unfailingly tuneful. Perhaps they also appeal to British audiences because of their sophisticated flippancy. They are, however, built on a solid musical foundation.

Arthur Sullivan (1842–1900) studied at the Royal Academy of Music and at the Leipzig Conservatory, and composed much music of serious intent. The Savoy operettas are usually beautifully constructed and some, such as *The Gondoliers*, have fully worked out opera buffa finales; they also abound in precisely judged parody as in the Mad Meg music of *Ruddigore,* the recitatives for Lady Jane in *Patience,* or the Waltzing Song in *The Pirates of Penzance.* But they also contain many songs which are musical gems in their own right.

Although the texts of these operas bristle with contemporary allusions, as musical works for the stage they have not dated.

Folk Song

Meanwhile in the English countryside at the turn of the century certain enthusiastic collectors were busy noting down the already fast-disappearing body of national folk songs. The most active of these was **Cecil Sharp** (1859–1924) who between 1904 and 1919 issued several volumes of *Folk Songs from Somerset*. He later collected folk songs in the Appalachian mountains of the USA where he was surprised to discover that some tunes bore a marked similarity to those he had already collected in England.

But serious composition in the late nineteenth century was not neglected. Several composers were active whose music was of sufficient importance to be regarded as forming an English musical Renaissance, a reference to the fact that no outstanding English composer had appeared since the death of Purcell in 1695. Among these were **Sir John Stainer** (1840–1901) whose Easter Passion *The Crucifixion* was immensely popular during the first half of the twentieth century and can be performed by an average church choir; **Charles Villiers Stanford** (1852–1924), a prolific composer and a teacher who had an important effect on musical education in the early twentieth century; and **Sir Hubert Parry** (1848–1918), perhaps the outstanding composer of this group. His choral music remains effective and the splendid Ode *Blest Pair of Sirens* remains firmly in the repertoire.

But it was in the twentieth century that the English musical Renaissance was finally effected, appearing in the work of Elgar, Delius, Vaughan Williams and Holst.

Elgar

In **Edward Elgar** (1857–1934) England produced a composer of international stature. Elgar was largely self-taught; his music derives from both Wagner and Brahms but its individual sound in unmistakeable, with an opulent dignity which is frequently tinged with melancholy. His orchestral scoring is rich and sophisticated; instruments tend to play short fragments which are woven together to form a continuous orchestral texture. His melodies often move in wide leaps and are formed from repeated rhythmic phrases. They frequently contain falling 7ths, as occurs in 'Nimrod' from the *Enigma Variations* (1899). It was with this work that Elgar first came to prominence. A year later with *The Dream of Gerontius* (1900), an oratorio in the English tradition, he achieved international fame.

Elgar's other two oratorios, *The Apostles* (1903) and *The Kingdom* (1906) are equally compelling although not so frequently performed. He wrote two symphonies, the first of which, in A♭ major, appeared in 1908. This work opens with a slow, broad melody which acts as a motto theme for the whole symphony. The two inner movements are thematically related since the theme of the third movement is a much slowed down version of that of the scherzo which precedes it. The Second Symphony, in E♭ major (1910), is a musical valediction upon the Edwardian era. Its slow movement propounds the pomp and ceremony of a royal funeral.

Elgar's Violin Concerto, in B minor (1910) is a fine example of a late

Romantic concerto in which the solo part interacts with the main orchestral sound with no sense of strain. Similarly successful is the Cello Concerto in E minor of 1919, reflecting the subdued postwar feeling; this was Elgar's last major work. Among Elgar's other fine works are the symphonic study *Falstaff* (1913) and the *Introduction and Allegro* (1905) for string quartet and string orchestra, a latter day concerto grosso. Elgar's favourite performing instruction is *nobilmente*, an Italian sounding word which he seems to have invented.

Delius

The most forward looking of English composers of the early twentieth century was **Frederick Delius** (1862–1934). Delius loved the English countryside; but he also spent several years as the manager of an orange grove in Florida and lived for the last ten years of his life, blind and paralysed, in France. Much of his music is concerned with the feelings evoked by nature. He developed a rich and highly individual harmonic style which owes something both to Grieg and to the Blues chords of jazz. His harmony moves quite slowly and his music is rarely disturbed by positive rhythmic activity. His best works are for orchestra or for voices and orchestra. Among the former are *Appalachia* (1905), *Brigg Fair* (1907), *On hearing the first cuckoo in Spring* (1912) and *Summer Night on the River* (1912). His last works were written down with the help of his wife and the Yorkshire-born musician, Eric Fenby.

Vaughan Williams

Ralph Vaughan Williams (1872–1958) was brought up in the German tradition but it was English music which influenced him most. He was very active in the folk song movement and was devoted to the music of the Tudor church composers, both of which idioms pervade his style. A familiar work in the latter vein is the *Fantasia on a Theme of Thomas Tallis* (1910). Much of Vaughan Williams' music reflects the contemplative and mystical side of his nature but it can also be ebullient and very forceful. He wrote nine symphonies of which the earlier ones, *A Sea Symphony, A London Symphony* and *Pastoral Symphony* are programmatic; these three works were composed between 1905 and 1910. The Fourth, Fifth, and Sixth Symphonies of 1935, 1943, and 1948 respectively contain the essence of his musical thought.

Vaughan Williams also wrote several choral works among which are *Sancta Civitas* (1925) and the *Benedicite* (1930). The breadth of his outlook is apparent from the fact that late in life he wrote the music for the films *49th Parallel* and *Scott of the Antarctic*.

Holst

A contemporary of Vaughan Williams and a collaborator of his in the folk song movement was **Gustav Holst** (1874–1934). Holst was attracted also to Indian mysticism, an influence which can be seen in such works as the chamber opera *Savitri* (1908) and four sets of choral hymns chosen from the Hindu epic Rig Veda (1908–12). During the early years of the century Holst taught at St Paul's girls' school for which he wrote the *St Paul's Suite* (1913) for string orchestra. The *Planets Suite* (1914–16), composed for a very large orchestra, justly retains its popularity; The *Hymn of Jesus* (1917) is a short work for double chorus and orchestra with some fine harmonic writing. Holst himself considered his best work to be the tone poem *Egdon Heath* (1925). This is a musical evocation of the bleak landscape which forms the setting of Hardy's *The Return of the Native*. Both Holst and Vaughan Williams had a sensitive feeling for orchestral colour and an imaginative way of setting words to music.

PART TWO

Two-Part Writing: One Note Against Another

We saw in Chapter 16 that melody and harmony are interdependent. Two-part writing is related to four-part harmony in a similar way. The problem in two-part writing is to choose an acceptable succession of intervals between the two parts and at the same time to make sure that each part is interesting in its own right. All intervals are possible between the parts; but if we consider a four-part chord it is clear that some intervals are basic to two-part writing. These are: unison, 3rd, 4th, 5th, and 6th.

In two-part exercises either the upper or the lower part may be given. It is often preferable to keep both parts on the same stave but they may well be written on two staves each with a separate clef. Two-part writing brought to perfection may be studied in Bach's two-part Inventions. When adding a part to a given part *do not alter the part which is given.*

1. *The beginning* of a two-part piece: make sure that the key is established.
   The Example 18.1 implies V Ib. *A perfect 5th* may be used at the beginning,

KEY C MAJOR

18.1

implying either I or V, as in Example 18.2. *An octave* may be used effectively at the beginning and the end of a piece – Example 18.3.

18.2

18.3

2. *The end* of a two-part piece: the final notes must suggest the tonic chord in its root position. The last Example above suggests a perfect cadence in C major.
3. *The middle* of a piece:
   (a) *3rds and 6ths* are the mainstay of this type of writing; but it is somewhat unadventurous to use only these. In any case do not use more than three consecutive 3rds or 6ths. Avoid using two major 3rds which between them encompass a tritone (see Chapter 13, p. 144) as demonstrated in Example 18.4. But the pair of major 3rds in Example 18.5 in C minor is quite acceptable because they encompass a *perfect* 4th.

KEY C MINOR

18.4   **18.5**

   (b) *the octave* may be used just as it occurs in the outer parts of a passing six-four chord (Chapter 10, p. 110). The octave is the middle interval of three whose parts are moving in contrary motion in Example 18.6. An octave may also be used when other parts of the same chord have just been sounded as in Example 18.7.

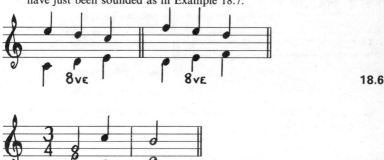

18.6

18.7

   (c) *a 5th* is effectively used where the upper part moves up the scale with the lower part forming the sequence 6th, 5th, 3rd, below it. This has the effect of a hunting call, shown in Example 18.8. This works equally well in the minor.
   (d) *a 4th* effectively occurs where the two parts in (c) above are inverted. The effect of a hunting call remains (see Example 18.9).

Example 18.10 contains the above uses of intervals.

Discords which are Prepared: Suspensions

A powerful way of making music move forward is by striking a *discord* on the strong beat of a bar (see Example 18.11). This causes the hearer to listen

18.8

18.9

KEY C MAJOR

UNISON   8ᵥₑ   6ᵀₕ 5ᵀₕ   3ᴿᴰ   5ᵀₕ **18.10**

18.11

forward for the discord to be *resolved*, as in Example 18.12. Sudden discords
have at various periods of musical history seemed objectionable. The objection
disappears if the note causing the disruption has just been heard as part of a
concord on a weak beat, as in Example 18.13. This note is said to cause a
suspension. Suspensions can resolve upwards but by far the greater majority
of suspensions ever written move downwards.

   To write a suspension into an existing piece of music:

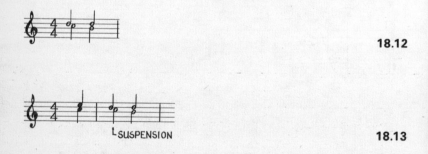

18.12

SUSPENSION   18.13

1. Find a passage in which a note in a chord on a weak beat falls by step on
   to the next strong beat, as in Example 18.14.
2. Instead of allowing the note to fall, repeat it on strong beat either by
   striking it afresh or by tying it over (see Example 18.15). At this point it
   causes a discord with a note in the existing chord. It therefore *resolves* by
   moving down a step, now appearing as the original strong beat note. The

18.14

18.15

timing of the bar must be adjusted to accommodate the extra note. In order to savour the full effect of the discord, the suspended note must be at least of equal length to the note of resolution.

In four-part harmony make sure that the note of resolution is *not present in another part of the chord* carrying the suspension or the effect will be very harsh as in Example 18.16. But this harshness is not apparent if the note of resolution is in the *bass*. It is, therefore, perfectly possible to write as shown in Example 18.17.

18.16

18.17

Exercise

1. Rewrite the passages in Example 18.18, introducing suspensions.

18.18

Suggested Further Reading

Clapham, John. *Dvořák* (Newton Abbott: David and Charles, 1979).

Clapham, John. *Smetana* (London: Dent, Master Musicians, 1972).

Horton, John. *Grieg* (London: Dent, Master Musicians, 1976).

Howes, Frank. *The English Musical Renaissance* (London: Secker and Warburg, 1966).

Kennedy, Michael. *Elgar Orchestral Music* (London: BBC Music Guides, 1970).

Layton, Robert. *Dvořák Symphonies and Concertos* (London: BBC Music Guides, 1978).

Layton, Robert. *Sibelius* (London: Dent, Master Musicians, 1979).

Palmer, Roy. (ed.) *A Touch on the Times* (London: Penguin, 1974).

Reed, W. H. *Elgar as I knew Him*, (London: Gollancz, 1978).

19

PART ONE: FROM ROMANTICISM TO POST-ROMANTICISM

As the nineteenth century passed into the twentieth, music moved from a period of late Romanticism into one which may be termed Post-Romanticism. As the twentieth century progressed, Romanticism ceased to be the dominant style in Western music although it has remained a distinguishing feature of much of the century's music. The characteristic features of Post-Romanticism are: rhythmic complexity, tonal instability, i.e., a weakening of the key structure in music, harmony used in an increasingly individual way rather than forming a common language, excess of time-scale, of dynamic range and emotional intensity, and an exaggeration of the elements of Romanticism to a point of disintegration.

The evolution from Romanticism to Post-Romanticism is clearly seen in the music of a series of South German and Austrian composers whose work spans from about 1850 until well into the twentieth century. The first of these is Bruckner.

Bruckner

Anton Bruckner (1824–96) is chiefly remembered as a symphonist, although he wrote some fine choral music. He was born nearly ten years before Brahms but started writing symphonies seriously even later than Brahms did; consequently his work belongs to the late nineteenth century.

Bruckner wrote eleven symphonies. Ten of them are numbered, from No. 0 ('Die Nullte') to No. 9, the remaining one being a student work. Bruckner was devoted to the music of Wagner whose influence is seen in his harmony. As a symphonist he starts from the position of Beethoven's Ninth and inherits the Romantic features of Schubert. Historically, it is necessary to disentangle him from Brahms on the one hand and from Mahler on the other, for a Bruckner symphony provides a most satisfying and exhilarating musical experience in its own right.

Bruckner as a symphonist is stylistically and structurally consistent and his musical thought is not difficult to follow. All of his symphonies have four movements which appear in the traditional order of allegro, slow, scherzo, finale. He uses recognizable versions of standard sonata form and his scherzos and trios contain the traditional repeated sections.

A Bruckner first movement typically begins with the music arriving out of nowhere and coming into focus as a strong theme based upon a triad or upon the interval of a 5th. He is fond of the rhythm in Example 19.1. His second

19.1

subject groups are expansive and aria-like, but nevertheless fit easily into the structure. One reason for this may be that Bruckner avoids transition passages; when he has completed one section the music just stops, and starts again straight into the next section complete with new material, new scoring and new key. Many of Bruckner's movements contain chorale-like tunes, which sometimes form closing themes. His recapitulations are often shortened and make way for a grand coda.

Bruckner's music moves in unhurried, granite-like chunks. His slow movements proceed with the greatest unconcern for the exigencies of the passage of time, the most celebrated of these being the second movement of the 7th symphony. His scherzos move, by convention, faster than the other movements, but remain expressions of staid joy.

Bruckner was persuaded frequently to revise and alter his work so that several versions of the symphonies exist. It is now customary for the composer's original thinking to be heard in performance. He was for many years a professional organist, at the monastery of St Florian and at the cathedral in Linz. From 1869 he worked as a professor at the Vienna Conservatory. His vision of God was firm and untroubled by doubt; it is this vision which he celebrates in his music.

Bruckner's symphonies are as follows: No. 0 in D minor, No. 1 in C minor, No. 2 in C minor, No. 3 ('Wagner Symphony') in D minor, No. 4 ('Romantic') in E♭ major, No. 5 in B♭ major, No. 6 in A major, No. 7 in E major, No. 8 in C minor, No. 9 (unfinished) in D minor.

Wolf

Also stemming from the Viennese tradition of Schubert but in a very different manner was the music of **Hugo Wolf** (1860–1903). Wolf composed opera, chamber music, and symphonic poems but his reputation rests almost entirely on his songs with piano accompaniment. They number about 250 and were composed in short bursts of intense activity followed by uncreative periods during the years 1887–97 when Wolf became incurably insane.

Wolf's achievement was to fuse the ideals and methods of Wagner onto the existing forms of the German Lied. The results of this are that his songs are not set in verses but are through-composed; that the voice part often proceeds in a sort of declamation but is nevertheless always melodically of great consequence; and that the function of the Wagner orchestra is fulfilled by the piano which provides a constantly unfolding atmospheric background to the vocal line.

Wolf was the most discerning of the nineteenth century songwriters in his choice of poets, for he wished above all to express the *quality* of a poem in music and was not so much concerned with the details of its expression. His work is published in six collections, each devoted to a single poet or group of poets, as follows: 53 songs to poems of Eduard Mörike (1889); 20 of Eichendorff (1889); 51 of Goethe (1890); 44 to German translations of Spanish poems, the *Spanisches Liederbuch* (1891); 46 to translations of Italian poems, the *Italienisches Liederbuch* (Part 1 1892; part II 1896) and three songs to poems of Michelangelo (1898).

Wolf was entirely successful in his aims, for his songs express a masterly insight into the poet's vision. He works with musical patterns of an infinite variety but at the same time concentrates the poetic image into a single musical stroke. By condensing the music he heightens its intensity.

Mahler

The song also forms the basis of much of the music of **Gustav Mahler** (1860–1911) but Mahler's method is to allow his musical thought to expand so as to encompass every detail of the idea upon which he is working. He is fascinated by the soul of man, by suffering and death, but also by the mystical glory of the natural world.

Mahler was a professional orchestral conductor of outstanding ability. His methods were rigorous and uncompromising and were carried out often in the face of hostile criticism. He called himself a 'holiday composer' and much of his music was composed in the intervals of a busy professional life. To his great knowledge of orchestral scoring he brought a natural gift for instrumentation. His scores abound in the minutest of performing details; in this respect they fully represent the Romantic composer's assumption that the score is sacrosanct and is a blueprint for an ideal performance, in contrast to the Baroque position, and one common in our own day, which allows a certain amount of licence to the performer on the grounds that each performance is a separate recreation of the musical score.

Mahler's work consists almost entirely of songs and symphonies. There are four song cycles for solo voices and orchestra and nine symphonies, with a tenth incomplete. Mahler's chief source of inspiration for his vocal music was the early nineteenth-century anthology of German folk-poems, *The Boy's Magic Horn* (*Des Knaben Wunderhorn*). His work may be divided into three periods. The first includes the Symphonies Nos. 1–4, the 'Songs of a Wayfarer' (*Lieder eines fahrenden Gesellen*) (1883) and the song cycle from *Des Knaben Wunderhorn*. The second period reaches a climax with the Eighth Symphony and includes also the *Kindertotenlieder* (Songs on the Death of Children). In the third period are the Ninth and Tenth Symphonies and 'The Song of the Earth' (*Das Lied von der Erde*).

Four of the symphonies include parts for voices: No. 2 in C minor, known as the *Resurrection Symphony* brings in voices at the end in the manner of Beethoven's Ninth; No. 4 in G major is scored for small orchestra and includes a soprano solo in the final movement; No. 3 in D minor has parts for solo contralto, for a women's choir and for a boys' choir; No. 8 in E♭ major, known as the *Symphony of a Thousand* consists of two vast movements including parts for eight solo voices, a double choir and a boys' choir. All of Mahler's music must be considered programmatic even when no definite clues as to the programme exist, as is the case with the middle group of symphonies, No. 5 in C minor, No. 6 in A minor, and No. 7 in D major, known as *The Song of the Night*.

For Mahler a symphony represents a vision of the world in its entirety. Since the world apparently consists of a series of unrelated events, so too in Mahler there is a frequent dislocation of ideas; and if the world is sometimes uncomfortable to be in this too is reflected in Mahler's music, for there are often passages of sarcastic, sardonic and devilish irony, contrived with the composer's superb skill at orchestration. But the world also has moments of beauty, joy, and serenity and these too are found in full measure in Mahler.

Throughout his work there is fully apparent the weakening of the tonal system which led directly to the work of the Viennese composers Schoenberg, Berg, and Webern.

Strauss

Richard Strauss (1864–1949) chose to work in two fields of music completely different from one another: the symphonic poem, which he called *tone poem*; and opera. He is also a Lieder writer of some consequence. In his work he succeeded for the most part in bypassing the tonal revolution of the early twentieth century.

Strauss was born in Munich, son of the first horn player in the royal orchestra which took part in the first performance of *Tristan und Isolde* in 1865. Richard Strauss is not a member of the famous Strauss family associated with the Viennese waltz. Like Mahler, Strauss became a virtuoso international conductor. While in his teens he composed quite a few works which have endured, among them a Cello Sonata in F major, op. 5, the First Horn Concerto, in E♭, op. 11 and some fine songs including *Ständchen* ('Serenade').

After this early period his work divides with very little overlap into one period devoted to tone poems and another to stage works. The programmes of his tone poems are both literal, in that they imitate the sounds of things, and evocative, in that they deal with underlying ideas. His first success was with *Don Juan* (1889). This work brilliantly illustrates that hero's search for love and his final descent into hell.

Death and Transfiguration (*Tod und Verklärung*) written in 1890, conveys the oppressive sense of a sickroom in which the patient's heart can be heard to stop beating, after which he proceeds gloriously to a higher sphere. Much more extrovert is *Till Eulenspiegels lustige Streiche* (*Till Eulenspiegel's Merry Pranks*) (1895). Each prank is illustrated by a variation upon a double theme, although Strauss called the work a rondo. *Don Quixote* (1897) includes a wind machine, and the bleating of sheep is directly imitated by muted brass. This resulted in hostile critical reaction. Strauss replied the following year with *Ein Heldenleben* (*A Hero's Life*) in which the Hero is identified by quotations from Strauss's own works while his critics chatter inanely in the woodwinds. Strauss's orchestral writing is extremely colourful and depends for its effect in performance upon accuracy and precision of execution, particularly in the difficult string writing.

All but one of Strauss's operas date from the twentieth century. His first major successes were *Salome* (1905) and *Elektra* (1909). Both of these works startled the operatic world, the first by its subject matter and the second by its style. Salome, based upon a one-act play by Oscar Wilde, tells a violent and erotic story which is conveyed in splendid orchestral sound based upon descriptive rhythms and harmonies. *Elektra* is a story of hatred and revenge for which Strauss used a discordant style which seemed far in advance of anything yet heard.

With *Elektra* Strauss began a long and fruitful collaboration with the Viennese dramatist **Hugo von Hofmannsthal** (1874–1929). Their subsequent works concentrated largely upon the portrayal of an elegant and sunny world, decadent and slightly erotic, which is seen at its most complete in *Der Rosenkavalier* (1911). This opera evokes eighteenth-century Vienna in music of glittering sentimentality. In this and in subsequent works such as *Ariadne auf Naxos* (1912), *Intermezzo* (1923) and *Arabella* (1933) Strauss displays his superb ability to write for the soprano voice. This ability is heard on the concert platform in the *Four Last Songs* (1948). But Strauss's farewell to instrumental music was made in 1945 with the appearance of *Metamorphosen*, a work for twenty-three solo string instruments, ten violins, five violas, five cellos and three double basses. Strauss writes easily for the twenty-three parts in music which looks back nostalgically to a distant past and which is finally crystallized into the funeral march theme from Beethoven's 'Eroica Symphony'.

Reger

A composer who succeeded in adapting Wagner's harmonic vocabulary to formal compositional methods of the late Baroque era was **Max Reger** (1873–1916). His output is large and includes all types of composition; his music is nonprogrammatic. He is important in the history of nineteenth-century organ music, having written over 100 organ pieces using such forms as the chorale prelude, fugue, toccata, and canon. Of his orchestral music the *Variations and Fugue on a theme of Mozart* (from the piano sonata in A major K.331) are sometimes heard.

Post-Romanticism in Italy

Italian music in the late nineteenth century continued to be dominated by opera. The achievement of Verdi was succeeded by a style of operatic writing known as *verismo* (truth to life). The plots of such operas were concerned with dramatic but plausible incidents from the seamier side of contemporary life. The style did not last long but from it two short operas have survived. Happily they together form an agreeable evening's entertainment; they are familiarly known as 'Cav and Pag'. *Cavalleria Rusticana* ('Rural Chivalry') (1890) was the first opera by **Pietro Mascagni** (1863–1945) and tells, in one act, the story of a tragic village love affair against the background of a Sicilian blood feud. Its partner, *I Pagliacci* ('The Clowns') (1892) by **Ruggiero Leoncavallo** (1858–1919) is in two short acts. It concerns a group of travelling players and points up the difference between their real lives and their stage lives.

Puccini

The operas of **Giacomo Puccini** (1858–1924) have always been subject to stern critical appraisal, in the teeth of their immense popularity. It is sometimes said that his acute commercial sense, which allowed him to acquire several expensive motor cars and a small fleet of motor boats, was exercised at the expense of his artistic integrity, in that his music is often more extravagantly emotional than the plots of his operas demand. However that may be, Puccini's gift for memorable melody and his dramatic awareness are undeniable. He has too a precise feeling for orchestral colour and often handles his orchestra with reticence. This gives greater impact to the climatic melodies which clinch his love duets, usually sung by tenor and soprano. At such moments both voices unite while the orchestral strings support them up and over the climax, a practice which is also found in Verdi.

Puccini's first success was with *Manon Lescaut* (1893). This was followed by *La Bohème* (1896), *Tosca* (1900), and *Madame Butterfly* (1904), all of which were, and have remained, extremely popular. *The Girl of the Golden West* was staged in 1910 and in 1918 appeared three one-act operas under the title *Il Trittico* ('The Triptych'). These works form an admirably contrasted sequence: *Il Tabarro* (The Cloak), *Suor Angelica*, a tragedy set in a convent, and *Gianni Schicchi*, Puccini's only comic opera. Puccini's final opera, *Turandot*, remained unfinished at his death; it is a work in which it is generally agreed that the music matches the demands of the drama.

PART TWO

Two-Part Writing (2) – Decorated

In Chapter 18 we saw how to write in two parts with both parts moving together, note for note. Either part may be decorated to provide interest to the whole composition. Even the most simple passage may be decorated in several ways, by the use of harmony notes, passing notes and auxiliary notes. Example 19.2 shows a two-part passage and two of the many possible ways of decorating it.

a) PASSING NOTE
b) HARMONY NOTE
c) AUXILIARY NOTE

19.2

Suspensions may also occur in a two-part passage, as in Example 19.3. A suspension is a *prepared discord* (see Chapter 18). Some discords are *unprepared* and may occur as the result of using non-essential, i.e., non-harmonic, notes. Among these are the *Accented Passing Note, Appoggiatura*, and *Acciaccatura* (for the pronunciation of the last two words see Appendix II).

19.3

Accented Passing Note

Like an unaccented passing note this occurs between two harmony notes a 3rd apart, but an accented passing note *falls on the beat*. Example 19.4 contains

19.4

214   *Music*

an unaccented passing note. It is joined to the *first* of the two notes which form
the interval of a 3rd. The same note used as an accented passing note belongs
to the *second* of these two notes, as in 19.5.

19.5

Therefore in order to write an accented passing note work as follows:

1. Keep the first note of the interval of a 3rd as it is.
2. Put the passing note in the place of the second note of the 3rd.
3. Now join the second note of the interval of a 3rd on to the passing note,
   splitting the time value of the original second note between itself and the
   passing note.

The passage in Example 19.6 is worked with (a) unaccented passing notes and
(b) both unaccented and accented passing notes.

a)

b)

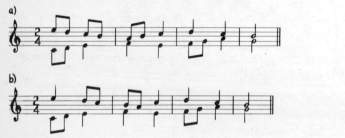

19.6 a/b

Appoggiatura
An appoggiatura acts like an accented passing note but is arrived at by a leap,
as shown in Example 19.7. The appoggiatura is used frequently in music of all

a) UNACCENTED PASSING NOTE
b) APPOGGIATURA
c) ACCENTED PASSING NOTE

19.7

styles. In the eighteenth century it was of particular importance and was the
subject of two distinct performing conventions:

1. It was approached by a leap and was often shown as a small note as in Example 19.8. Its exact value varied in performance, for it is an *expressive*

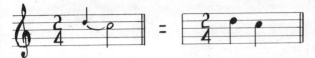

19.8

device. The standard interpretation of the appoggiatura is that it takes half the value of the note which follows it: in triple time it is played as shown in Example 19.9.

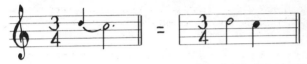

19.9

2. In certain passages, notably in recitative but also in an aria, it was sung, at the end of a phrase, as if it were an accented passing note. It was not shown at all, but its presence was inferred from the melodic shape. The passage from Mozart's *The Marriage of Figaro* in Example 19.10 may well be sung as in Example 19.11.

19.10

19.11

Acciaccatura

An acciaccatura is an appoggiatura played as quickly as possible. It is written as a small note with a line through it as in Example 19.12.

Sometimes a note is *anticipated* on the previous weak beat. It may cause a discord but is not usually felt as such, for its function is to call attention to the accented note which follows it – see Example 19.13.

19.12   **19.13**

Changing Notes

These are purely a method of decorating a single note and have no harmonic
implications. The note to be decorated moves above and below itself and ends
where it started, as in Example 19.14. A particular form of changing note was
much used in sixteenth-century choral polyphony and is shown in Example
19.15. It carries the Italian term for changing note: *nota cambiata*.

19.14

19.15

With accented passing notes and appoggiaturas as with suspensions, avoid
writing the note of resolution inside the discord. It is quite acceptable as the
bass note, as in Example 19.16.

HARSH   GOOD   **19.16**

Suggested Further Reading

Barford, Philip. *Bruckner Symphonies* (London: BBC Music Guides, 1978).
Barford, Philip. *Mahler Symphonies and Songs* (BBC Music Guides, 1970).
Carner, Mosco. *Puccini* (London: Duckworth, 1958).
Kennedy, Michael. *Richard Strauss* (London: Dent, Master Musicians, 1979).
Mitchell, Donald. *Gustav Mahler*, 2 vols. (London: Faber, 1979).

20

PART ONE: FRENCH MUSIC FROM 1870

During the earlier part of the nineteenth century French music was largely dominated by opera. Paris was the operatic capital of Europe and Rossini and Meyerbeer, both foreigners, were its two most important operatic composers. In the middle of the century the tradition of opera passed to French composers, notably to Bizet and Gounod. At about the same time there arose a succession of notable French composers who were active in all branches of composition and who established a renaissance in French music which was to lead to the commanding figure of Debussy. The influence of Debussy has extended throughout the twentieth century up to our own day. In addition, before and after World War I Paris again became an international centre for schools of composition and for the exchange of ideas relating not only to music but to all aspects of western and eastern culture.

Mid-nineteenth-century Opera

Two main types of French opera were inherited from the eighteenth century: grand opera, with its serious subjects, spectacular effects, choruses, and ballets; and opéra comique, a much more lightweight, but not necessarily lighthearted, entertainment which allowed spoken dialogue. To these forms a third was added by the German born **Jacques Offenbach** (1819–1880) which he named *opéra bouffe*. This is to be distinguished from the Italian *opera buffa* and is characterized by wit, buffoonery, and irreverence. It included spoken dialogue and its English equivalent is operetta. Offenbach wrote over one hundred such works between 1840 and 1880, turning them out at enormous speed. The most famous is *Orpheus in the Underworld* (1858) and perhaps the most familiar is *La Belle Hélène* (1864), both of which poke malicious fun at classical mythology. In a much more serious vein is *The Tales of Hoffman* which was produced in 1881, after Offenbach's death, and must be classed as a true opera. Offenbach was a competent cellist; his characteristic charm and wit find expression in a series of cello duets which are well within the capabilities of the average player.

    Charles Gounod (1818–1893) was a more serious composer. His music lacks the abrasiveness of Offenbach's and does not always avoid sentimentality. However, with *Faust* (1859) he wrote the best-known lyric opera of the period. The plot is taken from Goethe's drama, and Gounod wisely concentrated on the tragic love affair of Gretchen and Faust in Part I of that work and so avoided writing an opera based on metaphysics.

    As an opera, *Faust* is completely consistent in style and its succession of fine melodies and sturdy choruses have assured its popularity over a long period. Gounod wrote a great deal of religious music of various kinds, but a very attractive instrumental work is the *Little Symphony for Wind Instruments* (1879). A rather more spirited composer of the middle of the century, perhaps

because of his Spanish ancestry, was **Edouard Lalo** (1823–1892). He is best
known today for the violin concerto under the title of *Symphonie Espagnole*
(1873). His opera *Le Roi d'Ys* (1888) was immensely successful until well into
the twentieth century and is still performed in France.

But the outstanding French opera of the mid-nineteenth century and perhaps the greatest example of opéra comique is Bizet's *Carmen*, first produced
in 1875. The most important music of **Georges Bizet** (1838–1875) was written
during the last four years of his rather short life. His music is marked by its
wit, its freshness of invention, and the clarity with which his ideas are presented. But it was not these qualities which caused *Carmen* to achieve immediate fame. Its subject matter caused a scandal with the first scene in particular causing distress to its viewers, for the heroine is seen coming out of a
cigarette factory and throwing a flower, uninvited, at a waiting soldier. Such
scruples, however, were quickly dispelled by the quality of the opera itself and
its worth has been recognized continuously throughout the world. Bizet wrote
equally well for the voice, the piano and the orchestra. His suite for piano
duet, *Jeux d'enfants* (1871) rightly takes its place amongst a number of fine
nineteenth century pieces for and about children. The immediate appeal of
Bizet's music is heard in the familiar suite from the incidental music to
L'Arlésienne (1872). The orchestral suite *Roma* (1868) takes the form of a
symphony, but Bizet is remembered by another symphony, in C major,
composed in 1855 when he was seventeen. This was not first performed until
1935 since when its originality and sparkle assure it a firm place in the repertoire.

The Renaissance in French music

The renaissance in French music gathered increasing momentum after the
Franco-Prussian war of 1870. The establishment of the National Society for
French Music in 1871 gave encouragement to both composers and performers
and resulted in a marked rise, both in quality and quantity, in the composition
of works other than opera. The composers concerned with this development
may be loosely divided into two groups, although their work is naturally
interdependent and shares many common features. On the one hand was a
group following the German tradition and influenced by Wagner: this was
established by César Franck and included in due course Chausson, D'Indy,
Duparc, and Dukas. Deriving from this group is the work of two twentieth-
century composers, Honegger and Roussel. The earlier members of this school
were antipathetic to what they saw as the narrow outlook of the Paris conservatory. In 1894 they helped to establish the Schola Cantorum with a more
broadly based musical education.

The other tradition stemmed from Saint-Säens and his contemporaries, and
included Chabrier, Fauré, and Ravel, and Debussy may also be thought of as
a member of this group. These composers were much more idealistic in their
outlook than the followers of Franck and they were in a sense nationalistic in
that they sought to re-establish the traditional qualities of French music. They
were concerned with the Classical ideals of restraint and balance and their
music is lyrical and dance-like rather than epic and grandiose. They paid
great attention to detail and to the expression of emotion in a subtle rather

than in an obvious way. Their vocal music is an expression of the French language itself, with its restraint and its closed vowel sounds.

Standing apart from these two traditions and yet influencing them both is the figure of Eric Satie. Some of the technical aspects of his music are said to have influenced Debussy, and the twentieth-century composers Milhaud and Poulenc both owe something to him. Satie also provided a point of reference for various groups of composers during the first part of the twentieth century, among them Les Six, La Jeune France and the School of Arcueil.

The German Tradition

Franck

César Franck (1822–90) was in fact Belgian. As a youth he achieved a reputation as a virtuoso pianist. His influence upon the course of French music begins with his appointment as organist at Ste Clothilde in Paris in 1858. Here he began to gather about him a group of pupils who became his disciples. In 1872 he was appointed organ professor at the Paris Conservatory and it is from this date, in his fiftieth year, that his important works begin. Franck was an instrumental rather than a vocal composer. He is not generally concerned with programme music although his work includes some symphonic poems. His music is noted for its chromaticism, in the melody rather than in the harmony; he is fond of writing music in canon, and it is to Franck particularly that the term *cyclic form* is applied, implying that material from one movement of a work is transferred to other movements in order to bind the whole work together. In this respect it is similar to the *idée fixe* of Berlioz and to the metamorphosis of themes of Liszt, but it differs from the Wagnerian *Leitmotiv* whose function is rather to draw attention to a nonmusical idea.

Among the works in which Franck employs cyclic form are the symphonic poem *Le Chasseur Maudit* ('The Accursed Huntsman') (1882), a very loud work; the Piano Quintet in F minor (1879), a work notable for the symphonic effect of its scoring; and the Symphony in D minor (1886–88). Franck's only symphony is in three movements which, though they move at different speeds, share a mood of weighty seriousness. The first movement is long because its opening *lento* section is repeated further on. The second movement shocked Gounod because it includes prominent parts for harp and cor anglais. The third movement is splendidly rousing and quotes from the other two. In common with much French nineteenth-century orchestral music cornets are used in addition to trumpets.

The most successful of Franck's large-scale instrumental works is perhaps the *Symphonic Variations* for piano and orchestra (1885). The piano part is thoroughly integrated with the orchestra and not felt to be antagonistic to it, as in the Romantic piano concerto; Franck's handling of his two themes is masterly. Another cyclic work is the Violin Sonata in A (1886). It is a large-scale work with four movements, the second of which is the main one. The Finale is a canon at the octave between violin and piano. Two notable works for piano solo are *Prelude, Chorale, and Fugue* (1884) and *Prelude, Aria, and Finale* (1886). A similar fine work for organ is *Prelude, Fugue, and Variation*.

Other Composers in the German tradition

Franck was by nature gentle, but lively and firm. He was revered by his pupils
the most important of whom was **Vincent d'Indy** (1851–1931). D'Indy was
aristocratic, independent and given to strong likes and dislikes. He used his
wealth and influence to further causes to which he was attracted. He was
devoted to the music of Franck, whom he likened to Beethoven, and was
averse to that of Debussy and Ravel amongst others. In his work he incorporated traditional French melodies, as in the 'Symphony on a French Mountain
Tune' (1886) which uses a piano in the manner of Franck's *Symphonic
Variations*. Perhaps his most successful work is the Second Symphony in B♭
(1904) in which he handles the problems of cyclic form with complete assurance and success.

One of Franck's earliest pupils was **Henri Duparc** (1848–1933), whose reputation rests entirely upon fourteen songs which are all generally agreed to
be masterworks. He destroyed most of the other music he had written. The
songs are of the type known as *Mélodies*, a form which Duparc helped to
create. Two of the most outstanding are *L'Invitation au voyage* and *Phidylé*.

Another song writer was **Ernest Chausson** (1855–99) who was a pupil of
both Franck and Debussy. He is remembered for the lyrical piece for violin
and orchestra, *Poème* (1896) and for a fine symphony in B♭ (1890). **Paul
Dukas** (1865–1935) was a follower of the Franck/d'Indy school; his tone poem
The Sorcerer's Apprentice (*L'Apprenti Sorcier*) (1897) is a fine example of how
to translate into purely musical terms a story with vivid factual details.

A further pupil of d'Indy but one whose work belongs properly to the
twentieth century was **Albert Roussel** (1869–1937). Roussel came to music
late, having served in the navy until he was twenty-five. From d'Indy he
inherited a feeling for order and restraint but his travels caused him to be one
of the composers who were influenced by the East, particularly by India.
These characteristics all appear in the opera-ballet *Padmâvatî* (1914), an exotic
but restrained entertainment. After the first world war Roussel adapted his
style to the prevailing *Neo-classicism* which characterizes such works as the
Orchestral Suite in F (1926) and the *Sinfonietta* for strings (1934).

Composers who followed the French tradition

One of the founder members of the National Society for French Music of
1871 was **Camille Saint-Säens** (1835–1921). Saint-Säens was a prolific composer who wrote in a variety of forms. He took a detached view of music
which differed from the general Romantic idea that the composer should
become closely involved in his art. His importance lies not so much in the
music of his which has survived as in the inspiration he gave to other composers concerned with the renaissance of French music and the impetus he
gave to the movement which carried it well into the twentieth century. His
style is most clearly seen in his most familiar work, *The Carnival of Animals*
(1886), a parody which pokes fun at Rossini and Berlioz amongst others. But
his disengagement is also seen clearly in such programmatic works as the
symphonic poems *Le Rouet d'Omphale* (1871) and *Danse macabre* (1875). The
only one of Saint-Säens's thirteen operas which is still current is *Samson et*

Dalilah whose voluptuous mezzo-soprano solos suggest a certain involvement on the part of the composer after all.

Like Saint-Säens **Emmanuel Chabrier** (1841–94) was a deft musical parodist. He was nearly forty when he decided to devote himself to composition, after hearing a performance of Wagner's *Tristan und Isolde*. But Chabrier is no Wagnerian. His music is exuberant, colourful, very rhythmical, and not without its brash tunes. His output is small and his reputation rests on the fine orchestral scores of *España* (1883), a musical travel diary; and *La Marche Joyeuse* (1890) which fully lives up to its title.

Gabriel Fauré (1845–1924) became the establishment figure of the French musical renaissance. Like his teacher, Saint-Säens, he was a founder member of the National Society for French music and from 1905–20 was the director of the Paris Conservatory. His music is so essentially French that it is an acquired taste; often it appeals to those who do not like Wagner. It is completely unprogrammatic and is characterized by elegance, intimacy, and serenity.

Fauré was not interested in orchestral colour and often entrusted the scoring of his work to others. His melodies are long, their phrasing unpredictable. His harmony is modal and owes something to Gregorian chant. He is fond of chords of the 7th used in succession, either minor, e.g., (C E♭ G B♭) or major (C E G B) and when he writes in minor keys the leading note is often flattened. Most of Fauré's music is couched in the smaller forms; he is a superb writer of chamber music, piano music, and, above all, songs. Even an extended work such as the *Requiem* (1877) does not give the impression of being on a large scale.

His principal chamber works were all written late in his career: the second Violin Sonata (1917), Second Piano Quintet (1921) and String Quartet (1924) are all outstanding works. His piano pieces derive from Chopin and are given noncommittal titles such as Barcarolle, Nocturne or Prelude; they are often formed from restrained melodies surrounded by arpeggiated chords. Among his most delightful music for piano is the suite *Dolly* (1894) for four hands at one keyboard.

Fauré's songs are settings of contemporary French poets. They are both evocative and restrained, partly as a result of the sound of the French language. Among the most haunting are 'Lydia' (1865), 'Après un Rêve' (1865), the ten songs of *Le Chanson d'Eve* (1910) and the four of *L'Horizon Chimérique* (1922). Fauré's style is very personal but his influence is seen most clearly in the work of his most gifted pupil, Maurice Ravel.

With the music of Saint-Säens and Fauré the character of traditional French music was fully re-established. But its course was to be somewhat diverted by the music of **Eric Satie** (1866–1925), who had an attitude to music somewhat akin to that of Chabrier in his high spirits and tendency to make fun of the past, a tendency which he carries to the point of eccentricity. This is seen from the titles of some of his works 'Truly Flabby Preludes', 'Cold Pieces', 'Three Pieces in the form of a Pear'. But this levity is used to cover up an essential seriousness of purpose. He was concerned to use *sound* in an abstract way, an idea which has been of immense importance in the music of the twentieth century. He used discords which do not resolve and in *Gymnopédies* (1888) writes parallel 4ths which may have influenced Debussy. His style may

be traced in the work of such twentieth-century composers as Milhaud and
Poulenc.

Debussy

The break-up of the tonal system had been threatening throughout the nineteenth century. It had taken a lurch forward with the music of *Tristan and
Isolde*, and had more or less become a reality in the work of the Post-
Romantics. In the early twentieth century it was subject to two revolutions,
one in Paris with **Claude Debussy** (1862–1918), and the other in Vienna with
Schoenberg. Debussy did not so much cause the tonal system to disintegrate;
rather he sidestepped it. He did this in two ways, one of them technical and
the other aesthetic.

Debussy's technical innovations were in his use of scales, intervals and
chords, and in his part-writing. Instead of the major and minor scales of the
tonal system, Debussy favoured the whole tone scale and to a lesser extent the
pentatonic scale. The *whole tone scale* divides the octave into six notes each a
tone apart (see Example 20.1). It is impossible to notate this scale in whole

20.1

tones; at some point a diminished 3rd must be written. The scale exists at only
two pitches since each note is two semitones apart from its neighbour. The
augmented 5th is a common ingredient of the scale and the harmonies which
arise from it give an impression of vagueness. Its use was pretty well exhausted
by Debussy. The *pentatonic* scale happens to coincide with the intervals
produced by the black notes on a piano. Aside from the use of these scales
Debussy's music often moves in parallel 4ths, 5ths or octaves. He is also fond
of a series of chords of the ninth and eleventh which often move in parallel
motion.

Aesthetically, Debussy did not conceive of chords as combining to form an
overall structural pattern. In this way he discarded not only the tonal system
but its formal structures as well, the sonata principle in particular. Instead he
imagined each sound as an entity in itself, having its own colour, harmony,
and rhythm. This is not to say each sound is disconnected from its neighbour;
on the contrary, the music of Debussy is highly organized into phrases, paragraphs, and periods.

The influences upon Debussy are many, but they are all absorbed into his
own style. He had a formal musical training at the Paris Conservatory, win-
ning the Prix de Rome; he worked for a time in Russia and was attracted to
the music of the Russian nationalists, particularly that of Mussorgsky; a visit
to Bayreuth in 1888 caused him to come under the spell of Wagner which he
later rejected; a year later, in 1889, he heard performances in Paris given by
an Indonesian *gamelan* orchestra, music based largely upon a variety of percussion instruments; also from the East he was attracted to the prints of the
eighteenth-century Japanese artist Hokusai; the sights, sounds, and scents of
the Iberian peninsula also attracted him; above all he was influenced by the

ideals of the Impressionists in painting (Manet, Monet, Renoir, Degas, Cézanne, and Seurat) and by the Symbolists in poetry (Mallarmé, Baudelaire, and Verlaine). Both of these groups sought to create in their art the impression of a fleeting image as they themselves – rather than the world in general – experienced it. Debussy, together with Delius, and to a lesser extent Ravel, represents *Impressionism in music*.

Debussy's style, thus compounded, shows a continuous development. His earliest work betrayed the influence of other composers, even of Wagner, but by 1890 his own style was fully established. Among his earliest works are the *Prélude à 'L'après-midi d'un faune'*, (1894) and the three orchestral *Nocturnes* (1897–99): 'Nuages' (clouds), 'Fêtes' (festivals), and 'Sirènes' (sirens). But Debussy's most important work during this period was his only opera, *Pelléas et Mélisande*, first produced in 1902. This is sometimes regarded as one of the most outstanding achievements of twentieth-century music. In this work Debussy creates a misty, dreamlike atmosphere which remains unbroken from start to finish. The vocal parts proceed in a kind of nebulous declamation undisturbed by arias or by a chorus; they are supported by a continuous orchestral commentary. The partnership between words and music is as complete as in any opera.

During the early part of the twentieth century Debussy broadened his technique in such orchestral works as *La Mer* (1905) which consists of three tone pictures of the sea in its immensity and in its sparkling detail, and *Ibéria* (1912), from the orchestral suite *Images*, which evokes precisely the ethos of Spain.

Debussy's piano music is amongst the most important of the twentieth century. For Debussy the instrument was not percussive, but sonorous. He revolutionized the use of the sustaining pedal and evoked from the instrument all the resonant possibilities of which it is capable. Among Debussy's various sets of piano pieces are 'Estampes' ('Engravings', 1903), 'Children's Corner Suite' (1908), 24 Preludes (1910–13), a prodigious collection of what the composer called 'sketches', and finally twelve Études (1915) which pose, and deal with, every problem the pianist is likely to encounter. In his late works Debussy's style underwent a change towards abstraction which occurs particularly in the ballet score *Jeux* (1912).

Debussy's influence upon twentieth-century music is incalculable. A list of those who would acknowledge their indebtedness to him in one way or another would include Scriabin, Reger, Strauss, de Falla, Puccini, Janáček, Stravinsky, Bartók, Berg, Webern, Bax, Respighi, and Orff.

Ravel

Impressionism as a musical style was shortlived. It is seen in some of the early work of **Maurice Ravel** (1875–1937). Although Ravel was influenced by Debussy he is more indebted to his teacher, Fauré. Ravel tended towards clarity and precision where Debussy inclined to a sort of sensuous haze. Ravel also differs from Debussy in basing his work upon traditional tonality even though he freely uses chords of the 9th and 11th. He was attracted to dance music of various types and his later work shows the influence of jazz.

Ravel was essentially a composer for the piano and of music for the stage. He had a gift for brilliant orchestration; of his *Bolero* (1928) he said that it consisted of orchestral effects without music. Mussorgsky's *Pictures at an Exhibition* is usually heard in the orchestral version of Ravel.

Ravel's Impressionist phase includes the piano works, *Jeux d'eau* (1901), the five pieces entitled *Miroirs* (1905) and the three entitled *Gaspard de la Nuit* (1908). Impressionist orchestral music includes the suite, *Rhapsodie Espagnole* (1907) and the ballet score, *Daphnis and Chloë* (1911). His attraction towards dance music is seen in the *Valses nobles et sentimentales* (1911) and the choreographic poem, *La valse* (1920). His two operas, *L'Heure espagnole* and *L'Enfant et les sortilèges* (1925), show great mastery in writing for the stage. Both of Ravel's Piano Concerti, one in G the other in D, date from 1930/31 and both show the influence of jazz. The D major work, for left hand alone, is of considerable difficulty; it was written for the pianist Paul Wittgenstein who had lost his right arm in World War I.

Ravel composed a handful of chamber works, all of them charming and attractive. Among them are the String Quartet in F major (1903), Introduction and Allegro for harp, string quartet, flute, and clarinet (1906), Piano Trio in A minor (1914), and Sonata for Violin and Piano (1927). In this last work the influence of George Gershwin is seen in the second, 'Blues', movement.

Musical Societies

In 1904 Ravel was one of a group of musicians, which also included de Falla and Stravinsky, who formed a rebel group called the *Société des Apaches*. This society was dedicated to promoting the ideas which were then new.

Composers who worked in Paris seemed often to feel the need to band themselves together in sometimes quite arbitrary groups to further a cause. A recent association is IRCAM – Institut de recherche et de co-ordination acoustique (musique) – which occupies a series of laboratories and electronic studios at the Georges Pompidou Centre in Paris. The Institute was inaugurated in 1977 under the direction of Boulez. Earlier in the century Satie had formed the *School of Arcueil* and later, in 1936, came the group known as *La Jeune France* whose most distinguished member was **Olivier Messiaen** (*b.* 1908). Perhaps the most famous of such groups was *Les Six*. The aims of Les Six were dictated by the views of the dramatist, Jean Cocteau: members of the group were anti-Wagner, anti-Debussy, and anti-Impressionism; they were to cultivate music which was light, witty, sardonic, and jazzy. Two of the six soon ceased to compose, **Louis Durey** (1888–1979) and **Germaine Tailleferre** (*b.*1892); a third, **Georges Auric** (*b.* 1899), made a successful career as a writer of film music. The remaining three were **Darius Milhaud** (1892–1974), **Arthur Honegger** (1892–1955) and **Francis Poulenc** (1899–1963).

Milhaud wrote a great quantity of music in every vein possible. His style of writing was to pile up one triad upon another until the music moves in several keys simultaneously (*polytonality*). Two of his most outstanding works are *Scaramouche* (1937) for two pianos and the ballet score, *La création du monde* (1923), both of which make extensive and subtle use of jazz.

Honegger's music bears little relation to the aims of Les Six. His later works are dramatic, religious, ceremonial, conceived on a large scale, and sharply dissonant. But he is remembered especially for the more modest chamber oratorio, *King David* (1921), and for the railroad tone poem of 1923, *Pacific 231*.

Poulenc's natural style was witty and popular and thus enabled him to remain faithful to the aims of Les Six. He was a remarkable pianist who caught the public eye in his youth. His ballet, *Les Biches* (1924), and his *Concerto for Two Pianos* (1932) both achieved a popular success. His later works are more profound and include the two operas, *Dialogue des Carmélites* (1957), and *La voix humaine*, and the popular *Gloria* (1960).

PART TWO: HARMONY

Extensions of the Dominant Seventh

Chords of the 9th, 11th, and 13th

These chords are usually formed from the dominant seventh although they may be built on other degrees of the scale such as I, II, or IV. As the name suggests, a note lying a 9th, 11th, or 13th from the root is added to the V_7 chord. In C major V_7 = GBDF, i.e., a chord formed by the successive addition of 3rds. This process of adding 3rds upwards is continued in the case of the 9th, 11th, 13th, thus GBDF + A(9th) + C(11th) + E(13th) (see Example 20.2). This collection of notes is reduced in four-part harmony as follows. The

20.2

5th of V_7 is left out, leaving the root, 3rd and 7th only (GBF). To these three notes is added either the 9th, 11th, or 13th, as follows:

V_9 consists of root, 3rd, 7th, and 9th as in Example 20.3
V_{11} consists of root, 5th, 7th, and 11th as in Example 20.4
V_{13} consists of root, 3rd, 7th, and 13th as in Example 20.5

20.3   **20.4**   **20.5**

The dominant extensions stop at V_{13}. A 15th above the root is the same note as the root, two octaves higher.

V_9 and V_{13} can be either major or minor, for the topmost 3rd of each chord is a major one and can be flattened. In Examples 20.3–20.5, the flattened 3rd is shown in brackets. The topmost 3rd of V_{11} is a minor one and the chord generally exists in only one form. The topmost 3rd, however, can be sharpened to make it a major one, the sharpened 3rd is shown above in brackets. This chord is used in jazz and is known as the augmented 11th.

The 9th, 11th, and 13th of these chords usually resolve downwards as if they were appoggiaturas, for they make a dissonance with the bass note – see Example 20.6.

V^9 V^7 V^{11} V^7 V^{13} V^7 I

20.6

The Chord of the Diminished Seventh

If the root of a dominant minor 9th (in C major = GBDFA♭) is omitted, the remaining four notes form a chord consisting of three minor 3rds placed one above the other. This is the *chord of the diminished 7th*. It is formed on the leading note; in C major it therefore consists of BDFA♭. Another way of arriving at the same chord is to add a minor 3rd above the diminished triad formed on the leading note. The top note of the diminished 7th chord *sounds* yet another minor 3rd below the tonic above it (the interval between the two notes is theoretically an augmented 2nd; in C major A♭ – B♮). An arpeggio of diminished 7th chords therefore sounds as if were composed entirely of minor 3rds, detaching it from the sense of the key to which it belongs. Therefore, if the chord is used injudiciously it can give the harmony a sloppy effect, although there are countless fine examples of its use. But its very ambiguity makes it an excellent chord as part of a modulation.

The lowering of any of the four notes of a diminished 7th chord by a semitone results in a dominant 7th, as follows:

Key = C major Diminished 7th chord = BDFA♭

          B lowered to B♭ = V_7 of E♭

          D lowered to D♭ (C♯) = V_7 of G♭ (F♯)

          F lowered to E (A♭ = G♯) = V_7 of A

          A♭ lowered to G = V_7 of C.

The four tonic notes of the new keys themselves form a diminished 7th.

The Supertonic Seventh

V_7 is the *primary* chord of the seventh. Seventh chords on all other degrees of the scale are *secondary*. The most commonly used secondary seventh chord is II_7, the supertonic seventh. II_7 may be major or minor and because it consists of four notes it has three inversions. II_7 is a splendid chord in whatever form it is used; it has many virtues (see Example 20.7). *All* chords of the seventh are *figured* in the same way because they are all formed in the same way (see Chapter 14, p. 154).

    7   6   4   4

          5   3   2

   II^7 II^7b II^7c II^7d

20.7

When resolving a secondary seventh chord, the 7th must fall as is the case with V_7, but the 3rd need not rise, since it is not the leading note. II_7 in its root position and II_7b are frequently used as part of a *cadence*, being stronger versions of II–V–I or IIb–V–I (see Example 20.8). II_7b is very common in the

                                                                      20.8

cadences of Bach's chorales (see Chapter 23, p. 251). The 7th in this case is usually prepared by being sounded in the previous chord. II_7c is not often used but can create a fine effect, as in Example 20.9. In II_7d the bass note,

                                                                      20.9

being the 7th, must fall to the 3rd of the dominant causing Vb or V_7b. It is not, therefore, a cadential chord in the same way as II_7 or II_7b – see Example 20.10.

                                                                      20.10

As a means of *modulating*, II$_7$ forms an excellent pivot chord. It can lead to any one of the five nearly related keys, i.e., from C major it can lead to D minor, E minor, F major, G major, and A minor. All that is necessary in order to effect any of these modulations is to alter one or more of the notes of II$_7$ chromatically to form the dominant seventh of the new key, as seen in Example 20.11.

20.11

Finally II$_7$ makes an excellent starting point for the consideration of *chromatic harmony* (see Chapter 21).

Suggested Further Reading

Cox, David. *Debussy Orchestral Music* (London: BBC Music Guides, 1974).

Davies, Lawrence. *Franck* (London: Dent, Master Musicians, 1973).

Davies, Lawrence. *Ravel Orchestral Music* (BBC Music Guides, 1970).

Dawes, Frank. *Debussy Piano Music* (BBC Music Guides, 1969).

Dean, Winton. *Bizet* (London: Dent, Master Musicians, 1977).

Lockspeiser, Edward. *Debussy* (London: Dent, 1979).

Nichols, Roger. *Debussy* (Oxford OUP Studies of Composers, 1973).

21

PART ONE: MUSIC OF THE TWENTIETH CENTURY

The terms 'nineteenth century' and 'twentieth century' when applied to music refer not so much to periods of time as to styles of writing. The nineteenth century was almost exclusively the era of Romanticism and many of its distinguishing features are to be found in twentieth-century music. The twentieth century, on the other hand, presents a greater variety of styles than does any other time in musical history. For after the tonal system ceased to be the central basis of composition composers have felt constrained, on the one hand, by the need to find an acceptable alternative to it, but free, on the other hand, to experiment, particularly with the opportunities for musical expression presented by technological developments. This resulted, particularly in the middle of the century, in a division of interest between the composers, who were working in these new areas, and the music-loving public, who gave the allegiance rather to music labelled classical, popular, 'pop', or jazz. However as the century nears its end the boundaries of music acceptable to popular taste have considerably widened and the barriers which have separated music of different sorts, from the Middle Ages to our own day, are fast disappearing.

The Second Viennese School

The revolution which finally displaced the system of tonality from the centre of the European musical stage was effected in Vienna. It was brought about mostly by three composers, Schoenberg and his two disciples, Berg and Webern, both of whom he outlived. Together they form the *Second Viennese School*.

Schoenberg

Arnold Schoenberg (1874–1951) was thoroughly trained in the Germanic tradition of Bach, Beethoven, and Brahms. From them he acquired the ability to manipulate large-scale formal structures, a love of counterpoint, and a deep insight into the development of the tonal system. He inherited a tradition which was at the time dominated by the ideals of Wagner who, together with the post-Romantic composers had brought the tonal system to a point of disintegration. Schoenberg carried this process to its logical conclusion and developed from the resultant fragmentation a new basis for composition which not only produced important works in its own right but was able to point a way forward for mid-twentieth-century composers.

Schoenberg's work falls naturally into four periods. The first period, which lasted until 1905, contains works written in the post-Romantic style, and includes the String Sextet *Verklärte Nacht* ('Transfigured Night'), of 1899, which stems directly from the music of *Tristan und Isolde*. With the *Gurrelieder* (1901) for solo voices, chorus and orchestra, Schoenberg outdid anything by Mahler or Strauss in vastness of conception and execution.

His second period from 1905–12 shows a marked change both of compositional technique and of style. For in the final movement of the Second String Quartet, in F♯ minor, a work which includes a part for soprano solo, Schoenberg shook himself free of the tonal system and wrote without reference to a key centre. This method of writing in which the composer forms the music out of a continuous chromatic scale has become known as *atonality*. Perhaps its most successful application is seen in Schoenberg's *Pierrot Lunaire* ('Moonstruck Puppet') of 1912, a setting of twenty-one songs for female voice and eight instruments. In this work Schoenberg developed a technique of vocal writing known as *Sprechstimme* or *Sprechgesang* in which the voice glides in and out of the written notes in a cross between singing and speaking.

Closely linked with Schoenberg's use of atonality is the style of writing known as *Expressionism*. This term, like Impressionism, was originally applied to painting. Impressionism tries to capture a fleeting moment of experience; Expressionism tries to convey exactly what that experience does to the artist's emotions.

After 1913 no new work appeared from Schoenberg for nearly ten years; and in 1923 his style entered its third and most decisive period. For the continuous chromatic scale of atonality became organized and controlled into a system based upon the twelve semitones which go to make up a single octave. The method of composition which results from this is known variously as *twelve-tone* music, which is American; *twelve-note* music, which is British; *dodecaphonic* music, from the Greek word for twelve, and *serial* music.

The system is as follows. The twelve notes are arranged in a fixed order using each note once. This is called a *tone (note) row*, or *series*. The composition is made up entirely of successive appearances of this row or series. The row may be used in four ways: frontwards, backwards (*retrograde*), upside-down (*inversion*) and upside-down and backwards (*retrograde inversion*). The row may appear at any one of the twelve pitches available within the octave. This gives to the composer at any one time four dozen possible melodic units by which to move the composition forwards. More than one note of the row may be used up at the same time to form a chord. In Schoenberg's system such aspects of the composition as rhythm and instrumentation remain within the composer's discretion.

To a serial composer the limitations which this method imposes are no more inhibiting than is the intractability of a system based upon major and minor scales. The first work in which Schoenberg deliberately employed his new system was the *Five Piano Pieces* of 1923. The system appears fully developed in the *Third Quartet* (1926) and *Variations for Orchestra* (1928). Schoenberg's most important work in this style is the unfinished opera *Moses and Aaron*.

Schoenberg spent his last years in America and during this time his style entered its fourth period, becoming somewhat more relaxed. He turned again to a more tonal idiom and the fierce astringency of some of his earlier work was softened by a Romantic warmth. Works of this period include a *Suite for String Orchestra* (1934) and *Theme and Variations for Band* (1943).

Both **Alban Berg** (1885–1935) and **Anton Webern** (1883–1945) accompanied Schoenberg in his move to atonality and thence to serial music. But within this framework they developed in entirely opposite directions and produced completely different sorts of music. Berg is expansive and lyrical and employs serial techniques in such a way as not to lose sight of the tonal tradition; Webern, on the other hand, refines the serial process and extends its application so that it leads directly into the earlier work of Boulez and Stockhausen.

Berg

Berg is the most accessible member of the Second Viennese School. His technical fluency as a composer is remarkable. He studied with Schoenberg, who was a most excellent and thorough teacher, from 1904 to 1910. He is the most outstanding example of an Expressionist composer and his lyricism totally absorbs the mathematical complexity of his work. His output is not large and his most important works date from after the introduction of the twelve-note system. Among them is the *Lyric Suite* (1926) for string quartet. This is in six movements of which only three are serial, but the mixture of styles does not affect the unity of the work. Berg's Violin Concerto (1935) is another work where serial technique is relaxed to take account of tonality. The tone row is very carefully devised so that the key of D is apparent and with superb assurance Berg uses it to harmonize a Bach chorale in the last movement. Berg wrote two operas, *Wozzeck* (1917–21), and *Lulu* which remained unfinished at his death. Both are Expressionist works and are remarkable for their psychological penetration. In these operas Berg's music ensures that the sordidness of each of the plots becomes a matter of sympathy for the hearer; and both works employ Leitmotiv and Sprechstimme. *Lulu* is the more strictly serial of the two, for *Wozzeck's* fifteen scenes are cast in a variety of Classical forms and idioms.

Webern

In spite of its extreme compression, or perhaps because of it, the music of Webern is not difficult to come to grips with. His works are numbered from op. 1–31 and total less than four hours of music. In fact many movements last much less than a minute. Webern's output consists of vocal and instrumental music in roughly equal measure; he wrote no opera. He strove for extreme economy of both texture and instrumentation. His melodic line is deliberately arranged to avoid any sense of tonality, with wide leaps and dislocated rhythms. There is little or no repetition since each element of a composition has a single, complete function.

Often the music is of such delicacy as to be scarcely audible and rarely does it rise to a forte. The music is laid out in such a way that it passes rapidly from one instrument to another, quite often with each instrument playing only a single note of a phrase. Webern called this procedure 'melody of sound colours' (*Klangfarbenmelodie*). In this respect he extended the serial idea to the realm of instrumentation. Because of its extreme compression Webern's music demands great concentration on the part of the listener. A good starting point is the *Five Pieces for Orchestra*, op. 10.

Stravinsky

The figure of **Igor Stravinsky** (1882–1971) relates to most aspects of twentieth-century music, for his earliest works were written in the late nineteenth century and he continued composing almost to the end of his long life. His music passes through several styles but it is basically tonal even when he is writing in the serial idiom. One of his main preoccupations during the early part of the century was to restate the importance of rhythm.

The main influences upon Stravinsky were all Russian, although as a composer he was cosmopolitan. He was a pupil of Rimsky-Korsakov, whose exotic style and brilliant orchestration were absorbed into Stravinsky's thought. He was also influenced by the Russian folk idiom and above all by the music of the Russian Orthodox Church to which he remained devoted all his life. His first important works were three ballet scores for the impressario Diaghilev, for performance in Paris.

These are *The Fire Bird* (1910), an exotic, oriental fairy tale deriving directly from Rimsky-Korsakov, *Petrushka* (1911), one of the most masterly of twentieth-century scores, and *The Rite of Spring* (1913) ('Le Sacre du Printemps'), an epoch-making work which precipitated a riot in the theatre at its first performance. These scores, like many works immediately preceding World War I, are planned on a large scale and extravagant in the number of forces employed.

This process was reversed after the war when both the scale of the music and the scoring contracted. In Stravinsky this process manifested itself firstly, in an interest in jazz with such works as *Ragtime* (1918) for eleven instruments and the *Piano Rag-Music* of 1920, and secondly, in the adoption of the style which became known as *Neo-classicism*. Stravinsky wrote mainly in this style from the composition of the ballet score *Pulcinella* of 1919 until the opera *The Rake's Progress* of 1951. During this period Stravinsky often based his work upon the style of earlier composers; *Pulcinella* is greatly indebted to the music of Pergolesi (1710–36), while the ballet *Le Baiser de la Fée* (The Fairy's Kiss) draws on the music of Tchaikovsky. This period also includes two large-scale choral works: *Oedipus Rex* (1927) and *The Symphony of Psalms* (1930), the latter a masterpiece of invention, structure, and religious devotion. Both these works have Latin texts, a language chosen for its non-emotive quality.

From the 1950s Stravinsky used the method of serial composition, adapting it to his own ends, in such works as the ballet *Agon* (1954–57). This style is heard in its most extreme form in *Movements* (1959), for piano and orchestra, which stands in apposition to the work of Webern.

The full impact of Stravinsky's achievement is perhaps not yet apparent, for much of his music is deliberately cast in an unemotional and almost offhand manner so that what the composer has to say strikes the hearer only later.

Hindemith

An even more deliberately tonal composer than Stravinsky and the most important German composer of the first half of the twentieth century was **Paul Hindemith** (1895–1963). Hindemith's earliest works, dating from the 1920s, appear violent and aggressive but during that decade Hindemith became ever more disturbed at the gulf which separated composers from the public. For him music was a social activity and should be available for use (*Gebrauchsmusik*). Allied to this was his belief that the tonal system provided the natural basis for composition. Hindemith was himself a remarkably fluent composer and was able to put his ideas into practice, writing a great quantity

of music which entered the performing repertoire of the day. He wrote numerous sonatas, for all instruments including some of the most unlikely, for
example the tuba and viola d'amore. His most successful and best-known
work was the opera *Mathis der Maler* ('Matthias the Painter') of 1934. The
orchestral suite from this work has achieved much popularity.

Hindemith was a renowned teacher and a viola player of distinction. During
the earlier part of his career he wrote a number of works which were capable
of being performed by amateurs and at the same time intended to provide
teaching material for the professional instructor. Hindemith called this type
of work 'Music to Sing and Play' (*Sing- und Spielmusik*). An example is the
children's opera, *Let's Build a Town* ('Wir bauen eine Stadt') of 1930. His
thoughts on the place of music in society are set forth in *A Composer's World*.

Eastern Europe

The course of early twentieth-century music was affected by the revolutions
of Debussy in Paris and of Schoenberg in Vienna, as well as by the Neo-
classical reaction to them. Another major development was the emergence of
a national style from Eastern Europe, the main protagonists of which were
the two Hungarians: **Béla Bartók** (1881–1945) and **Zoltán Kodály** (1882–1967);
and the Czech composer **Leoš Janáček** (1854–1928).

Bartók and Kodály

Bartók and Kodály worked together in the earlier part of their career collecting and publishing nearly 2,000 Hungarian folk tunes. They collected the
tunes by means of a recording apparatus which meant that they did not have
to adapt what they heard to the existing system of notation but could analyse
the scales and rhythmic patterns of the tunes later with some precision. Their
findings were very influential, particularly upon the music of Bartók himself.
The influence upon Kodály resulted in the formulation of his views upon
musical education, which, he felt, should be based upon a regulated course of
singing. This principle has spread far beyond his native Hungary and the
Kodály method of singing is now studied and applied throughout the world.

Kodály's best-known music is the suite derived from the musical play *Háry
János*. This begins with a musical sneeze and ends with an attractive movement
which features the Hungarian cimbalom.

Bartók was a powerful virtuoso pianist and a large amount of his work is for
piano solo or includes a part for piano. His early music was influenced by the
revolution of Debussy which affected his harmonic vocabulary without im-
pairing his natural exuberance of invention. In the early 1920s Bartók was
influenced by the Second Viennese School. His style became astringent and he
wrote at this time small-scale works for groups of instrumentalists. Bartók's last
years were spent in America, where he died famous but poor and neglected.
During this period he achieved much popular acclaim with a series of orchestral works in a style both uncompromising and appealing. Amongst these
works may be classed the *Music for Strings, Percussion and Celesta* (1936), the
Divertimento for Strings (1939), and the *Concerto for Orchestra* (1944).

Of great importance is the collection of 153 piano pieces (1926–37) with the
title of *Mikrokosmos*. These are of graded difficulty and collected into six
books and they form a summary of Bartók's own style and are at the same

time a compendium of many of the developments of early twentieth-century music. In these works and in his three piano concerti, Bartók views the piano as a percussive instrument rather than as a lyrical or resonant one.

Central to Bartók's output are the six String Quartets, which he wrote between 1908 and 1939. In them the three periods of Bartók's stylistic development are clearly outlined. The quartets compose a stylistic arch, a structural form of which the composer was fond. Bartók's quartets are generally regarded as the most important contribution to the medium since Beethoven, for apart from their intrinsic worth they greatly extend the technique of string quartet writing.

A particularly fascinating brand of music which Bartók invented he called *Night Music*, an evocation of the night-time sounds of the Central European countryside. Examples are found in the Fifth String Quartet and the *Music for Strings, Percussion, and Celesta*.

Janáček

A completely individual voice during the early part of the century was that of Janáček. He is remembered chiefly as an opera composer although his work includes Sinfonietta (1926) and two string quartets: 'Kreutzer Sonata' (1923), and 'Intimate Letters' (Listy důvěrné, 1928). It was not until Janáček was fifty in 1904 that he achieved recognition, with the opera *Jenufa*.

Janáček's method of composition is to build up blocklike musical paragraphs from small and often repeated melodic fragments. These melodic snippets are closely related to the inflections of the spoken Czech language, making them difficult to translate into other languages. Janáček's music is powerful and original; it includes the operas *Kaťa Kabanová* (1919–21), *The Cunning Little Vixen* (1921–23), *The Makropoulos Affair* (1923–24), *From the House of the Dead* (1928), the *Glagolitic Mass* (1926), and the two String Quartets.

Italian Music of the Twentieth Century

The establishment of the Baroque and Classical traditions in the seventeenth and eighteenth centuries had been greatly indebted to Italian composers. During the nineteenth century in Italy those traditions had been discontinued in every field except that of opera, but with the beginning of the twentieth century there occurred a renaissance in other forms of music in Italy. This was achieved by a succession of Italian composers, some of whom form a group because of their common aim, although they cannot be regarded as a national school. The first of these, **Ferrucio Busoni** (1866–1924) spent most of his professional career in Berlin strongly influenced by the German tradition. However, by his remarkable writings about music he helped to diffuse the new ideas about composition formed at the beginning of the century. Outstanding among his writings is the *Sketch of a New Aesthetic of Music* (1907) which comments on the waywardness of regarding the octave as consisting, for harmonic purposes, of twelve equal semitones.

The establishment of symphonic music, tonally based, was effected by the work of **Ottorino Respighi** (1879–1936) whose tone poems, *The Fountains of Rome* (1916) and *The Pines of Rome* (1924) have achieved wide popularity. With **Alfredo Casella** (1883–1944) Italian music began to come to terms with the works of Debussy and Schoenberg. Casella was by nature anti-Romantic and it was to Neo-classicism that he was drawn in the 1920s. He forms a group with **Ildebrando Pizzetti** (1880–1968) and **Francesco Malipiero** (1882–1973). Malipiero was the most important of these, a scholar as well as a composer, and he was much concerned with editing and publishing Italian music of the past. In consequence his compositions, which include a large number of both stage and instrumental works, are influenced by older Italian music, especially that of the seventeenth century.

The influence of the work of Schoenberg is finally seen in the music of **Luigi Dallapiccola** (1904–1975), who succeeded in adapting the techniques of twelve-tone composition to innate Italian operatic lyricism, with particular success in the opera *Il Prigioniero* (1948).

American Music

The first important American composer and the first composer of Western music to work apart from the mainstream of European culture is the remarkable figure of **Charles Ives** (1874–1954). His father was a bandmaster and Ives was trained firmly in the tonal tradition of nineteenth-century band music. But his idea of what a musical composition should sound like was of the broadest, he was constantly searching for new ideas and anticipated many of the compositional techniques which have since become important parts of twentieth-century music. In his music he adhered to no one particular style, not even in the same composition: and he rightly judged that his ideas would not find immediate acceptance. In the meantime, he made a fortune as an insurance broker.

Most of Ives's music was composed between 1890 and 1922. It includes five symphonies and a number of programme works for small orchestra. For Ives, music was not to be listened to but was to be performed, and if the audience could be persuaded to join in so much the better. Certainly it is difficult for an audience not to take part in *Three Places in New England* (1914) if only with reactions of delight.

A more consciously avant-garde composer was the French born **Edgar Varèse** (1883–1965) who arrived in New York in 1915. Varèse viewed music as consisting of isolated blocks of sound which are used in contrast to build up a recognizable form and which are given coherence by rhythmic propulsion. He achieved fame with *Ionisation* (1931) which is scored entirely for percussion including chains, anvils, sirens, and bells. In his later work he adopted electronic composition.

Henry Cowell (1897–1961) was interested in arriving at new sounds by conventional means. He is particularly associated with the tone-cluster, a 'sound formed from the playing together of several adjacent notes which becomes a musical unit in its own right. He also contrived to produce new sounds from conventional instruments, for instance the effect gained from plucking, scraping, and strumming the inside of a piano. In this respect he anticipated the 'prepared piano' of John Cage (see p. 240). These advanced techniques go beyond the resources of conventional notation; Cowell was a pioneer in devising new methods of indicating the composer's intentions.

Meanwhile mid-century American music has included several figures who have continued to work in the tonal, Neo-classical idiom without at the same time abandoning experimentation. Important in this group are the works of

Virgil Thomson, (*b.* 1896) **Aaron Copland** (*b.* 1900), and **Roy Harris** (1898–1979).

A composer who spent most of his time in America and yet cannot be considered an American composer is **Ernest Bloch** (1880–1959). He employed a late Romantic style derived from Debussy, Strauss, and Mahler which he brought to bear upon Hebrew melodies, American folk songs, and jazz. His personal idiom was strong enough to stamp itself upon these various elements.

British Music

The generation which succeeded Holst, Elgar, and Vaughan Williams produced several composers whose music, although influenced by European developments, has remained largely within the tonal idiom. The most persistently Romantic of these was **Arnold Bax** (1883–1953) whose prolific output includes seven symphonies. His best-known work is the tone poem *Tintagel* (1917). **William Walton** (1902–1983) achieved international fame with *Façade* (1922), a witty setting of poems by Edith Sitwell for spoken voice and chamber orchestra. Walton's oratorio *Belshazzar's Feast* (1931) combines an almost Handelian breadth of style with the violence of twentieth-century rhythm and the astringency of twentieth-century harmonies.

Britten and Tippett

The best-known and the most successful of mid-century British composers was **Benjamin Britten** (1913–1976). Britten composed music in every form and in many different styles but he is particularly associated with writing for voices, whether in opera, cantata, or solo song. His skill lies in his ability to find the precise music to fit any situation and he can convey in musical terms human thoughts from the most trivial to the most profound. He also has a sure grasp of structure and is equally at home composing music on a small scale such as *A Ceremony of Carols* (1942) and on the scale of the *War Requiem* (1962), a complex choral and orchestral work. Perhaps his ability is seen most clearly in his operas, equally in such tragic and large-scale works as *Peter Grimes* (1945) and in the chamber opera buffa *Albert Herring* (1947). Britten's style is gathered from many sources, amongst them Purcell and the English choral tradition, the Neo-classicism of Stravinsky, and the twelve-tone music of the Second Viennese School.

An equally important composer but one whose characteristic mode of expression is both more complex and more introspective is **Michael Tippett** (*b.* 1905). Tippett is deeply concerned with social injustice and with human suffering, feelings which expressed themselves in the oratorio *A Child of Our Time* (1942) but which are equally apparent in his operas for which he writes his own libretti. Tippett's music is characteristically polyphonic and rhythmically complex. It is nowhere abrasive but expresses itself in a tough lyricism.

Russian Music

Apart from Stravinsky two composers of importance have arisen in twentieth-century Russia: **Sergei Prokofiev** (1891–1953) and **Dmitri Shostakovich** (1906–1975).

Prokofiev's career may be divided into three periods, the second and third of which are connected with political developments inside Russia. Prokofiev's idiom throughout his career is basically tonal and his music is cast into the traditional forms of symphony and concerto, ballet and opera. His works combine originality of thought with a distinctive style. One of his fingerprints is his habit of side-slipping at points of cadence from the expected key into a distant one. Prokofiev's first compositions, during the final years of Tsarist Russia, are characterized by a highly dissonant texture carried forward with great rhythmic drive. This style reached a peak in the *Scythian Suite* of 1914 which has parallels with Stravinsky's *Rite of Spring*.

Prokofiev left Russia in 1918 and worked in Paris in the 1920s, continuing to compose symphonies, piano concertos, and ballet scores in a brilliant and powerful style which does not, however, sustain the level of his works written in Russia. In 1934 he returned to Russia and adapted his style to accord with prevailing political and artistic theory, writing music overtly tonal and Neo-classical. To this period belong the popular *Peter and the Wolf* (1936), the film music for *The Queen of Spades* (1936) and for *Alexander Nevsky* (1938), and the ballet *Romeo and Juliet* (1935). Prokofiev's output includes six symphonies and five piano concertos.

Shostakovich, unlike Prokofiev, remained in Russia all his life and devoted his energies to the composition of music for Soviet Russia. His efforts were not always attended by success and he more than once suffered stern official criticism. On the other hand he received the highest honours which the State was capable of giving him. Whether from these causes or not Shostakovich's music shows startling divergencies of quality, moving, even in the same work, from passages of the highest excellence to others of banality and triviality. His style is based on an interesting contrast between sentimental lyricism and mordant wit. He came to prominence with his First Symphony, written at the age of nineteen, which may be regarded as amongst his best works. Of his other symphonies, the Fifth is a consistently fine work and the Seventh, 'Leningrad', owes its fame to the circumstances of its composition during World War II. His fifteen string quartets constitute a fine body of work for the medium. Shostakovich was thus the foremost Soviet composer.

Messiaen

Olivier Messiaen (*b.* 1908) is an important, highly original and quite un-classifiable composer. One of the original members of the French group known as La Jeune France, Messiaen has since 1931 been the organist at La Trinité in Paris. A mystical religious devotion is one of the many influences upon his work. Others are the music of the East and the songs of birds. Messiaen is an accomplished amateur ornithologist, and has made extensive transcriptions of birdsong, which form the entire basis of two of his piano works, *Oiseaux exotiques* and *Catalogue des Oiseaux*. Messiaen early developed a style which is completely free from any suggestion of tonality, but which presents a wholly integrated sound world, complete in itself.

One of Messiaen's chief concerns is with colour in his music. This is apparent in his long series of organ works of which *L'Ascension* (1933) may be taken as typical or in the vast ten-movement *Turangalîla Symphony* of 1948. Messiaen is also fascinated by the subject of rhythm which in his work becomes independent of other elements of composition. He has been immensely important as a teacher and his work has led directly to the late twentieth-century musical avant-garde.

The Post-war Avant-garde

Late twentieth-century avant-garde music may be thought of as dating from the end of World War II. With the passage of time the avant-garde in any age gradually becomes transformed into the traditional, and this has already happened with some postwar avant-garde music.

The point of departure for postwar music was the serial technique as used by Webern who had extended the idea of the fixed tone row to include other aspects of music, notably instrumental colour. From this technique emerged the concept of *total serialism*, in which all the basic elements of music are subject to an independent but interacting series of predetermined events. The first such work was by Messiaen, entitled *Mode de valeurs et d'intensités* (1949) for piano solo. This technique was adopted by two of Messiaen's pupils, **Pierre Boulez** (*b*. 1925) and **Karlheinz Stockhausen** (*b*. 1928). During the 1950s and 1960s both these composers were active and influential, but since the 1960s Boulez has devoted himself more to conducting than to composition, while Stockhausen has continued to be one of the most potent forces in contemporary music. Total serialism was refined and relaxed in one of the most important works of this period, Boulez's *Le marteau sans maître* ('The masterless hammer') of 1955. This is a work lightly scored for flute, viola, guitar, a varied group of percussion instruments, a vibraphone and a xylorimba (a cross between the xylophone and the marimba), and a contralto solo. In its nine short movements Boulez creates a fascinating, translucent web of sound.

Stockhausen during the same period created a series of works which carried serialism to its limits, turning his attention to such factors as density, complexity, arrangement of instruments in space and symmetry of presentation. Among the works of this period are *Gruppen*, *Carré*, and *Momente*. This last piece is for chorus, keyboard, percussion, and brass instruments, and involves its performers in various kinds of singing, speaking, whispering, babbling, hand-clapping, banging and foot-shuffling.

Musique Concrète

Meanwhile the technological revolution had affected music with the introduction of electronic devices. Once more the development of these new resources came from France, in the form of *Musique concrète*. This is a method of composing with prepared tapes. Sounds of everyday life were prerecorded and then manipulated in various combinations, at different speeds, to form a work of art. The resultant work is completely controlled by its composer and never varies in performance. The first such composition was issued in 1948 by Pierre Schaeffer at the French Radio. But electronics can be used to create a much more interesting and varied collection of sounds than can be recorded in real life. Not only is there the possibility of creating new timbres by this method but the idea of separate pitches, i.e., semitones, gives way to that of a single continuously alterable pitch (*pitch continuum*). The idea of *spatial relationships* of different sounds also plays an important part the development of electronic music. A composer who has evolved a distinctive style in this medium is the Rumanian-born **Yanni Xenakis** (*b*. 1922).

Indeterminacy

Meanwhile the idea that all aspects of a performance may be controlled has given way to a method of composition in which none of them is controlled. The chief exponent of this type of composition is **John Cage** (*b*. 1912). The name given to this type of music is *aleatory*, from the Latin for 'dice', or as Cage prefers, *indeterminacy*. Cage's method may be seen in *Concert for Piano and Orchestra* (1958), a work which combines percussive sounds, electronic sounds, and aleatory music. The pianist's part is made up of 84 different compositions which he is free to play in any order, in whole or in part or not at all. Occasionally he goes under the piano to thump the instrument from below. The orchestra can consist of any number of players (or none), playing, with or without instruments, any of the pages of the instrumental music. But some specific directives are given to conductor and orchestra, e.g., that a wind player performs on two tubas at once. Cage's most famous composition is *4' 33"* which consists of a complete absence of sound for that length of time. Both in his writings and in his compositions Cage has caused the musical world to consider its art afresh.

Side by side with the development of electronic and aleatory music there has been a return to large-scale, live, fully composed works which take advantage of avant-garde developments. A strong school of such composers has emerged in Poland. Of the older Polish composers **Witold Lutoslavski** (*b*. 1913) has achieved recognition for such atonal works as the *Concerto for Orchestra* (1954). The best-known of the younger generation is **Krzysztof Penderecki** (*b*. 1933) who creates intense and dramatic effects from an interesting juxtaposition of sound-masses, in such works as *Threnody for the Victims of Hiroshima* (1960) and *St Luke Passion* (1966) whose music has found a large audience.
  Certain works of the avant-garde, for example *Le marteau sans maître* have already become part of history; much remains experimental and addressed to a limited audience.

Pop Music

Postwar music for a mass audience is found in the pop culture which arose in the 1960s. Rock and Roll was based upon a strong social awareness. It made use of traditional tonality but was much indebted to the new technologies with its use of electric instruments, synthesizers, live amplification and use of multi-track recording media. It was given reality by a series of composer–author–performers who combined a high level of melodic invention with a sophisticated handling of the basic rhythmic pulse. *The Beatles* were crucial to its development. Their range of composition extended to all forms of pop music combined with elements of chamber music and of vaudeville. Their songs combined memorable melodic invention with an individual, yet precise, feeling for tonal harmony. With the breakup of the Beatles the classical period of pop music may be said to be at an end; since then it has existed in a variety of styles and has profited by the continuing interaction between 'straight' and popular music.

PART TWO

Chromatic Harmony

A chromatic chord is one which does not belong to the prevailing key. It is used only for effect and not with the intention of causing a modulation. If many chromatic chords are used in a passage the sense of key will become confused. Because of this it is often possible to label a chromatic chord in more than one way.

1. *Supertonic Chromatic Concord.* A major chord formed on the supertonic. The supertonic triad, DFA in key C, is a minor one. If it is given a major 3rd the resultant chord, D F♯ A in key C, is the Supertonic Chromatic Concord. The chord is used in the standard harmonization of 'All Through the Night', shown in Example 21.1. The key is G major. The supertonic chromatic concord is A C♯ E.

21.1

2. *Supertonic Chromatic Seventh.* This is the chord above with the addition of the minor 7th, D F♯ A C in key C. The passing note, G, in the version of 'All Through the Night' above turns the chord, at that point, into the supertonic chromatic seventh.
3. *Neapolitan Sixth.* This chord is formed on the flattened supertonic with a major triad built above it; e.g., in C major the Neapolitan sixth is D♭ F A♭. This chord is used in its first inversion and resolves on to the dominant, as shown in Example 21.2.

I   V   I
└ NEAPOLITAN
    6ᴛʜ

21.2

4. *Chord of the Augmented Sixth* This chord exists in three forms: the *Italian Sixth, French Sixth, and German Sixth.* Of these the most commonly used is the German Sixth. The chord of the augmented sixth is usually formed on the flattened submediant, A♭ in the key of C, with an augmented sixth above it, F♯ in key C. The three versions of the chord are as follows:

Italian Sixth: root plus 3rd plus augmented 6th, see Example 21.3

French Sixth: root plus 3rd plus *augmented 4th* plus augmented sixth, see Example 21.4

German Sixth: root plus 3rd plus *perfect 5th* plus augmented 6th, see Example 21.5

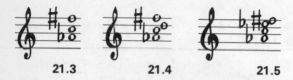

21.3   **21.4**   **21.5**

These chords may all be preceded by IVb. They resolve naturally on to the cadential six-four formula, Ic–V, which produces a feeling of relief from tension. They may also resolve straight to the dominant. But a German Sixth which resolves to the dominant carries with it built-in consecutive 5ths and is best avoided – see Examples 21.6 and 21.7.

GERMAN SIXTH

21.6

ITALIAN SIXTH

FRENCH SIXTH

21.7

Suggested Further Reading

Ewen, D. *The World of Twentieth Century Music* (Hale Books, 1969).
Griffiths, P. *Concise History of Modern Music* (London: Thames and Hudson, 1978).
Hitchcock, H. W. *Music in the United States* (New Jersey: Prentice-Hall, 1974).
Salzman, E. *Twentieth Century Music, an Introduction.* (New Jersey: Prentice-Hall, 1974).

22

JAZZ

A Definition

Jazz may fairly claim to be the most durable and persistent of twentieth-century musical styles. Although its influence is seen in many straight compositions, and although jazz itself has increasingly drawn upon other twentieth-century techniques of composition and performance, it has nevertheless throughout the century maintained a vigour and consistency of style which mark it off from all other developments. Although the presence of jazz is very potent in twentieth-century music, it has always been a minority interest among musicians, but its devotees may be drawn from any musical culture or from none; it appeals equally to the layman and to the professionally trained musician.

The elements which constitute jazz are clearly defined. It is first and foremost a style of *playing* rather than a style of *composition*. In classical music the composition is the end product towards which the composer works and which when completed becomes a fixed part of the corpus of music. In jazz the composition is the starting point for stylistic treatment and individual interpretation. The result of this is that the names associated with jazz are not so much composers as performer/interpreters. This also means that the history of jazz could easily become merely a record of names, anecdotes, and critical reviews. However, this is not so, for by chance the history of jazz coincides with the history of recorded sound and recordings of jazz performances from its earliest days give substance to an otherwise ephemeral art. Jazz, moreover, is the subject of a continuous living tradition which today shows no sign of diminishing.

The second important constituent of jazz is the element of *improvisation*. Jazz has thus developed a tradition of performance whose conventions are not necessarily apparent from the printed page. In this respect it resembles the music of the Baroque. In particular the jazz musician has a special relation to the pulse of music, defined as *swing*. It is the element of improvisation which distinguishes one performance from another and which has caused the most dominant performers to impose their style upon the prevailing idiom and so to divert the course of jazz. Largely for this reason, the history of jazz exhibits a startling rapidity of stylistic change. The instruments of jazz are mostly woodwind, brass, and percussion, with the addition of a string bass. The piano occupies a special and important place as a solo instrument or in combination.

The jazz sound arises as a result of a confrontation between tonal Western music and indigenous African Negro music. From the Western tradition jazz takes its instrumentation, melody and harmony; its rhythms, phrasing, and production of sound are derived from African music.

244

The Blues

The most important Negro contribution to jazz is the *Blues*. The term 'blues' refers both to an expressive mood and to compositional devices associated with that mood. The mood is usually one of melancholy, initially related to slavery but transferred in jazz to express the general suffering of mankind. Blues as a style figures prominently in the whole of jazz even when its compositional techniques are not used. Technically the blues consists of a twelve-bar harmonic sequence and of a melody formed from bending the diatonic major scale. The blues harmonic sequence, usually in a major key, is formed of tonic, dominant, and subdominant chords, as shown in Example 22.1. These

KEY C MAJOR

22.1

chords are arranged in three phrases of four bars each, for the sequence was originally used to accompany a vocal verse three lines long. The verse was made up of two rhyming lines, with the first line repeated, for example:

Blues, Blues, Blues, why did you bring trouble to me?
Yes, Blues, Blues, Blues why did you bring trouble to me?
O Death, please sting me and take me out of my misery.

The singing of the words usually takes the singer up to the third bar of each phrase. The remaining one and a half bars of each phrase form the basis of an instrumental improvisation called a *break*. The blues break is the basis from which jazz improvisation as a whole springs.

The blues scale is a version of the major scale and consists of flattening the 3rd and 7th degrees of the scale. The flattening is an expressive device and consequently in, for example, C major consists of a B flattened and an E flattened rather than of B♭ and E♭. These blues notes are, however, generally notated as in Example 22.2. The general effect of the blues notes is to push

22.2

the melody downwards and they are usually used in a descending melodic phrase. On a wind instrument it is possible to bend the blues notes to accord with vocal practice. On the piano, however, the desired effect is often obtained by playing both the diatonic and the flattened notes together, e.g., E♮ and E♭, or by making one an acciaccatura to the other. The use of 'blue' notes does not affect the blues chord sequence. The result of this is that it is possible to hear a major 3rd or 7th sounded against the same note flattened, an effect which contributes to the mood of the blues. In the 1940s a flattened 5th was also added to the blues notes. The result of incorporating these three blues

notes in a melodic line may be heard in the very common blues sequence
shown in Example 22.3.

22.3

In addition to the blues, basic jazz material may be drawn from a variety of
sources, the most common of which are popular tunes which become known
as *standards*. One of the fascinations of jazz in performance is the built-in
tension between the demands of solo improvisation and the give and take of
group playing. Before a jazz performance can take place the music has to be
organized in an arrangement. An *arrangement* may consist of fully written out
parts but may equally well take the form of a verbal agreement between the
players as to the course of the music.

History

Jazz originated in America and has largely developed there. Negro songs
formed its most important antecedent. These existed in the form of work
songs, play songs in which the blues were prominent, and religious songs
which included the spiritual. Another direct antecedent of jazz was ragtime,
the leading exponent of which was **Scott Joplin** (1868–1917). Ragtime was
piano music, fully composed, its structure deriving from European piano
music. In ragtime the left hand plays chords with the bass note on the beat
and the remaining notes of the chord at some distance away off the beat; this
is the *stride* style; the right hand plays a syncopated running melody. **Jelly
Roll Morton** (1885–1941) claimed that he had introduced the idea of jazz by
adding improvisation to ragtime.

By 1900 in New Orleans the jazz style was fully apparent. This style which
lasted until about 1920 is now known as *traditional jazz*. It was played in
small groups the main members of which were one or two cornets or trumpets,
a trombone, and a clarinet. These instruments were not regarded as solos but
formed an instrumental group. In traditional jazz the pulse of the $\frac{4}{4}$ bar carries
its natural accent on the first and third beats. The style of playing is 'hot' a
term which indicates intensity of feeling, firm attack, and use of vibrato.

During the second half of this period arose the style known as *Dixieland*.
This was performed by white musicians; the style is more bland than that of
traditional jazz and is technically more precise.

In the 1920s the New Orleans musicians moved to Chicago taking their
style with them. But there developed an extrovert and forceful Chicago style
which made use of both ensemble and solo playing, with the solo usually
placed in between an ensemble beginning and end. From this time dates the
introduction of the saxophone into the jazz ensemble. The playing of solos
resulted from the appearance of a number of outstanding individual musicians
who had a marked effect upon jazz styles. Chief amongst these players was
Louis Armstrong ('Satchmo', 1900–71) who is generally regarded as one of the

foremost of all jazz musicians. The Chicago style is admirably represented in the series of recordings which Armstrong made with groups called The Hot Five and The Hot Seven. The most outstanding white player of this period is the cornet player **Bix Beiderbecke** (1903–1931) who cultivated a soft tone and a cooler style of playing. Beiderbecke was an extremely sensitive musician whose career was short but lively.

The 1920s is also the period of Boogie-Woogie, a blues-based piano style which has become somewhat debased through overfamiliarity. In this style the left hand plays conventional rhythmic patterns over which the right hand introduces variations, as shown in Example 22.4 and 22.5.

KEY C MAJOR

22.4

22.5

The 1930s is the era of *Swing* and of the *Big Band*. 'Swing' in this sense does not denote the rhythmic element common to all jazz, but derives from the rhythm in which all four beats of a common time bar carry an accent, although the first and third still bear the stress. A Big Band contained no more than 12–15 players but this was sufficient to form certain instruments into sections, as: three trumpets, two trombones, one clarinet, two alto and two tenor saxophones, piano, guitar, string bass, and drums. Such bands were used, as was the Dance Band, to meet the strict demands of formal ballroom dancing. This resulted in the appearance of the professional arranger, though improvisation was still possible from the use of the *riff technique*, whereby a rhythmically based motive was repeated and built up by various sections of the band. Jazz harmony at this time was extended to include unresolved chords of the dominant 9th, 11th, and 13th.

The style is marked by syncopation with much use of the rumba rhythm, i.e., a bar of eight quavers arranged as if it were a $\frac{9}{8}$ bar with the last quaver missing. The 1930s was also an age of outstanding soloists such as the clarinettist **Benny Goodman** (*b.* 1909), the tenor sax players **Coleman Hawkins** (*b.* 1904), and **Chuck Berry**, the drummers **Gene Krupa** (*b.* 1909) and **Cozy Cole** (*b.* 1909), and the pianists **Fats Waller** (1904–1943), and **Teddy Wilson** (*b.* 1912). For it was at this time that jazz piano playing first gained prominence. The style had been developed from the stride method of ragtime and had reached a point of sophistication in the playing of **Earl Hines** (*b.* 1905). It was further developed by one of the most influential figures in the history of jazz, **Duke Ellington** (1899–1972). Ellington was a pianist/band leader and also an arranger and jazz composer with an unparalleled mastery of jazz orchestral textures. In Ellington the tension between jazz as improvisation and jazz as composed music finds its synthesis, and it is due to him that the piano found its proper position as a member of a jazz ensemble. For as part of a group the piano for Ellington was both supportive and subordinate while extending its full range during breaks.

With the 1940s came the birth of modern jazz, though this development did not gather strength until the 1950s. The movement started as a reaction against the Swing era with its commercialization and the smoothness of the Big Band. The new style used smaller groups with sustained opportunities for improvisation. It became known as *Bebop* and one of its main centres was at Minton's Playhouse, a nightclub in New York. Behop added the flattened 5th to the two existing blues notes; it also included the complete range of chromatic harmony. It produced some outstanding musicians, among them **Thelonious Monk** (*b*. 1920), piano, **Kenny Clarke** (*b*. 1914), drums, **Dizzy Gillespie** (*b*. 1917), trumpet and above all **Charlie Parker** (1920–1955) who with the alto sax was able to convert the complexities of the new harmony into melodic patterns of great beauty, based on an astonishing technical ability allied to a captivating tone.

Meanwhile the reaction against Swing had also manifested itself in a revivalist movement which was interested in traditional Dixieland New Orleans jazz. The movement was widely adopted and became commercially successful. In the 1950s the reaction against Swing reached a turning point in the style known as *cool jazz*, an allusive style based on understatement and a relaxed rhythm. Its chief exponents were **Miles Davis** (*b*. 1926), a trumpeter who infused coolness into music of exquisite melancholy, and **John Lewis** (*b*. 1920) whose Modern Jazz Quartet has produced austere music based on the European tradition. Confronting this development was a dynamic type of jazz known as *hard bop*. Its exponents were based in New York, musically highly trained and technically of great competence. At the same time there was a split amongst jazzmen in the USA between those on the East Coast and those on the West Coast, who were attracted to Hollywood. Much of their work was experimental and combined jazz with various avant-garde straight styles. The result is known as *Thirdstream*. The East Coast musicians were more traditional in outlook and were associated with the developments in New York. It is, however, not profitable to press the divisions between the coasts too far for many jazzmen worked in both areas.

Jazz developed in the 1960s from Thirdstream into what has become known as *free jazz*. The movement was pioneered by **John Coltrane** (1926–67), until his death, and by the saxophonist **Ornette Coleman** (*b*. 1932). In free jazz there has been a disintegration of the various elements which go to make up jazz as there had been in straight music earlier in the century. The movement has continued during the 1970s and into the 1980s; some of its concerns are as follows:

1. use of atonality;
2. adoption of musical styles from other cultures, e.g., the *tala* and *raga* of Indian music;
3. a greater use of sound as an end in itself;
4. an intensity of expression which seeks its end in physical rather than in emotional reactions;
5. a merger between jazz and rock music;
6. electric jazz.

The history of jazz is short, fast-moving, and always continuous. It is possible that it is still moving forward in an integrated and positive direction.

Improvisation

Improvisation at the piano, or on any instrument, needs a basic vocabulary of rhythm, melody, and harmony. Each of these can be taken to an advanced stage but there is much first-class music in all styles and periods formed from the simplest means. What the performer adds to the basic ingredients is *imagination*; this is already present in all of us and cannot be learnt.

When learning to improvise, relax at the instrument and do not hesitate to play the same thing over and over again, however slowly and haltingly at first. Most jazz is notated in $\frac{4}{4}$ time. Often it is syncopated and contains dotted rhythms. If you have difficulty with the syncopation it might be helpful to split the bar into quavers so that the off-beat note can be played in its proper place. This method, however, will not catch the feel of the music; it is perhaps better to tap out the basic pulse with your foot and catch the disturbed rhythm emotionally. Jazz dotted rhythms are lazy, not crisp. It would be possible, but cumbersome, to notate the basic $\frac{4}{4}$ bar as $\frac{12}{8}$, with a dotted quaver and semiquaver pair appearing as a crotchet followed by a quaver.

Apart from playing it one of the best ways of getting the feel of jazz is to listen to it. Recordings of jazz in all styles are readily available. Examples 22.6, 22.7, and 22.8 show a selection of basic rhythmic, melodic, and bass-line patterns. They can be played separately and in several combinations. Relax and keep on playing them; when these, and such patterns become second nature, your imagination will join in.

Bass Patterns. These can include the Boogie woogie bass on p. 247 and the notes of the blues sequence on p. 246 split up in different rhythms.

22.6

Rhythmic Patterns

22.7

Melodic Patterns

22.8

Suggested Further Reading

Berendt, Joachim. *The Jazz Book* (London: Paladin Books, 1976).
Collier, Graham. *Jazz* (Cambridge University Press, 1977).
Dankworth, Avril. *Jazz: An Introduction to Its Musical Basis* (Oxford University Press 1966).
Harris, Rex. *Jazz* (London: Pelican, 1952).
Harvery, Eddie. *Jazz Piano* (London: Hodder & Stoughton, 1974).

23

HINTS FOR EXAMINATION CANDIDATES

Many students are not at all sure that the sounds which they have written down bear an exact relation to those to which they aspire.

Basic Chord Progressions

1. The following sound effective:
   (a) Chords whose roots move by a 4th or a 5th. Distinguish between the *root* and the *bass note*, e.g., I–IV II–V V–I.
   (b) Chords whose roots fall by a 3rd, e.g., I VI VI–IV.
   (c) Chords whose roots rise by step, e.g., I–II V–VI. Be careful over consecutive 5ths. Remember that in the progression V–VI in the minor you must double the major 3rd of VI.

2. Chord VII, and II in the minor, are both formed from a diminished triad. They are best used in the 1st inversion with the *bass note* doubled, i.e., in C major the triad of VII is BDF; the D is the bass note and it is doubled. The commonest progression in the major is VIIb–Ib. IV–VIIb–I is also a fine progression.

3. The progression I–III–IV makes a good harmonization for the beginning of the descending major scale.

4. The descending melodic minor scale can be harmonized by I–VIIb–IV–V . . .

5. If you find that all four parts of two successive chords move in the same direction look carefully for consecutive 5ths and octaves.

Four-Part Harmony

Carry out the following *in the order given*:

1. Establish the key by looking at the key signature, the first bar, and the final cadence.

2. Write out the triads for that key.

3. Identify the phrases of the passage and if necessary insert phrase markings.

4. Deal with the final cadence. If it is plagal use IV–I in root position; the best approach chord is VI. If the cadence is perfect check back from the end for VI–IIb–Ic–V–I. This formula may well spread over two or three bars. Remember the procedure for dealing with the cadential six-four (Chapter 8).

5. Look for modulations and carry them out (Chapters 15 and 17).

6. Deal with the remaining cadences.

7. Now fill in the remaining chords using 'Basic Chord Progressions' above as a guide.

8. Add interest to the piece but do not drown it.
   (a) use unaccented and accented passing notes, auxiliary notes, additional harmony notes, and a sparing use of the appoggiatura.

(b) The harmony can be enlivened by the addition of a dominant 7th and a secondary 7th. Both of these can be found in a final perfect cadence: II_7b–V–V_7–I.

(c) A suspension, correctly contrived, will usually add greatly to the effectiveness of the piece.

9. Finally check for consecutive fifths and octaves. If you find any do not be dismayed to discover that you may have to unravel two or three chords either side in order to get rid of them.

Bach Chorale Harmonization

The harmonization of Chorale melodies in the style of Bach is a frequent examination requirement, particularly in Diploma work. The harmonization may be required in open score, on four staves. It is often best to work the exercise on two staves and then transcribe it. Remember that in open score the tenor part is transposed up an octave and written in the treble clef, in order to avoid ledger lines. The standard collection of chorales harmonized by Bach is that by Albert Riemenschneider (1941), published by G. Schirmer.

1. *The final cadence.* This is the most characteristic part of the harmonization. It is normally a perfect cadence; 94% of all cadences in Bach chorales are either perfect or imperfect; 2% are plagal; only 1.5% are interrupted and the rest are the subject of special treatment. Bach shows a marked preference in the final cadence for II_7b–V–I, as shown in Example 23.1. Notice that the discord is formed between the soprano and alto and that the discordant 7th is prepared in the previous chord. The II_7b chord may be altered chromatically as shown in Example 23.2. It is wise to learn this progression by heart; decorations of it may be studied in Riemenschneider. Further considerations concerning the final cadence are:

23.1

23.2

(a) The final chord is always major and it always consists of four parts. This means that the leading note will often fall to the dominant or, more rarely, rise up to the third in the tenor part.

(b) The final chord rarely contains a suspension.

(c) The final cadence proceeds at the same pace as the remainder of the chorale, i.e., normally in crotchets and quavers.

2. The treatment of the chorale melody is harmonic, not contrapuntal, i.e., it avoids fugal devices such as imitation.

3. The parts move mostly in crotchets and quavers, with occasional minims and semiquavers.

4. The pulse is very steady, no faster than 60 crotchets to the minute.

5. Chorales were always accompanied, either by organ or orchestra or both. This means that the bass line is doubled at the octave beneath it and if it appears to go above the tenor it still sounds below it. The effect to aim for is one of sonorousness.

6. The tenor part is usually kept high, often moving in the range of Middle C and above. On the other hand the alto part is fairly low and it is not unusual for tenor and alto to cross. The bass line is strong, moving frequently by step, but emboldened by leaps of a 4th, 5th, and octave.

7. The harmony which Bach uses is unsophisticated but it sometimes moves towards a modulation in mid-phrase without actually arriving at a new key.

8. The sonorous effect of a Bach harmonization is derived largely from the use of unessential notes. Passing notes are common with the accented ones sometimes causing considerable discord. Anticipation is sometimes used in the soprano part of the final cadence. *There are no appoggiaturas.* There are no rests.

9. Suspensions are common in all parts, including the bass, and are found in both crotchet and quaver movement. When using suspensions, especially if they are tied, make sure that you have enough notes to fit every syllable of the words.

10. If a chorale starts with an anacrusis, Bach prefers the tonic rather than the dominant on the upbeat, i.e., I–I, not V–I.

11. Bach does not hesitate to double the major 3rd, particularly in a 1st inversion chord, with the other 3rd in the soprano part.

12. Bach prefers the passing six-three (I–VIIb–Ib) to the passing six-four (I–Vc–Ib).

13. Do not add indications of speed or dynamics to the finished exercise.

Writing for String Quartet

The style is usually that of mature Haydn and Mozart.

1. General Remarks:

(a) Strings are much more flexible than voices. String writing employs wide leaps, rapid movement and a wide range of decoration.

(b) Examination passages for completion are often taken from minuets and slow movements, rather than from the outer, faster-moving movements of a quartet.

(c) It is possible in this sort of test to write in short score and transcribe the parts afterwards, but a much more convincing texture is likely to result if you work in open score. Remember to score the viola part in the right octave (see Example 23.3—*Middle* C) and not the one below it.

(d) Mature Haydn and Mozart both use a sophisticated harmonic vocabulary including chords of the augmented 6th and the Neapolitan

23.3   **23.4**

6th. Chromatic melodic decoration is also common and this may tend to obscure the harmony.

(e) As a guide to the basic harmony see 'Basic Chord Progressions' above.

(f) Appoggiaturas and passing notes are frequently used in the melody especially in such figures as shown in Example 23.4.

(g) The use of both tonic and dominant pedal points is quite common.

(h) Haydn and Mozart rarely employ tremolando figures.

2. The Texture:

(a) *The main point* about writing for string quartet is that the texture changes frequently; the same rhythmic and melodic patterns are rarely repeated for more than three bars and a glance at any late quartet by Haydn or Mozart will reveal changes of texture much more frequent than this. This means that in a 12- or 16-bar exercise the student should have at least three or four different sorts of texture to work from.

(b) Rests are frequently used and occur at different times in the four parts. It is rare to find a passage of more than three bars without a rest or rests. Sometimes one or more parts stop completely for a bar or more.

(c) There are only three ways of combining the four instruments: all together, in pairs or three against one. Each of these three ways should be used when varying the texture.

(d) A favourite device is to start a melody and let the harmony join it at the half beat or one beat later.

(e) accompanying parts in late Haydn and Mozart are often of great interest in themselves, and passages are not uncommon where all parts are of equal importance.

3. Conventions of String Writing:

(a) It is not necessary to use signs for upbow and downbow.

(b) But bowing (phrasing) marks must be added. If these are omitted the player will take a separate bow for each note, or, more likely, lean forward and add his own bowing marks.

(c) Dynamic marks, e.g., p, mf, ff, cresc., must be added.

(d) Special types of bowing must be shown if they are applicable (see Example 23.5).

23.5

Textural Patterns are very numerous and endlessly varied. A representative selection may be culled from the score of any mature quartet by Haydn or Mozart (see Chapter 11).

A Note About Suspensions

Suspensions in diatonic harmony are mainly of three kinds. They are identified by the intervals which the suspended note and its resolution make with the bass note: 4–3, 7–6, 9–8.

1. In all cases the preparation chord should be a root position or a 1st inversion.

2. 4–3. This is the most common kind of suspension. The chord below the suspended note should be in its root position with the 3rd left out, for this is the note upon which the suspension resolves (see Example 23.6).

4   3

23.6

3. 7–6. This suspension resolves onto a chord in its 1st inversion, as the resolution, 6, implies. The 5th from the root should be doubled, as shown in Example 23.7.

7   6
3

23.7

4. 9–8. This suspension is found above a root position chord complete with 3rd and 5th. The note of resolution is already present as the bass of this chord (see Example 23.8).

5. The 9–8 and 7–6 suspensions may effectively be used together, as in Example 23.9.

9   8

23.8

9   8
7   6

23.9

POSTSCRIPT

What Next? A Word About Examinations

British Examinations in music are conducted by a variety of institutions and range from the most humble to the very exalted. They can be taken in theory, performance, harmony, counterpoint, composition, teaching, psychology, history, set works, and aural perception. 'O' Level and 'A' Level in music are offered by most of the national examining boards. They can be prepared for and taken at many Further Education establishments. Many schools also offer facilities for external candidates to sit 'O' and 'A' Level exams. Both practical and theoretical exams are offered by the Associated Board of the Royal Schools of Music and by the Colleges of Music in London and in the provinces. The requirements for a Diploma in Music vary from one establishment to another; given the right degree of proficiency it is possible to find a syllabus which will suit most musical aptitudes.

The Open University also offers courses in music for Associate Students, that is those who are not necessarily taking a degree course. Thus, if you are interested in gaining a musical qualification there is plenty to choose from. Prospectuses and syllabuses for courses are available upon request, from the relevant institutions.

APPENDIX I

SOME SIGNS, ABBREVIATIONS, AND ORNAMENTS

D.C. (Da Capo): repeat from the beginning and continue to the word *Fine*.
D.S. (Dal Segno): repeat from the point marked by the sign 𝄋 and continue to the word *Fine*.
G.P. indicates a bar during which all performers are silent.
sf or *fz* (sforzando) indicates a forceful accent, dying away immediately, on a given note.
Reiterated notes: a note with a line or lines below it or through its stem is to be repeated as long as the value of the note itself. The lines represent the tails of quavers or semiquavers and indicate the pace at which the repetitions are to be played (see Example S.1).

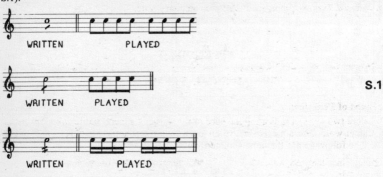

S.1

Alternated notes: see Example S.2.

S.2

Tremolando or *Tremolo*: notes to be alternated or repeated as quickly as possible are indicated as shown in Example S.3.

S.3

A broken, spread, or arpeggiated chord, starting with the lowest note is indicated in Example S.4.
Mordent or *Upper Mordent* consists of a note, the note above it and the note again, played as quickly as possible. This ornament is played on the beat but the accent stays

256

S.4

 S.5

with the principal note. *A Lower* or *Inverted Mordent* consists of a note, the note below it and the note again, as in Example S.5.

< >: get louder and then softer: commonly called 'hairpins'.

Trill: the rapid alternation of two notes which may or may not end in a *turn*. A trill is an expressive ornament; there is no general agreement as to which of the two notes was the starting note at various times in musical history.

Turn (Gruppetto) ⁓: consists of a four-note figure, the note above, the note itself, the note below and the note again. It is assumed that the upper and lower notes are part of the key of the piece unless an accidental appears above or below the sign to indicate otherwise. The sign may be placed above a note or between two notes. If it appears above a note the turn is played instead of that note. Where the sign appears between two notes there is no general agreement as to the positioning and speed of the four-note figure, after the first note has been played. However, if the turn is phrased with the note following the sign its manner of performance should become apparent.

An *Inverted Turn* ⌖ begins with the lower auxiliary note.

APPENDIX II

MUSICAL TERMS

A. Speed of Performance

There are two ways of indicating the pace of the music: a general indication often using an Italian word, and a precise indication given by a metronome marking.

1. The following are the most commonly used Italian terms:

Adagio – in a leisurely way
Allegro – lively
Allegretto – fairly fast and lightly
Andante – at a moderate walking speed
Grave – very slow
Largo – broadly

Larghetto – rather broadly
Lento – slowly
Moderato – at a moderate speed
Presto – very fast
Prestissimo – very fast indeed
Vivace – quick and lively

2. A *metronome* is a mechanical instrument which measures how many beats there are in a minute at any given speed. It was invented by Maelzel in 1814, since when composers have been able to indicate, if they wish, the exact speed at which their music should be performed. They do this by indicating how many notes of a particular value there are in a minute, e.g., $\frac{1}{2}$ = 60 means that 60 minims take a minute to perform.

B. Terms which Modify the Speed of Performance

Accelerando (accel.) – getting gradually faster
Allargando – decreasing in speed, broadening
A tempo – return to the original speed
Calando – getting slower and softer
Doppio movimento – twice as fast
L'istesso tempo – retain the same pulse
Meno allegro – less quickly

Meno mosso – slacken the pace
Perdendosi – dying away
Più mosso – quicker
Ritardando (rit.) – getting slower
Rallentando (rall.) – getting slower
Ritenuto (rit.) hold back the pace
Stringendo – getting faster
Tempo giusto – in exact time
Tempo primo – return to the original speed

C. Terms Relating to the Intensity of Performance

Crescendo (cresc.) – getting louder
Decrescendo (decresc.) – getting softer
Diminuendo (dim.) – getting softer
Forte (f) – loud
Fortissimo (ff) – very loud

Mezzo forte (mf) – moderately loud
Mezzo piano (mp) – moderately soft
Piano (p) – softly
Pianissimo (pp) – very softly
Forte-piano (fp) – accent sharply

Vibrato – a controlled and more or less rapid fluctuation of the pitch of a note used for expressive purposes. It is produced on stringed instruments by the vibration of the player's finger stopping the string and on wind instruments by breath control; of the keyboard instruments vibrato is possible on the clavichord (Bebung). Vibrato may also be used by singers.

D. General Terms Relating to the Manner of Performance

A cappella – unaccompanied
Ad libitum – as the performer p'eases
Affettuoso – tenderly
Amabile – gentle
Animato – with spirit
Appassionato – with much feeling
Assai – very
Attacca – start right away
Ben marcato – each note distinctly
   emphasized
Cantabile – smooth and lyrical
Colla voce – follow the solo part
Con brio – vigorously
Con forza – with force
Con fuoco – with fire
Con grazia – gracefully
Con moto – with movement
Dolce – sweetly
Dolente – sadly
Espressivo – expressively
Furioso – impetuously
Giocoso – gracefully
Legato – smoothly
Leggiero – lightly
Ma – but
Maestoso – with dignity
Meno – less

Mesto – sadly
Molto – very
Non tanto – not so much
Non troppo – not too much
Parlando – as if speaking
Pesante – heavily
Piangevole – plaintively
Più – more
Poco – a little
Poi – then (next).
Pomposo – majestically
Portamento – glide from one note to the
   next
Quasi – as if
Risoluto – determined
Scherzando – playfully
Sempre – continuously
Senza – without
Sostenuto – sustained
Sotto voce – in an undertone
Staccato – detached
Strepitoso – noisily
Tempo rubato – disregard strict time
Tenuto – held on, sustained
Tranquillo – quietly
Troppo – too much
Volti subito (V.S.) – turn the page quickly

E. Italian Terms for String Players

Arco – play with the bow
Con sordino – with the mute
Senza sordino – without the mute
Pizzicato (pizz.) – plucked
Col legno – play with the back (wood) of the bow
Sul ponticello – play near the bridge
Sul tasto – play near the fingerboard
Sul G – play on the G string
Divisi – an instruction for two notes forming a chord to be played by separate players
   rather than by all players using two strings (= double stopping)
Spiccato – play with the middle of the bow and bounce it on the string; this may also be
   indicated by a slur with dots above the notes

Martellato – draw the string across the bow with hammer strokes

⊓ = a downbow ∨ = an upbow 𝄐 notes treated thus are to be played tremolando, i.e., with very rapid strokes of the bow; orchestral players call this 'scrubbing'.

Harmonics – by lightly placing his finger on the string the player can produce notes of the harmonic series. The sign for a harmonic is a small circle above the note. A diamond shape above a note means that the string has to be stopped with one finger and the harmonic produced with another. Such a note is known as an *artificial* harmonic.

F. How to Pronounce Italian Terms

The following points are not intended as a guide to the language but are meant to help English-speaking people who use Italian musical terms.

  (i) The pronunciation of the Italian language is straightforward. The same letters or combinations of letters always indicate the same sound.
 (ii) E at the end of a word is always pronounced, approximately as a sharp-*ay* sound, e.g. *andante* has three syllables.
(iii) The most troublesome letters are C and G.
      They can be hard: C as in cat, G as in gate;
      or soft: C sounds as ch as in church, G sounds as J as in just.
      They are pronounced the same way doubled as single.
      If either C or G is followed by E or I they are soft, e.g. dolce, adagio.
      If either C or G is followed by A, O, U, or H they are hard, e.g. attacca, fuoco, largo, largando, larghetto.
 (iv) The function of the letter I before another vowel is to point the vowel; I is then pronounced as a fast Y, e.g. sinfonietta, adagietto.
      The pronunciation of *appoggiatura* is then *apojyatura*; of *acciaccatura* is *achackatura; stringendo* does not have the English -ing sound but is pronounced *strinjendo*.
  (v) The word *tacet* is Latin (= is silent) and the C is usually pronounced as S.
 (vi) The letter Z (or ZZ) is pronounced DS (often TS) e.g. *senza, mezzo.*
(vii) *Più* = pyoo.

G. Italian Terms for Pianists

Ped. or *Pedale*: use the righthand (damper) pedal; this raises the dampers and allows the struck strings to vibrate freely. The point at which the pedal is to be released is marked by an asterisk *.
Una corda (one string) and *Con sordino* (with mute): use the lefthand pedal. This instruction is cancelled by the corresponding *Tre corde* (three strings) and *Senza sordino.*
mano destra (*M.D.*): use the right hand.
mano sinistra (*M.S.*): use the left hand.

H. German Musical Terms

Anhang – coda
ausdrucksvoll – with expression
Bebung – vibrato
bewegt – moved
Bratsche – viola
feierlich – ceremoniously
Geige – violin
gemütlich – cheerfully
getragen – sustained
heftig – impetuously
heimlich – mysteriously
herzlich – tenderly
leicht – lightly
leise – gently softly
linke Hand – left hand
mässig – moderately
munter – lively
mutig – boldly
ohne – without
Partitur – an orchestral or vocal score
rasch – fast
rechte Hand – right hand
ruhig – calmly
sanft – softly

hervortretend – prominently
immer – continuously
innig – heartfelt
kräftig – vigorously
langsam – slowly

schnell – quickly
schwermütig – sadly
sehr – very
Vorspiel – prelude
wenig – a little
zögernd – hesitating

I. French Musical Terms

à deux – for two instruments or voices
à deux mains – for two hands
archet – a bow
assez – enough, quite
aubade – morning music
cuivré – brassy tone of a stopped horn
doux, doucement – gently
main droite (M.D.) – the right hand
main gauche (M.G.) – the left hand
douleur – grief

étude – a study, exercise
pot-pourri – a musical medley
reprise – 1. chorus of a song
            2. a repeat
sans – without
sec – dry, unornamented
sourdine – a mute
touches – keys of a piano
très – very
voix – voice

Opus

Latin for 'a piece of work', i.e., a composition. Strictly the 'o' is short (as in hot) but the word is frequently pronounced with a long 'o' (as in go). Opus numbers, e.g., op. 59, give a rough guide to the order in which a composer's works appeared but there are many kinds of exception, e.g., a composer may issue a composition some years after he has written it or he may number some works and not others. In some cases a single opus number comprises a group of works in which case the number is subdivided e.g. op. 59, No.2.

APPENDIX III

BEETHOVEN'S MAIN WORKS

Op. No.	Title	Date
1	3 Piano Trios: E♭ Maj. G maj. C min.	1793–95
2	3 Piano sonatas: F min. A maj. C maj.	1795
5	2 Cello sonatas: F maj. G min.	1796
7	Piano sonata: E♭ maj.	1796
9	3 String trios: G maj. D maj. C min.	1796–98
11	Clarinet trio: B♭ maj.	1798
13	Piano sonata Pathétique: C min.	1798
14	2 Piano sonatas: E maj. G maj.	1795–99
15	Piano Concerto No. 1: C maj.	1797
18	6 String Quartets	1798–1800
19	Piano Concerto no. 2: B♭ maj.	1795
20	Septet: E♭ maj.	1799
21	Symphony No. 1: C maj.	1799–1800
22	Piano sonata: B♭ maj.	1800
24	Violin sonata: F maj.	1801
26	Piano sonata: A♭ maj.	1801
27	2 Piano sonatas: E♭ maj. C♯ min., 'Moonlight'	1801
28	Piano sonata: D maj.	1801
30	3 Violin sonatas: A maj. C min. G maj.	1802
31	3 Piano sonatas: G maj. D min. E♭ maj.	1802
33	7 Bagatelles for piano	1799–1802
35	'Prometheus' Variations for piano	1802
36	Symphony No. 2: D maj.	1802
37	Piano Concerto No. 3: C min.	1800
40	Romance for violin: G maj.	1803
43	Overture 'Prometheus'	1800
47	Violin sonata 'Kreutzer': A maj.	1803
49	2 Piano sonatas: G min. G maj.	1796
50	Romance for violin: F maj.	1802
51	Rondo for piano: G. maj.	1802
53	Piano sonata: C maj., 'Waldstein'	1804
54	Piano sonata: F maj.	1804
55	Symphony No.3: E♭ maj., 'Eroica'	1803
56	Concerto for piano, violin, cello: C maj.	1804
57	Piano sonata: F min, 'Appassionata'	1804
58	Piano Concerto No. 4: G maj.	1805–6
59	3 String Quartets: F maj., E min., C maj., 'Rasumovsky'	1806
60	Symphony No. 4: B♭ maj.	1806
61	Violin Concerto: D maj.	1807
67	Symphony No. 5: C min.	1805–7
68	Symphony No. 6: F maj., 'Pastoral'	1807–8
69	Cello sonata: A maj.	1808
70	2 Piano trios: D maj., E♭ maj.	1808

Op. No.	Title	Date	Op. No.	Title	Date
72	Opera *Fidelio*	1803–5	109	Piano sonata: E maj.	1820
73	Piano concerto No. 5: E♭ maj., 'Emperor'	1809	110	Piano sonata: A♭ maj.	1821
74	String Quartet: E♭ maj., 'Harp'	1809	111	Piano sonata: C min.	1822
78	Piano sonata: F♯ maj.	1809	113	Overture 'Ruins of Athens'	1811
81	Piano sonata: E♭ maj., 'Les Adieux'	1809	117	Overture 'King Stephen'	1811
84	Overture 'Egmont'	1810	119	11 Bagatelles for piano	1820–22
86	Mass: C maj.	1807	120	'Diabelli' variations for piano	1823
90	Piano sonata: E min.	1814	123	Missa Solemnis	1818–23
92	Symphony No. 7: A maj.	1812	125	Symphony No. 9: D min. 'Choral'	1823
93	Symphony No. 8: F maj.	1812	126	6 Bagatelles for piano	1824
95	String Quartet: F min.	1810	127	String Quartet: E♭ maj.	1824
96	Violin sonata: G maj.	1812	130	String Quartet: B♭ maj.	1825
97	Piano trio: B♭ maj., 'Archduke'	1811	131	String Quartet: C♯ min.	1826
101	Piano sonata: A maj.	1816	132	String Quartet: A min.	1825
102	2 cello sonatas: C maj. D maj.	1815	133	String Quartet 'Grosse Fuge'	1825
106	Piano sonata: B♭ maj., 'Hammerklavier'	1818	135	String Quartet: F maj.	1826

APPENDIX IV

The Circle of Fifths

The relationship of each key to every other key is often shown as a circle with a starting point of C major (A minor) having no accidentals in its key signature. The circle moves clockwise in 5ths with each successive key adding an extra sharp until the point is reached where every note of the scale is sharpened. But at the key of six sharps (F♯ major) it is convenient to relabel the key signature as six flats (G♭ major) and to continue notating in flats which become one fewer with each successive 5th. Eventually the circle arrives back where it started at C major (A minor) with no accidentals shown.

However, if the procession of keys is shown not as a circle but as a straight line a curious fact emerges. From the accompanying diagram it can be seen that if you start at C and move through twelve successive 5ths you arrive back at C seven octaves later.

Now, if a stretched string vibrates at x times a second, each separate half of the string will be found to vibrate at twice that number, i.e., $2x$ times a second, and each half of the string will sound an octave higher than the whole string by itself. The relationship of a note to the note an octave below it is therefore 2:1. If the string is divided into three the interval of a 5th emerges and the relationship of a note to the note a 5th below it is 3:2. As the diagram overleaf shows, the seventh octave above a C (or above any other note) is the same note as the twelfth 5th above it. In other words $2x^7$ should equal $\frac{3}{2}x^{12}$. But it doesn't. The resulting discrepancy is known as the *Comma of Pythagoras* and is expressed by the ratio 531,441:524,288.

1. The order of sharps in the key signature is by rising 5ths; the order of flats is by falling 5ths. One is the reverse of the other: ♯⟶FCGDAEB⟵♭
2. In the sharp major keys the keynote is immediately above the last sharp.
3. In the flat major keys the keynote is a 4th below the last flat, i.e., at the pitch of the last flat but one.
4. Minor keys have the same key signature as the major key three semitones higher.

The Circle of Fifths

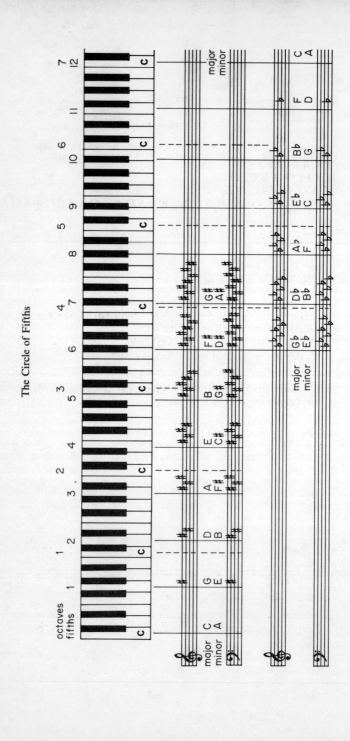

APPENDIX V

Answers to Exercises

Chapter 2
1. G A B C D E F♯ G
2. D E F♯ G A B C♯ D
3. E♭ F G A♭ B♭ C D E♭
4. C G A G F♯ G C G G A B C B C B A A G A A G A F E C B A G A F D C

Chapter 3
1. D A
2. G A
3. A E♭
4. B C♯ E

Chapter 4
1. (a) perfect 5th; (b) perfect 5th; (c) perfect 5th; (d) augmented 4th; (e) minor 3rd; (f) diminished 5th; (g) perfect 5th.
2. (a) D; (b) E♭; (c) F; (d) G♭; (e) A♯; (f) B♭
3. (a) C; (b) D♭; (c) E♭; (d) F♭; (e) G♯; (f) A♭

Chapter 6
1. (a) C major; (b) F minor; (c) D major; (d) G minor; (e) B♭ major; (f) E major; (g) A♭ major; (h) F major.
2.

Chapter 7
1.

263

2.

3.

4.

Chapter 8
1.

2.

IIb V I IIb V I

3.

Ic V I Ic V I Ic V I

Chapter 9

1.

a) b) c)

I V I V

2.

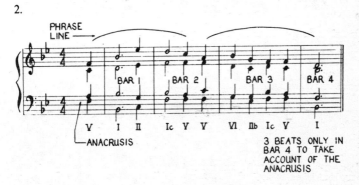

PHRASE
LINE →

BAR 1 BAR 2 BAR 3 BAR 4

V I II Ic V V VI IIb Ic V I

ANACRUSIS

3 BEATS ONLY IN
BAR 4 TO TAKE
ACCOUNT OF THE
ANACRUSIS

Chapter 10

1.

2.

3.

Chapter 11

1, 2, and 3.

4.

I   IV II VI VI II V I

Chapter 12

1.

VIOLA

CELLO

2.

VIOLA

CELLO

Chapter 13

1.

1)   2)   3)   OR

Chapter 14

1. (a) G B D F; (b) A C♯ E G; (c) E G♯ B D; (d) F A C E♭; (e) B♭ D F A♭;
   (f) E♭ G B♭ D♭.

2.

3.

Chapter 15

1. As this question was designed for experimenting, no answer has been
   given.
2. (a) A minor, B minor, C major, D major, E minor; (b) G minor, A minor,
   B♭ major, C major, D minor; (c) E minor, F♯ minor, G major, A major, B
   minor; (d) C minor, D minor, E♭ major, F major, G minor.

3.

4.

Chapter 16
1.

2.

3.

Chapter 17
1.

A.27

2. As this question was designed for experimenting, no answer has been given.

Chapter 18
1.

Index